AF574545

Butterfly Tears

Stories of Entrapment to Empowerment

Wil Drouin
Managing Editor

Jennifer Thomas
Editor-in-Chief

Published by

Butterfly Legacy

Tustin, California

Published by Butterfly Legacy, 14081 Yorba Street, Suite 101, Tustin, CA 92780; www.butterflylegacy.com. Contact: info@butterflylegacy.com

The stories in this book are true. However, some names, locales, and descriptive details have been changed to protect the privacy and safety of the Pathways to Independence clients and some individuals whose lives have intersected with their own.

ISBN: 978-098342180-1 Hardcover

Library of Congress Control Number: 2011925174

First edition published in 2011
Printed in the United States of America

A portion of all proceeds directly benefit
the Pathways to Independence Foundation

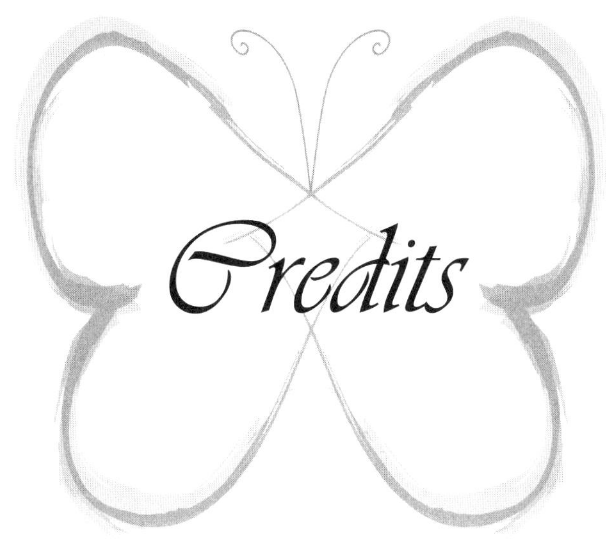

Credits

Managing Editor	**Wil Drouin** *Pathways Benefactor*
Editor-in-Chief	**Jennifer Thomas** *Beyond Words Editing*
Contributing Authors	**Bill Hayes** **Candice Hessel** **Melanie Launius** **Tracy Lisauskas** **Jennifer Thomas** **with Dave Bishop,** *Pathways to Independence Founder*
Design & Layout	**Jennifer Thomas** *Beyond Words Editing*
Cover Artwork	**Jamie Grace Davis** *Fine Artist*
Jacket Photographs	**Christine Fay** *Photographer*

"You can't live a perfect day until you do something for someone who will never be able to repay you."

—John Wooden

This book is dedicated to

Dave Bishop

Founder of Pathways to Independence

...for your many perfect days

Contents

Part 2
Outside the Cocoon

Amazing success stories from women who have completed the Pathways program and soared into a brighter future.

Preface

"I have a dream!" Dave Bishop, founder of the Pathways to Independence Foundation, said to me.

Since 1991, Pathways has offered a unique support program to over 250 young women in need. Women who have suffered early-life domestic trauma—abuse, neglect, addictions, and worse. Under Dave's leadership, this successful program has been a powerful lifeline, enabling a profound transformation in women's lives.

"We need to expand our financial base in order to serve more girls," Dave continued. "Our waiting list has over fifty applicants eager to start today, but we don't have the funds for them. It breaks my heart to turn them away."

I nodded. It broke my heart too.

"My dream is to do a book about Pathways," Dave explained. "It would help spread the word of who we are and how we so effectively help these young women. Proceeds from book sales and reader donations would increase our funds."

Dave smiled.

"What do you think about the idea?"

"It's a *great* idea!" I enthused. "A book would move Pathways to a higher level of awareness and support."

After a moment of reflective silence, Dave asked softly, "Wil, would *you* produce the book?"

For twenty years, Dave Bishop has tirelessly and passionately devoted his life to leading struggling and despairing young women toward a better life. He has been there for them in their darkest moments. How could someone *not* say "yes" to a request from this man—this Mother Teresa?

"Of course I'll do the book," I replied without hesitation.

Butterfly Tears was born.

—Wil Drouin, Managing Editor and Publisher

Acknowledgments

The day Wil Drouin invited me to undertake this project, I was ecstatic. I've had a lifelong passion for empowering women, and the Pathways to Independence Foundation sounded amazing.

I had no idea *how* amazing.

I had no idea how much every client I met—every person I interacted with throughout this process—would impact my life.

Meeting the young women of Pathways, hearing their stories firsthand, and—most of all—witnessing them *shine* after all they have been through...it goes beyond inspiration.

Interviewing the generous benefactors and volunteers, learning how much they all genuinely *care,* has a been a revelation.

And it's been an honor to meet Dave Bishop himself, to see the love and support he generates through his humble spirit and superhuman effort.

Pathways to Independence truly *is* a family. A loving cocoon that allows hope and healing to emerge. I am grateful to Wil and to the rest of the Pathways family for welcoming me in. This has been a blessing to my life.

—Jennifer Thomas, Editor-in-Chief

Our profound gratitude to all the generous and talented people who helped make this inspiring dream a reality. It has been an incredible journey, and the hard work, commitment, and sharing of love from every individual involved has been overwhelming.

A heartfelt thank you to each of you.

Special thanks to...

Contributing authors Candice Hessel, Melanie Launius, and Tracy Lisauskas, for their time, talent, and dedication.

Jennifer's invaluable writing and editing partner, Bill Hayes, for his creativity, support, and input.

Dave Bishop for his insightful contributions to the book and for all he does.

Icy Smith for her publishing expertise.

Jamie Grace Davis for investing her heart and soul into creating beautiful and impactful artwork for the cover.

All the generous supporters of the Pathways to Independence Foundation. What you do does matter.

Our deepest thanks to the courageous young women in these pages who were willing to share their stories with us ...and with the world.

You truly are a miracle.

A special thank you to Jennifer Thomas, Editor-in-Chief

I am especially grateful to Jennifer Thomas for her amazing dedication, passion, and professionalism in pulling together the many people and pieces involved in this comprehensive undertaking, and for completing the manuscript, chapter by chapter.

Dave and I conceived the idea for *Butterfly Tears,* but it was Jennifer who went through the hard labor pains of delivering our dream. As *the* driving force behind this monumental project, she nurtured it along from concept to first draft to final edit, and then through its beautiful design and layout. It was a challenging task well done.

Jennifer has created a compelling masterpiece that the Pathways family can all take great pride in.

Thank you, Jennifer, for helping give birth to Dave Bishop's dream.
You are a special gift to the Pathways family and to me.

—Wil Drouin

"Welcome to my world.
I am twenty-five years old and I have spent most of my life dead.

This is my story and the stories of other young women like me,
who have fought tremendously with the world and with life.
Courageous young women—
willing to share all they've endured; how they survived;
and how they finally began to live.

Today I am ALIVE!
This is my story and this is my truth."

—Kaysie, Pathways Client

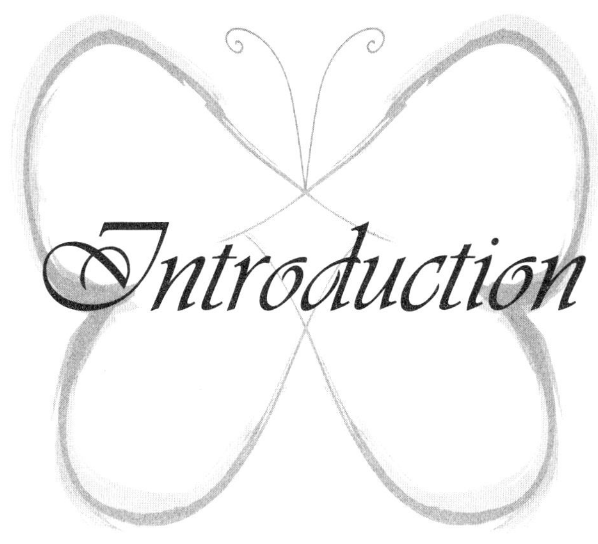

Introduction

"Today is the day that I will end my life."

These are harsh and horrible words.

This is a harsh and horrible desire.

But extreme cruelty in lives of the young can cut with enough harshness and horror to turn the beauty of life into a wish for numb refuge—an end to the pain at any cost.

The young woman who wrote that line—who so deeply felt that desire—was sadly willing to pay that highest of prices to escape the abuse and the addictions that crushed her childhood. She was willing to pay that price to rid herself of the haunting mental images of a family and a life that turned so twisted and wrong.

Ending one's life is a path. Everything we do ultimately takes us on a path to some end. Life is indeed a series of meandering trails. Some of those trails are in the blind dank wilderness; others have the benefit of light and signposts, placed there by experienced guides who offer direction.

Dave Bishop is such a guide.

And he has the experience.

That young woman's life did not end that day. As she came to that vicious fork in the road, she was guided to another path—the path out. A pathway to independence.

When Dave Bishop became that special guide—the guide who formalized the name, goals, and passion of the foundation that is Pathways to Independence—he had already traveled down many "dark roads" himself. He'd suffered familial terror. He'd sequestered himself behind the doors of seminary. He'd been drafted—but remained stateside—during the Vietnam War. He'd been mired in addiction. In fact, he'd been as lost as the women he now dedicates his life to helping.

Today, like the weathered and wizened Sherpa guides who lead the willing to the top of Everest, Dave has helped hundreds of women rise from the bottom of life to its summit.

Butterfly Tears is not just the story of Dave Bishop and the evolution of Pathways to Independence. No. It is the stories of the abused women and the kinds of harshness and horror that were the catalyst for Dave's dedication to a constant climb up some of life's steepest mountains.

These true stories are stark examples of heroism and despair. They generate every emotion from shaking anger to tearful joy. They are the real lives of real young women, who have been guided away from the suffocating quicksand of complete resignation. They have been guided to the bright white light of becoming lawyers, teachers, social workers, business professionals, nurturing mothers, and other wonders that now allow them to hold their heads high.

They are also stories that prove *no* path is an absolute dead end.

There *are* guides out there. For all those who exploit and victimize, there are also those like Dave Bishop and the generous supporters of his foundation who care deeply.

There *are* ways out.

There *is* Pathways to Independence.

—Bill Hayes

The Story of the Butterfly

A man found a cocoon of a butterfly.

One day a small opening appeared.
He sat and watched the butterfly for several hours
as it struggled to squeeze its body through the tiny hole.
Then it stopped, as if it couldn't go further.

So the man decided to help the butterfly.
He took a pair of scissors
and snipped off the remaining bits of cocoon.
The butterfly emerged easily,
but it had a swollen body and shriveled wings.

The man continued to watch it,
expecting that any minute the wings would enlarge
and expand, enough to support the body.

Neither happened!

In fact, the butterfly spent the rest of its life crawling around.
It was never able to fly.

What the man in his kindness and haste did not understand:
The restricting cocoon
and the struggle required by the butterfly to get through the opening
was a way of forcing the fluid from the body into the wings
so that it would be ready for flight
once that was achieved.

Sometimes struggles are exactly what we need in our lives.
Going through life with no obstacles would cripple us.
We would not be as strong as we could have been
and we would never fly.

Life's cruelest hardships are often the powerful driving force
that empowers us to emerge
from the prison of entrapment—and soar.

Independently and successfully.

Each client of the Pathways to Independence program
is gifted with a personal crystal butterfly upon her graduation—
a powerful symbol of the miraculous transformation
she has achieved through her own commitment and hard work.

Part 1

Strengthening Their Wings

"The more difficulties one has to encounter,
within and without,
the more significant and the higher in inspiration his life will be."

—Horace Bushnell

O Starry Night

"No one knows I'm planning to kill myself as soon and as fast as I can."

—Kaysie

It's cold in here. I breathe in and I breathe out as I hear my own heartbeat pulsating through me. I can feel my clammy bare feet sticking to the tile floor. I can taste desperation and my own salty sweet sorrow. I can smell fear and anxiety.

I'm in the bathroom. I see myself in the mirror. I can't help but stare in awe. Who is this person staring straight back at me? Who is this person injecting a needle into my arm? I am no longer recognizable even to myself; because in my eyes I see nothing but emptiness. Profound and utter emptiness.

Nobody is home, and I'm so cold, and I can't help but wonder, *How the hell did I end up here?* Was it not just the other day, I spent my days dreaming of becoming a ballerina and riding horses? Was it not just the other day, I was at sleepovers, telling ghost stories and talking about boys? Was it not just the other day, I was at Sunday school learning Bible verses and writing away in my diary? What would my prominent religious family think? Because here I am, slamming heroin into my veins—into my soul—desperately seeking to feel anything other than myself and my broken heart. My head is spinning so fast and all I can think is, *How did I get here?*

To explain I must go back in time; I must go back to the stars.

What beauty and wonder lie within the stars—to me, they were my safe haven, my saving grace. I was a little blond-haired, blue-eyed girl who escaped to the stars…

You see, at nighttime, my monster would come into my room and touch me and himself in ways and places that shamed me to the core of my being, starting at about age five. This shame I carried with me for most of my life, like weight upon my shoulders. A weight so heavy I found it hard to breathe at times.

I was always told to be very quiet and was even hushed with a pillow over my face. When this happened, I learned how to physically and mentally leave my body. My bed was below a very large window, so I would look out and not be in my bedroom at all; I'd be far, far away in the stars.

As a child, I told myself to just stay in the stars, while I prayed for God to come get me. I was actually so positive that God would come, I would pack my favorite toys and dolls night after night because I wanted to be prepared to leave with Him.

The day I realized He was not coming was a very sad day. A shattering moment—when I gave up on the one thing and the one person I still believed in. I lost all the hope and wonder that every child deserves. I turned cold; my precious little heart becoming ice as I learned to function in survival mode only. Instead of loving God and praying, I learned to hate Him for leaving me where I was, enduring what I knew to be hell. I was in hell with a monster.

Let me tell you about my monster. He was a pastor in the Christian Church. He was a charismatic and brilliant man.

He was my father.

Both my parents attended seminary and held master's degrees in a religious field: my father in Theology and my mother in Christian Counseling. We were the picture-perfect family; everyone thought we had it all together. But little did they know the profound brokenness of our household.

I idolized my father and wanted to do anything in the world to please him—even give him myself, my small child body and soul. I always thought that if I could be better or prettier or smarter, he would stop hurting me in ways I knew were wrong.

My father was a monster for what he did and the hypocrisy he lived in. But you must understand that although I hated who he became and the things he did, I loved this man. I was willing to do anything to be loved, no matter what form it came in. And so I endured, and spent many nights soaring through the stars.

I grew older, and colder, and defiant and angry as I found there were nights with no stars at all. I acted out at home, becoming verbally and emotionally abusive to my mother and younger brother. I was hurting so badly inside that I hurt others to make myself feel better. At school, I was withdrawn and shy; I was afraid to talk.

As a family, we moved so much and I changed schools so many times, that I never really felt like I fit in or belonged. I always felt somehow dirty, walking around with so much carried shame. I thought no one would—or could—ever understand me.

I escaped in my writing—I could tell *anything* to my diary and journals. Writing is where I had a voice. I was silenced in so many ways, but I when I put my pencil to paper I found a certain strength and sanity.

I let my wounded soul spill over onto blank pages—clean slates that would fill with my silenced words.

I escaped into books as well. I read book after book, losing myself in others' worlds—worlds with fairy-tale love and happy endings.

At age ten, I matured earlier than the other girls in my grade and I was beyond humiliated. I was my full height and very filled out. I felt so confused and ashamed of myself and of my body. I consistently got unwanted attention from boys, and that only made me more self-conscious.

I knew what it was to be and feel like nothing more than an object. I learned very early on what males wanted from me. I had learned this from my own father and now from the many boys I came in contact with.

I was ten, depressed, and suicidal. And so confused. I was without any friends or parents to talk to. So I began to starve myself.

I completely stopped eating food.

I believe a huge part of this was a cry for help—to get a reaction out of my mother, who I thought lived on another planet for not seeing, or wanting to see, things right in front of her face. But another reason I developed an eating disorder so young, I think, is that my whole world seemed so completely upside down; what I did or did not put into my mouth was the only thing I knew how to control.

So this is how my very first addiction began.

Months passed, and reprimands were made, but nothing serious was ever done. Life went on.

At age eleven, I fell in love.

At school, I had heard that you could drink vanilla extract and become drunk. Being that neither of my parents drank alcohol or ever kept it in the house, I proceeded to drink an entire bottle of vanilla.

I remember falling in love with the feeling of feeling nothing. It numbed me so wonderfully that even though I became ill, I desperately wanted more and more of this substance that one day would almost end me and my life. I began drinking as often as possible, stealing alcohol from friends' parents and so forth.

When I was intoxicated was the only time I felt okay about myself. This was the first time I had felt bearable in my own skin, and I craved more and more.

The abuse was still occurring at night; it had just become sporadic. In a way, this almost made it worse, because I never knew when he would come. At one point growing up, my parents moved into a smaller bedroom across the house and moved me into the master suite. No explanation was given; it was something that was just done—my mother still oblivious to all that was around her.

At age twelve, I began smoking marijuana and my drinking increased even further. Looking back though, I can honestly say that while drugs and alcohol almost killed me, they actually saved me in many ways. I am grateful for the substances that kept me numb and from killing myself, until I was able to let go of them and begin to feel.

But at that age, I was nowhere *near* ready to face reality.

At age fifteen, my father quit the church and ministry field, and moved us once again to another state. I was angry at having to pick up and leave again, terrified to start high school as a freshman in a new state, not knowing anyone.

My father changed in many ways around this time. For one, we no longer went to church. Neither my brother nor I complained, because most of the time we hated going. But it was just so odd that something that had been so important in our lives was no longer even mentioned.

Also, my father started his own company. He started making a lot of money, and our lifestyle changed dramatically. We moved into a large house on a golf course, in an exclusive neighborhood. And for a while things seemed to be different.

My father was rarely home because of travel for work, so the abuse was very seldom. Even so, my drinking and drug use continued to progress. I remember always wanting a friend to spend the night when my father was in town, because then I knew he would not come into my room.

It was the most terrifying thing for me to wake up with him in my room. Years had passed, yet he was still the same monster.

Drugs and alcohol became my best friends. They numbed me enough to make it through the days and nights.

At age fifteen, I went to a house party with some college kids. I proceeded to drink too much. I had no idea whose house I was in—all I remember is that the room was spinning, so I went to a bedroom to lie down. As I lay drunk in an unknown bed in an unknown house, two guys appeared; they came into the bedroom and locked door.

Unfortunately I will never forget the things they both did to me, and the pain and shame I felt. And I never uttered a word. I never said no. So for many years I honestly believed it was my fault. They called me names, and sadly I believed them.

I never told a soul.

A part of me died that day. Just shut down and pretended—like everything else in my world—that my reality was not reality at all.

I began dating a nineteen-year-old drug dealer. At fifteen, I was still a little girl, but at the time I thought it was cool that an older guy liked me. Girls my age felt lucky just to have a guy, or to know someone who had a car. *My* boyfriend was college age and had his own apartment. It was very convenient for me, because he always supplied me with drugs and plenty of money. The problem was he was angry and controlling and involved with shady people. The drug-dealing business is dirty; I was exposed to massive amounts of drugs and to guys with guns and other weapons.

At age sixteen, I found out I was pregnant. I assumed it was my boyfriend's, though I could not rule out my father.

I was so terrified. But something happened when there was another life growing within me: I felt a connection I had never felt. And for the first time, I felt love for someone I had never even met. Nothing in my world made any sense except the knowledge that I could never love anything more than I loved my child.

I named my child Triston.

And then I made an appointment.

When I went to have it done, I had to lie and say I was older than I was, and I had to steal the money to do it. I never told anyone, not even a friend. My heart broke into a thousand sobbing pieces as I aborted my child.

I mourned for days and days over this loss that was so great to me: the loss of my child, the loss of my childhood, the loss of love.

Another dose of my harsh reality.

Finally, when I was still sixteen, my prayers were answered: my monster moved out.

My father and mother split up. But instead of relief, a part of me felt pain—and even missed him. This only left me more confused, even guilty, about my own feelings. So I pushed them down harder, with harder drugs.

My mother fell apart and became emotionally unstable. Her husband, whom she had built her entire life around, had left her penniless and jobless, with a huge house on a golf course and two teenage kids.

My mother cried all the time and would break down in front of my brother and me, even in public places. She would come to us for comfort, for us to hold her, and this enraged me. I would push her away, which only made matters worse. But at age sixteen, I looked at my mother as a poor, pathetic, dependent excuse for a woman, and I promised myself I would never be that. I would never cry and show weakness; I would never be poor; and I would never be left.

And my ticket to ensure this was my father.

So I went to the man who had abused me for most of my life. You see, my father had a fancy company and car and a new young girlfriend, and he lived the life I thought I wanted. And while I hated my father, the conflicting part was that I loved him too.

I vowed to use my father for financial reasons until I had enough money for a way out and to make it on my own. And so I did.

High school life was no longer worthwhile; I had bigger and better plans for myself. So I threw myself into studying, ignoring friends and normal high school activities, and was able to graduate the summer before my senior year.

I moved out of my mother's house. Actually she asked me to leave, and after that, I went months and months without speaking to her. So I rented a room in a house while I worked full-time for my father's software company.

I worked my way up to accounts payable and receivable. No one knew that I was only seventeen, and I played the part well. I was making decent money, so I bought nice clothes; I came to work dressed in suits and heels, and I carried a laptop.

And I was good at my job. I was smart and eager to learn, and more and more responsibilities were put upon me. My stress level went through the roof, and I found myself dependent upon sedatives to make it through the days.

On the outside, I looked very professional and put together. But if you looked real close—if you looked into my eyes (which not many did)—you could see that I was just a scared little girl. I was broken on the inside and hiding a significant drug addiction. Yet through all this, I still got up every morning (with or without sleep) and put on my makeup and heels and a fake smile, to conceal my bleeding and dying essence. I wonder now, how many times did I fix my hair rather than cry? How many times did I apply my makeup instead of screaming at the top of my lungs? And how many times did I do a drug instead of feeling the intense pain of my world and my reality?

During this time, I accompanied my father on business trips all over the world and was treated as his girlfriend. This felt very wrong to me, but it also made me feel special. I felt sophisticated and older than I was—drinking in bars, traveling to exotic countries. I thought this was the life I wanted. How terribly wrong I was.

The last time my father ever touched me was when we had traveled together to Portugal. I awoke from a blackout in the hotel room that we shared, with him on top of me and inside of me.

A huge part of me died that night.

There are no words to describe this, nothing I can say or share with you as a reader for you to understand. Nor would I want you to, for the truth of this matter is too incomprehensible. Shame is a funny thing; it is heavy. Especially after years and years of carrying it around. So for me, life continued in the same miserable drug-induced existence.

At age eighteen, I still worked for my father's software company, and my drug addiction had progressed. I lived in an apartment now, and my roommate consistently made comments to me about my drug use—which I consistently ignored. I honestly did not think I had a problem. Getting high was the only way I knew how to get by, to get me through the days.

Until it backfired.

My drugs led me to begin nodding off at work, and even sometimes while driving. I also found myself waking up in random parts of my apartment.

My roommate got scared for my health and my safety, and did the unthinkable: she called my mother.

My mother and I had not spoken for almost a year, and I was furious that my roommate had called her—especially to tell her I needed help. My friends and my mother did an intervention on me. They tried very hard with me, and at last I agreed to check myself into the hospital.

Like the good addict that I am, I got as blitzed as I could possibly get; packed my bags, stashing pills as I went; and checked myself into a detox/psychiatric unit at a hospital. And it wasn't just any hospital; it was the hospital where my mother was employed.

I remember waiting to be processed, sitting with my two best friends and my mother—my mother, who felt like a stranger to me and against whom I was harboring many resentments. I was clutching a bag of brownies my mother had made for me and trying to keep my eyes open through my self-induced drug haze.

When it was finally my turn, only my mother went with me, and as it turned out, she knew most of the staff attendants in the unit I was assigned to. My mother introduced me to every single one of them, announcing proudly and loudly: "This is my daughter!" again and again.

I have never been so blown away. Why was she not embarrassed of me? My mother's apparent pride floored me.

I don't remember much from that particular day, except the way those brownies tasted; the comfort I had in knowing I had secretly sneaked drugs into a detox facility; and that for the first time in a long time, my mother had shown up and stood up for me.

I got out of detox with no intention of staying sober. I went straight back to using, only this time more discreetly. I quit my job, and my mother was back in my life. I was ready to start over—or at least not end up like before.

My father called a few days after I left the hospital and asked me to have lunch with him. I agreed, and the next day I met with him and his girlfriend. They were so all over each other, it hurt my stomach. I hated her. I hated him. I hated the way my father talked to me like a child when he was with her, but like a woman when he wasn't. I was jealous of her. I shouldn't have been, but I so desperately was.

Lunch that day was the last time I ever interacted with my father on a personal level. And I didn't see him again for *years*. They got married (supposedly) and pregnant and packed up and moved out of state. There was no good-bye, no forwarding address, no anything. He was gone.

Once again I was torn about how to feel. I should have felt relieved, but why did I feel so sad? My head would spin and spin; I was consumed with love and hate and ultimately shame. For at this point, at age eighteen, I had still never spoken about the abuse. I was drowning—screaming for help—yet others just looked right through me.

My solution was to get high. Being high and drunk made me forget that I was drowning, made me feel like I could breathe. So I pushed more and more, because the same amount of whatever I was doing no longer granted me the satisfaction of not feeling anything.

And this is when I found the needle.

It came to me at a time when I felt I needed it. I perceived the needle as my lover; because I so desperately fell in love with and craved its very essence.

When the drugs wore off and the sickness came, I felt dirty. Not just from the drug-induced life I was living, but from inside my very being. Dirty all the way to my core. No matter how many showers I took, or how hard I scrubbed—the dirt, the filth, the shame would not go away.

I made a decision.

I called my mother and asked her point-blank what she knew about my father and the abuse. She did not by any means seem shocked or surprised that I was asking; and she answered all my questions to the best of her ability. She said there were always the signs—and that she may have suspected it at times—but she just could never believe it to be true.

Talking to my mother about my one huge, big dirty secret made everything too real for me. See, for so many years, we had walked around it like it was not there. It was the stench-ridden elephant in our living room. Now, after eighteen years of walking around the elephant, saying, "There is no elephant. I see no elephant. I smell no elephant"—to *talk* about the elephant was emotionally overwhelming.

So I did what I did best: stuffed all my feelings back down with a mind-altering substance. Except this time the drugs and the alcohol were not working the way they used to. I still felt the pain, the sting, of my elephant becoming real.

At this point I knew I needed help. I went back to the hospital and detoxed, but this time I stayed with it and went to rehab for an additional thirty days. This was my first introduction to a twelve-step program. And let me tell you, I shined.

This is the problem: I know how to say anything you want me to. I know how to look so perfect and put together. And I know how to keep secrets. I have been doing it my entire life. I said all the right words, did all the work, excelled, had others looking up to me, impressed my counselors, spoke at the meeting.

And the day I was released—the moment I was alone—I consumed an entire bottle of pills.

That's the problem, you see. It's that I'll put myself together so perfectly—the hair, the makeup, the clothes—and act with such precise etiquette and manners due to my upbringing, that no one even suspects I'm screaming bloody murder on the inside. No one knows I'm drowning. No one knows I'm planning to kill myself as soon and as fast as I can.

At this point, I decided to move once again, and that this would fix all my problems. So I packed my things and moved out to the West Coast. The problem with *that* was that *I* followed me. No matter how far I ran, place to place, city to city, state to state, I was still the same miserable person, consumed with a pain so great, so deep, it consumed me.

In California, I checked into another treatment program. But I failed to comply with the rules and was kicked out. This is when I met my second love (the first being drugs and alcohol, of course).

This one's name was Brad.

I met Brad within the rooms of my sobriety program and immediately moved in with him. I loved him fiercely and deeply—even when he became emotionally and physically abusive with me.

You see, I had never been hit before. And in a strange way, I almost welcomed it. It was an abuse I could take. It was an abuse that was explainable. And it was an abuse that physically healed.

After the latest detox, I was no longer using drugs, but had begun using alcohol to the same extent, so there was really no difference. Brad—who drank just as much as I did—would have blackout rage fits at me and do things that were beyond humiliating. He would throw things at me, destroy my belongings, spit on me, hit me, head-butt me, kick me down, and so forth. He would verbally attack me, putting down my looks and criticizing my genitals. Some of the things he called me would haunt me for years.

And more and more parts of me died with every emotional and physical blow I took.

Brad and I rarely had sex, and I was beyond happy about this. He was often unable to perform due to his drinking, and so I endured his rage. I never even considered leaving him, until the night he came home with another girl and not-so-nicely asked me to get out. I packed my bags through tears and left.

Fortunately I had a friend who let me sleep on her couch. I stayed there until I had enough money from working to afford a run-down apartment in a bad neighborhood. I felt more alone than ever and eventually went back to Brad, as unfortunately many of us do. (I did not move back in with him, however, as he was actually living with another girl.)

Within no time, I found out I was pregnant with his child. I was twenty years old and as scared as ever. But this time I was determined to bring my child into this world—even though it had been so unkind to me. I quit drinking, smoking, and doing all drugs; for the first time in a long time I felt I had a purpose.

I called my family back in Louisiana to tell them my news. Their reaction surprised me: my mother expressed anger towards me, and my brother, disgust. I was told that my child would not be accepted into the family and that I was making the biggest mistake of my life.

I felt more than betrayed: I felt shamed. And more alone than ever. I went to Brad (who coincidentally had gotten his current girlfriend pregnant as well), and he was incapable of even caring.

The day the bleeding started, I was taken to the emergency room. At four months, it was determined that my baby's heartbeat was too slow. My baby did not survive, and once again I grieved for days, feeling empty and purposeless.

I lost all will to live, to thrive. I began using cocaine, which eventually turned into smoking speed. I was either high or drunk every waking moment. It was the only way I knew how to exist.

I began doing things and going places I would never have before. I found myself in very bad situations with very bad people; but I didn't care as long as I didn't have to come down. I didn't care whether I was raped or beaten or killed, because I had given up so much. My only existence was that pipe.

I bounced from place to place, job to job, until I could not keep a job and no longer had anywhere to go. I started sleeping in my car and eventually a vacant house. After some time of this, I decided I no longer wanted to live. Getting high was no longer enough for me.

I got a bottle of tequila, a bottle of Tylenol PM, and a bag of speed. I did all of it together to kill myself. As I lay there with my heart racing faster than I knew it should, I gladly welcomed death.

I awoke the next morning, angry to be alive. Angry to see another day of my grim future. You see, I was physically alive, but so dead inside. So much of me had shut down.

So I did what I did best and continued getting high to not feel.

One night, I found myself so strung out I got scared. I drove myself to the emergency room and checked in. The ER doctor who attended to me asked me lots of questions. Of course, I lied to him about being under the influence—but for some odd reason I opened up to him.

My whole story came out to this doctor.

I can't explain it; it just came. I started talking and I couldn't stop. I started to cry. I realized how long it had been since I'd cried, or even talked to somebody other than my drug dealer—let alone tell my story. It felt strange to hear my voice, and even stranger to hear the words I was saying through tears, lying in a blue gown in a sterile hospital room.

I told the doctor about my dad, my family, my pregnancies, Brad, and about not having anywhere to go. The doctor stayed and listened to it all. He had the nurses bring me food, and I ate for the first time since I could remember. He tore up my chart because he knew I could not afford the charges, and he let me stay the night in the emergency room. I was coming down, but for the first time in long time I felt safe. In an uncomfortable plastic hospital bed, I was safe.

The doctor gave me his number and told me to call him when I woke up and left the hospital.

I almost didn't call.

I was very wary of what he wanted from me.

But I called him. He told me that his sister was on the board of directors for a program called Pathways to Independence. He said that if I was serious about turning my life around and had the desire to go to school, he could get me an interview. I gladly accepted, and an interview was set up for me with the director of the program and his wife.

I was very excited about this program called Pathways. But also apprehensive. As always, I was unsure of their motives. I showed up for my interview loaded, and I told my story and answered their questions.

I realize, now, how I must have looked. And just how much of a risk they took with me, given that I was completely unstable and still using. Dave Bishop accepted me into Pathways, and I can honestly say that he, along with the ER doctor, saved my life.

What Pathways did for me, to this very day, still blows me away.

First things first, I had to get sober. So I went once again into a treatment program—this time for six months. Immediately after treatment, Pathways provided a therapist, whom I met with twice a week.

They helped me rent an apartment—a place of my own—and gave me a car. All my classes, books, and school supplies were paid for. I had doctors, including a dentist, optometrist, and gynecologist, whom I could go to free of cost. I had a mechanic to work on my car. And I was honored enough to have as my mentor, Dave Bishop, the Pathways founder.

I was overwhelmed by all that Pathways gave me, and it took me a long time to realize that they truly did not want anything in return, other than for me to succeed. I stumbled upon Pathways at a time when I had completely given up not only on myself, but on other people. I honestly did not know there were still good people and goodness in the world.

Unfortunately, even this time having such a great purpose and so much to lose, I was once again unable to stay sober.

I was working with an amazing therapist who was firm yet loving with me; but I was still unable to talk about my past—about my father—without feeling very much out of control. So I began using alcohol to stuff and numb my feelings.

I am sorry to say that I used and drank and hid it dishonestly for a very long time.

I drank extremely heavily. I drank vodka so that no one would smell it, and I poured it into water bottles so I could take it everywhere with me and no one would notice. I drank from the moment I woke up to the moment I'd black out; and then I'd start all over again. I drank alone in my apartment, day after day, night after night. I drank before work, school, and therapy—the whole time carrying off the persona that I was sober.

I was a miserable, yet somehow functioning, drunk. I drank so much, but you wouldn't even know it. I was still attending my twelve-step meetings under false pretenses. I stashed alcohol everywhere and had an intense fear of running out. Finally, I began having seizures and health problems, and others started to catch on.

I jeopardized all that I had with Pathways, and they gave me an ultimatum. But it was an opportunity, and I took it.

I left the state—and Pathways—temporarily, and went to an intensive treatment facility in Arizona to work on my addictions and abuse. After two months there, it was recommended that I relocate to another facility in Florida to continue work specifically on my trauma.

So I got on a plane to the East Coast, with a layover in Las Vegas. The result was one that to this day I never want to forget: I never got on that plane to Florida the day of the layover—nor the next day or the ones to follow. I spent four days in a motel room in Las Vegas, drunk from morning until night...until I couldn't tell you if it was morning or night anymore.

On my third day of continuous intoxication, I couldn't put myself "together" enough to go to the bars; I was still so concerned about how I looked on the outside. So I decided to proceed to the nearest liquor store to buy that bottle I needed so badly and then to crawl back to my motel room. But for some reason I couldn't find a liquor store in downtown Vegas. So I had to keep walking. And walking. I had blisters on my feet that were exceptionally painful and began bleeding. Every single step I took in my own blood was excruciating as I trudged those blocks and blocks, searching for a store.

At this very moment of this very day, I knew beyond a shadow of a doubt that I would walk miles and miles if I had to, because I *needed* that bottle in that brown paper bag more than anything I have ever known. For the first time in all my years, I knew and realized alcohol's cunning grip on me. It possessed my heart and soul more than I had ever allowed myself to realize.

So I vowed to drink the bottle of vodka I purchased, but then to get on that airplane to Florida and rehab to finally get sober.

I made two more trips to that same store. I did the walk of shame and carried back my bottle in my brown paper bag.

I reached a point in my intoxication that the room spun too fast and out of control and I needed to vomit out all the alcohol that I needed and yearned for, which was poisoning me to a deathly point. I was not able not walk, only crawl, producing rug burns up and down my arms.

And I lay there in my hole of a motel room with the shades drawn, not knowing where exactly I was or even the day. Not one person I knew was able to reach me or even knew where I was located. As I lay in my shame, covered in vomit and blood, with scuffed up arms and sickness so great and vast, I did something I hadn't done in twenty years: I prayed.

Because at *that* moment, I realized just how sick I was. I realized how much I wanted to die and how close I was to succeeding. So I prayed a simple and very short prayer, asking for help.

Consequently, I did get on that plane to Florida. And to this day, that was the last time I ever put a drink or mind-altering substance into my body.

At age twenty-four, I entered my eighth facility. But this time I gave it *all* I had. Because I already knew that where I was headed was not pretty. I spent an entire year learning to live, because I had no idea how to. I needed the structure I was given, and I needed the therapy I was provided.

Little by little, I began to come alive. I started talking about things in short bits—nothing ever came all at once—and I experienced short bits of relief. It was only when I was able to see how *truly* broken I was—how much I had lost, how much I had endured, how much I had self-inflicted—that I was able to put some of the pieces back together.

At age twenty-four, I woke up. I opened my eyes for the first time and saw *me*. I saw all that I had spent years trying not to see. And even though it hurt—instead of turning away, instead of closing my eyes and going silent, I finally walked forward with my head up and eyes open.

I came to find out that my father had a daughter with his now ex-wife. My mother was contacted regarding the custody battle going on for my half-sister, who was then five years old. My father's ex-wife feared him getting *any* custody or overnight stays with my sister and asked if my mother or I could be of assistance to her.

So I went to court and testified against my father.

This was the hardest thing I have ever done in my entire life. But it was the best thing as well. I stood up for myself, spoke the truth, and was heard. I saw my father for the first time in seven years, and I sat on the witness stand and told my story right in front of him. He was looking me straight in the eye, and I did not look down. I held my head up high. I spoke loud and I spoke clearly words I had been screaming inside for years. I told the judge all the things my father had done to me, in detail, with a stenographer making it public record. And I endured cross-examination.

I am sad to report that the judge ruled in my father's favor. The judge deemed that I was unstable and that my history of drug and alcohol abuse impaired my judgment and memory. He also stated that the one clear and vivid memory I had testified to (when I was eighteen years old in Portugal) did not qualify in the courtroom because it had occurred on international soil and when I was no longer a minor.

My father was granted partial custody without supervision, and that is how it stands to this day.

My heart broke the day I found out.

But no judge can take away what I got *back* that day. I stood up for myself and faced my biggest fear. And as I result, I got *me*.

Today I am alive, as a sober, strong woman in recovery. Today I am more and more okay in my own skin. Today my body is not so heavy, and today I can hold my head up high. Today I have a purpose and a wonderful life beyond anything I could have dreamt for myself.

I am back full-time in Pathways. I have decided to pursue the medical field. I never thought I was worth anything, or capable enough to become a doctor, but through Pathways I am now able to chase my dreams.

I also have an amazing, healthy relationship with my mentor, Dave, who has loved me unconditionally through all of this. He has in many ways become my father, and he has taught me what real love is—how a father *should* love a daughter.

I am proud to say that my mother is a wonderful part of my life today. She is in a wonderfully healthy relationship but also so independent and strong herself, as she has grown so much in her own therapy and support meetings. Whereas my greatest fear before was to become like her, today I admire her and would be honored to become a woman such as she.

I do not attend or participate in any kind of church, as I am personally not in favor of organized religion. But I do believe. I believe with all my heart in prayer. I believe in the goodness in others. I believe each and every one of us has a purpose and a path. And I believe—for the first time ever—in myself. My path and my journey have only begun. You see, now I am not only surviving; I am thriving.

I still have my bad days, days I want use or drink, days I want to hide and close my eyes again, days I want to give up—but *working through it,* I *get* through it. And this time not alone. I know I still have so much more to do, but I am so grateful for this path that I am on.

Today if you see me, I'm the one with a twinkle and so much depth in my eyes, because I am so fully present in my body and so excited for the life that lies ahead of me. Today if you meet me, I'm the one wearing a small purple heart around my neck, which symbolizes that I was wounded but that I was so brave.

Today I no longer go to the stars, because today I carry them within me. Today I shine.

Today I am healing and I am whole.

Now I breathe in and I breathe out, at peace with myself and the world around me.

This is my story, this is my truth.

The Last Strike

"I was brought into this world by alcohol, anger, and hostility... eventually I landed a four-year prison sentence with an added bonus of two strikes."

—Paige

I feel shame, guilt, sadness, regret, and a little crazy when I tell and hear my own story.

There is not one moment I am proud of, or one memory in which I was really happy inside. I was always scared and angry, and looking for ways to express it.

My story begins before I was even born. There was no plan for me to be brought into this world, and I was reminded of this throughout my life.

I was conceived in Yosemite Park. My mother was in her tent, sleeping or getting ready to sleep (I try not to remember the details), and my father—who'd had too much to drink—wanted to have sex with her.

She didn't want to, so he raped her.

Nine months later, here I come—unwanted, unplanned, with resentments already placed on me by my "caretakers." Almost on a daily basis, I was called an idiot child, asshole, slut, bitch, and shit-for-brains…

I'm the third of four children. I am the "accident." I don't know if my brother after me was planned, but I do know he wasn't the product of what I was.

My mom had become pregnant again when I was about a year old—that's also when she found out that my father was cheating on her with the woman who is now my stepmother. He came home drunk one night, and she kicked him out of the house, hosed him off on the front lawn, and told him not to come back.

My parents' whole thing was always a mess; from the time they got together in high school. And they were *both* drinking that time in Yosemite.

My father was gone for seven years after that, and during that time he got married.

My father was never *physically* abusive—he just wasn't there. There was more nonexistence than abuse—I mean, I *was* just a year old when he left.

It's kind of funny how the story of my "origin" came out. I remember being at the Orange County Fair. We were walking through the vendor booths, and one stand had these little buttons that said, "I'm a Wanted Child."

My mother grabbed *three* of them!

It's funny now, but it wasn't funny then. That's when I found out how I came to be—that I wasn't a "wanted one." I don't know if she was trying to be funny or was serious, but that's how she ended up telling me. I was between five and seven years old.

And I was always reminded of it: *You're not supposed to be here.*

After my father left, my mother worked two jobs to try and support us, so my sister ended up being our caretaker. I think my sister has suffered a lot from this.

When my mom *was* home, she was physically violent. She came from an alcoholic father and an abusive mother, so she knew no other way to be. I do love my mother, but I was severely damaged by her. She had no resources, no help, a history of abuse, and was in no state of mind to raise her children. She was physically and psychologically and emotionally abusive.

I can never remember exactly *why* we were in trouble, but I remember always feeling like I was. Not one day went by in which someone was not turned into a punching bag or told some damaging things. She would hit us with her hands or a belt. She would punch, kick, throw things, shake us, or throw us into walls. And I do remember, vividly, how much it hurt.

And if one of us dared cry about it, we surely suffered the consequences.

Once, my younger brother had a black eye and we pulled him from school so my mother wouldn't get in trouble for how he looked. We were *all* pulled out of school at times so nobody would call child services on us.

But so much of it was between my older brother and my mother. He suffered the most from the abandonment of my father, and he started using pretty heavy drugs at age eleven or twelve. This created a lot of fighting between him and my mom.

I was the quiet child—at first.

I didn't cry when I was born; my mother thought I was a good kid. But I've learned that it was because there was so much abuse going on that I just sat back and watched.

Then I became a problem child.

I couldn't stand to see my siblings getting beat up. I felt the need to rescue them. So I would cause a scene to draw the attention onto myself. I would scream as loud as I could within a foot of my mother's face, and I would try to pull her off of them. When that didn't work, I threatened to call the police.

When I finally *did* get the "attention," my mom made *sure* I regretted it! She would hit and kick me, saying I did this to myself. Then, when I did not stop crying, she would pin me down on the floor and pinch my nose with one hand and cover my mouth with the other until I passed out.

Interestingly to me, the most damaging and long-lasting was the emotional and psychological abuse. Because of the daily hideous insults, I felt worthless and stupid. I hated myself.

The rest of my family wasn't doing much better.

My little brother hit his head against a wall in school and wound up in a coma. He came out of it, but sustained permanent brain damage.

Meanwhile, my older brother became *extremely* violent. He was so angry and hurt, the only way he knew how to handle it was to take it out on whoever was present. He'd just run into the room and beat the shit out of you. He beat the shit out of *all* of us—even my mother.

My mom kept trying to put him into boys' homes, but he would stay for a bit and then run away. And every time he showed back up, he was even *more* angry and hostile. It was really scary.

It got to the point that my mother told us not to let him in the house. He showed up outside my bedroom window one day when I was about five and asked to be let in. When I wouldn't, he proceeded to punch in the window! I remember lying on my bed as glass showered over me. He got in, and we all paid for it!

So that's how home was for my first seven years of life. We all fought like crazy.

I was in the fourth grade when I started to smoke pot and ditch school. I made my younger brother ditch, too. We never got in trouble for it, though—I learned how to forge excuse notes pretty early on.

My dad came back into the picture around that time.

I called him Clark—not "Dad" or "Father," just Clark.

Seven years earlier, my stepmother, Carrie, had actually given him an ultimatum: *Either me or your kids.* And he'd chosen Carrie. But I think he resurfaced because my older brother got sent to a treatment home, and my mother wanted financial help. I think that's how they wound up back in contact.

Next thing we knew, one or two of us at a time wound up living with him, a few cities away. "You just take turns going there and back," my mom said to us.

I was the first to go.

I actually thought it might be *good* to get away from my mother. But I hated it. I wasn't comfortable there. They were never abusive, but Carrie is manipulative and she lies.

Carrie is a "born again" Christian and a teacher. But she is very, *very* fake and presents a completely different picture to the outside world. Behind closed doors, it was whole other story, what with taking pills and so forth. And she and Clark were racist—talking shit about people, using racial slurs and things. It made me sick.

I was more used to up-front things—even up-front fighting. I wasn't used to being talked about behind my back. I would hear Carrie saying, "*Paige did this," "Paige did that."* I never really understood her anger towards me, but the feeling was *very* mutual.

My stepmother liked fancy things; but when it came time to get us school clothes, there was of course no money.

And she would force me to dress how *she* wanted me to. It was weird—*uncomfortably* weird. When I was in the fifth grade, she made me a French maid's costume for Halloween that was inappropriately revealing. I was humiliated and teased.

Things never felt right. Carrie would compare us kids to one another and talk horribly about my mother. At one point she wanted my help to sue my mom for back child support. I think she was trying to pull us apart and get us to hate our mother. But I was too young then to really figure all this out.

One issue occurred when Carrie asked me to move to a city several hours away, with her and Clark. I said no, I didn't want to leave my mom.

Carrie wanted me to call *her* "Mom," which I wouldn't do.

My one saving grace was that I was doing well in school. When I focused, I was a straight-A student. And when I was studying, everyone left me alone. I focused everything I had on my homework and essentially hiding from the world. I did well, but at the expense of not having anyone to talk to. Isolating myself was my way of dealing with things and people—and I was doing something that people considered *good.*

But then Carrie decided to start *forcing* me outside to play with the neighbor kids. As uncomfortable as our house was, I felt even *less* comfortable outside with other kids. But I would get in trouble or even grounded if I didn't.

I did not trust anybody, nor did I want to associate with them. So I got in trouble for being timid. My behavior was rude and disgusting, according to my stepmother.

So I put on a smile and acted like I was supposed to, while I was literally dying inside. I constantly had suicidal and homicidal thoughts.

I had first been abused, and then been abandoned here. Everyone tells me I have abandonment issues from my father leaving, but I honestly feel that's not the case. It was *this*—being abandoned at *his* house. My mom would come and visit, and I would beg her not to leave me there. And when she did, I would lock myself in the bathroom and cry.

Then things changed.

I started my drinking.

I was in junior high, and it was my turn to live with Clark and Carrie again. It was *terrible* moving back and forth between two completely different environments. Living with my mother was one thing, but Clark and Carrie were something else. And I never understood why they took *me* there, when I had siblings who *wanted* to go. Looking back, I suppose we *had* to switch for child support reasons.

My sister was with me, and one day we asked my dad if we could try a drink. He said yes. He made us shots of White Russians, and I liked them. They were warm going down and I got fuzzy-headed. I had quite a few and kept asking for more. He finally told me no.

From then on, I started sneaking them from him and also took to making my own. He would make himself both White Russians and Black Russians, and they became my drinks too. *Doubles.*

By then I was in the seventh grade, and I would drink vodka out of a Styrofoam cup on the way to school. One time, I was in one of my classes and I was already drunk. I had my sweater on my desk for a pillow and my head was down. I reeked of alcohol and I started puking. They sent me home, but I never got any lectures or help or anything. Back then, I don't think they knew what to do with kids like me. I guess there weren't that many kids drunk in the seventh grade.

Plus, I was living with a cop and a teacher! So I should have been alright—right?

Oops—did I mention that Clark was a *police officer*? Yes, a cop! A cop who raped his wife and was an alcoholic—and more.

A couple years later, I saw Clark having dinner with some woman—a woman he was cheating on my stepmother with. He's just a bastard all the way around. But I've run into people who've been arrested by him, and they all actually *like* him. He has a good sense of humor and I think he hides behind that. Everybody loves him—but they aren't related to him. He was a law enforcement officer, but he didn't discipline his own children.

I think Clark and Carrie *knew* that I was smoking and drinking, but because they were both doing it too, they couldn't say much. They just told me I shouldn't, and that was the end of that. I think they were trying to be my friend, but it didn't work.

Things got worse when my older brother came to live with us. He was still a mess.

He used to stalk me while I was taking a bath or shower. He would try to get me to touch him in inappropriate parts. During a family therapy session we later had at a treatment center, my brother apologized for it, and Carrie told us that she had always known something was going on. *But she never did or said anything!*

There were times when my brother was so violent and angry, he had to be tied to a tree. Nobody knew what to do with him. He'd been to treatment homes, but he kept running away. The environment was chaotic.

I became passive-aggressive. It was *my* way of reaching out. I would write "Carrie is a pig" on the bathroom mirror so that when she took a shower it would show up. I hated that she was a "fake" Christian—I knew what Christians were and she definitely wasn't it. (Of course, this was when we were all sharing a bathroom because their new master suite was being built—but we still had no money for school supplies!)

One time—actually a few times—I sprayed hair spray on my bedspread and lit it on fire to spell out "666." Doing stupid shit like that was my way of getting back at Carrie. It felt so good to see her expression; it was a huge slap in her face, which I inflicted without physically touching anyone this time.

Carrie actually threatened to hit me once—and have my father do the same—but little did she know that it was a welcoming invitation. I was much more comfortable with that than any kid should be. I laughed at her, and she just stormed off. She must have thought I was Satan's child.

But with my brother being up-in-your-face violent, she and Clark *really* had their hands full.

When I finally reached my fill of torture living at Clark and Carrie's, I ran away.

My mother had remarried and I called my stepfather. I think this was actually right after he and my mom broke up. He came and got me and took me back my mom's. Shockingly, she was not mad *and* she let me move back in with her. I think she finally understood that I would literally rather *die* than go back to Clark and Carrie's. She never made me go back after that.

I don't remember how long my mom and stepdad stayed together, but I remember him being very nice to me when I did see him. I was one of his favorites. My older brother, on the other hand, broke both of his legs at one point! Ultimately, I think we were too much for my stepdad and mom, and they broke apart from the stress of it.

My mom essentially gave up on me and my little brother. She already had enough problems with the other ones. My sister went to live with my aunt. Both my brothers went back to Clark's. And I stayed at my mom's.

My mom *did* pull me out of school and put me into a treatment home once, when I was in eighth grade. She thought I was on drugs. I had some of the same behaviors as my older brother, so she assumed I was doing some of the same things.

I was drinking all the time. I wasn't coming home. I stayed up late. At the center, they would do blood tests on me at four o'clock in the morning. But the alcohol was good enough for me—I didn't need drugs.

I did get some schooling there and some therapy. I also wound up meeting my very first boyfriend.

That, too, became a mess.

He was violent and crazy. He was seventeen and I was about fourteen.

After a few weeks, the money ran out, so I left the treatment center; also, the therapist said I wasn't "opening up," so it was useless for me to stay there.

I started high school at yet another new school. I was somewhat of a tomboy, as it was comfortable and easy to hide behind. I did poorly in academics, but great at athletics. I regret to say that had I continued, I would have gotten scholarships for college. But it is what it is.

In high school, I *did* start smoking marijuana in addition to drinking all the time. I don't remember too much of it.

I started doing so poorly in school and getting into so much trouble drinking that I got transferred to another high school. The principal there told the other students to stay away from me.

At that point, I decided I was going to drop out, and my mom let me. She was struggling financially, so she told me I could stay if I got a job.

So I got a job, and I gave almost all the money to my mother. But life was going my way. I didn't have to go to school; I could drink and smoke when I wanted to.

My mother was still abusive—she'd beat me up for the stupidest things. But it was all funny to me now. Plus, I was bigger, so I could fight back. We beat the shit out of each other. But I preferred that to the sneakiness of Carrie. The fights I could handle.

I actually moved in with my crazy boyfriend and his mother for a little while. His mother was a wild Mormon and we *all* fought like crazy—*physically* fighting.

I ended up moving back in with my mother.

So now I'm a high school dropout, but I do have a job. It was at Chuck E. Cheese, but that job was probably the best thing that happened to me for a very long time. I met Larry there; he was actually my boss. He has become the best friend I've ever known. I consider him more like family than anybody else I've ever had in my life.

We started dating and eventually moved in together. Larry came from a really good family, so I didn't know why he liked me. It was kind of weird. His family was *normal*—no abuse or anything!

I would bring him over to my mother's, and by then she had become a pagan. She would have rocks laid out in the shape of a pentagram, and these robed men and other people in black robes would be milling around the house. We would walk in and I could see Larry looking *around.* It was hard to explain!

We later moved into Larry's parents' house. He didn't completely understand my deal, and I couldn't quite understand being normal. I continued to drink.

I had quit my job when we started dating, and now I started going to clubs.

One of my best friends was a black man named Calvin. He was a skateboarder I'd met in the neighborhood before going into treatment. We used to just hang out and drink and do stupid shit.

Now we went to raves and clubs together. And I started doing acid—pretty much five nights a week. I'm very surprised I'm not completely fried from that. I drank and did acid every night. I got a job in a coffee shop and I had to be there at four-thirty in the morning, so I would go straight from the clubs to work.

I was just too wild for Larry, so we broke up. I moved out of his place, back in with my mom. She had only one bedroom at the time but she let me live there. I was still doing the whole not-sleeping-all-night thing. I did that for a long time.

I found myself just detached. I wasn't much for crying; I was simply *detached.* I really didn't care much about anybody or anything. Even Larry, who was the best thing that ever happened to me—I treated him like shit. And I did that to a lot of guys. I learned how to be mean, and I did to people what people did to me. I wasn't promiscuous or anything, but I wound up being mean.

I don't remember much emotion except for that same sense of abuse and abandonment—like back when I would lock myself in Clark and Carrie's bathroom and cry.

From day one, I had become used to the fighting all around me. That's what was normal. When it wasn't in any of my relationships, I brought it. It was much more comfortable for me.

So I was doing acid, working at the coffee shop, and coming home to my mother's house and camping out in her living room.

The whole dancing thing *was* fun. The friends I had then were actually good; I'm back in touch with some of them now—and some are even sobering up, too.

I wound up living with my sister and brother-in-law for awhile and then I moved into my own place.

And this is where Calvin comes into play.

Calvin and I were inseparable. Along with another girl, Shannon, we went everywhere together—all the clubs and everywhere.

But Calvin turned out to be the "Costa Mesa Rapist"—an infamous criminal.

The three of us were at a club. We took turns driving when we went out; the person who would drive home was the one who could see the "straightest." I'm ashamed of how much I drank and drove, and I'm grateful that I did not die or, especially, kill someone else.

This night, Shannon and I drank; Calvin didn't—so he was kind of out-of-sight, out-of-mind. After the club ended at two or three a.m., Shannon and I went out to Calvin's car. We couldn't find him, so we kept setting off his car alarm.

About an hour later, he finally showed up, but it was kind of weird: he had puke all over him—he reeked of it—but he really hadn't been drinking.

He wound up getting arrested.

I found out a few days later when the police called me.

Apparently, a man fitting Calvin's description had brutally attacked a woman with a knife after the club closed. He pulled her into a car and probably would have raped her, except that she puked on him and got away.

They told me Calvin was in jail and that I was the only person he would agree to talk to.

I said no.

Calvin's face was all over news after that because of the string of events he had evidently been involved in. He had also been exposing himself at high schools. The police had been searching for him for a long time.

I was very pissed off at him, and I didn't want to believe it for a while. But it did turn out to be true. And apparently he had been doing this for a long time. Getting caught was probably a relief for him, as well as for everybody else.

I guess the reason I didn't go see him is because I was afraid that the accusations *were* true and that he would admit something to me that I didn't want to hear.

At one point, a friend of mine told me that he'd been watching the news with Calvin when a police sketch of the Costa Mesa Rapist came up. "That looks like *you*!" he said to Calvin, and they both just laughed.

Calvin ended up dying in jail—people with his charges *usually* get killed while incarcerated. He was let into the general population and that's never good. He was strangled and was on the floor for quite a while before the guards got to him. By the time they got him to the medics, he was dead.

I didn't cry when I heard he'd been killed. I guess I felt it was somewhat deserved. But while I wasn't devastated, I did feel betrayed. And I felt bad for his parents—losing a son.

I looked back and saw that Calvin was very protective of me. If I left a club without him, he would follow me home and sit outside until the next day. I guess he was protecting me from people like himself.

He probably saved me from putting myself in some really bad situations. He would never let me leave drunk, even though *I* had no fear at all and would leave drunk and go anywhere.

When I lived with Larry, Larry wouldn't worry about me if I was with Calvin, because he knew how protective Calvin was.

After all of that with Calvin, I moved out of my little place and back in with my sister. I got a job at a nearby brewery. It was perfect. That was my dream job: I was drinking all the time, and there was a big party scene that I was a part of for way too long.

I loved being intoxicated and I loved my courage when drunk. I was a master manipulator, and I was abusive to the men I allowed in my life. I got a kick out of degrading and hurting others.

Then I met a guy who was in a pretty popular band. He was strung out on heroin—something he didn't hide from anyone. So here, *I* wind up with a man who *I* had to try to sober up and drag off to shows so that he could play.

And he was doing some other bad stuff.

He needed me to take him somewhere once to "take care of business." He came back with a bag with somebody's finger in it. I was down for doing pretty much anything, but I didn't get a lot of details. I learned later that the finger apparently belonged to a child molester—again, I didn't get all the *details.* He got paid a lot of money to do that kind of stuff.

When we went to hotel rooms, he usually did heroin, but sometimes speed as well. All I did was drink.

Until this one time, when I was coming down from the worst hangover ever—although they were all pretty bad. My friend Shannon, who still went everywhere with me, said, "Here, this will take care of the hangover..."

She gave me speed—and it worked. It definitely got rid of the hangover.

I didn't do it again for a day or two, but then I went to a hotel with another friend. I did speed again and something happened in my head. Something snapped. It was like an aneurysm or something. It was the worst pain I've ever experienced. I thought I was dying.

By now, my boyfriend was on the run from the law for all the shit he was doing, so he couldn't take me to the hospital. "Just take me home!" I told him.

I got out of the car and passed out on the lawn. I couldn't move. My head was exploding. So my boyfriend put me back in the car and took me to the hospital. He had to hide from all the policemen around there.

They knew I was loaded, so they gave me some Demerol or something to quiet me down, and then they sent me on my way.

I went through two very bad weeks because of that one incident. The speed put me through hell and dropped me to my knees. But I didn't go to any doctors or anything to find out what *really* happened.

And it didn't stop me.

After the horror of the two weeks went away, I did speed again immediately and smoked it more and more. It was a downward spiral. I continued to hang around with the band guy (although he wasn't really playing in the band during that time, because the law was on his tail), doing more stupid shit. He'd get mad at people who were giving me speed, but we were *all* getting high and everybody knew about it.

So we're all on speed, and Shannon is dating some guy named "Spider" who lives in a manufacturing warehouse kind of place with a bunch of people who are disgusting—the whole place was disgusting. Everybody in there was getting loaded.

So we pretty much moved in there.

We kind of just stopped living. Stopped having a home in general—even though I never really felt like I had one anyway.

We were anywhere and everywhere.

I really only did speed for a couple of years, but I went down fast and I went down hard.

I hate admitting it, but I started hanging out with people in white supremacist gangs—men and women. This was not my style (my own best friend had been black), but I'd found a group of people who all hated themselves and others as much as I did. We were all perfect for each other.

And they had the *good* drugs. And plenty of them. I started doing the same things as these people: stealing cars and breaking into houses. I wasn't afraid to do *anything*. I became a liar, a cheat, and a thief, with no conscious concern for my victims.

Chris, my soon-to-be codefendant, and I would steal the cars. He knew who to give them to. He'd tell me go get this one and take it here. Sometimes we would simply walk into a house and grab the car keys. We would go through open windows, opened doors, or through the garage.

When we broke into houses, we were mostly looking for car keys and things like phones or jewelry—anything of value. Wallets were good because Chris could do things with IDs. Any cars that were open, we would go through them.

Most of the time, I stayed outside while Chris went into the houses; I'd be the lookout. But I was part of all of it.

One night we went to the house of some couple he knew. I'll never forget walking into that house. It was one of the most disgusting moments of my life.

I hadn't showered for a couple of days and the couple had a dog—*and fleas by the millions*. I'm allergic to fleas. I had sat down, and when I stood up my legs were black with fleas. They bit me so many times, I was about to pass out. My legs were swollen and bloody and disgusting.

Places like this were what my environment had become. I was covered in fleas and I knew I had hit bottom. I was fed up with everything, and I just didn't care. All I was doing was getting high. That was my life, and I would rather have died. I didn't know what I needed to do, but I needed to go. I think some part of me even *wanted* to get caught.

I got my two strikes in that one night.

I said, "Let's go out with a bang. I'm up for anything. Where are we going?"

Where we went was to the hills of a well-to-do area—to rob houses.

The first house we targeted was actually the home of a friend we had given our German shepherd to. This one I feel *really* bad about. I feel bad about everything I did, but this one in particular.

Chris entered the garage. The garage was attached to the house, and since the house had people in it, this was later considered a violent strike. We stole a bunch of stuff from there—from our friend.

Then we went and hit a bunch *more* houses. It was like a spree.

We *both* got two strikes because of that night—one night that produced twenty or thirty felonies.

But we didn't get *caught* that night.

Prior to that night, I'd done a few terms in the county jail—all for stupid stuff: stolen property, using fake IDs, possession of drug paraphernalia, things like that.

But shortly *after* that night, I was caught driving a stolen car—someone we knew had reported it stolen. I actually *wasn't* the one who had stolen it, but I wound up getting like thirty days.

I was serving my time at "the farm" (the county's minimum-security jail) when the detectives came and wanted to know if knew about "anything else."

I ended up telling them *everything.*

Yup, I told on myself. This is how I got caught. They would have never known, but I wound up telling on myself because I just couldn't live like this anymore.

Of course, they already *suspected;* my description was out there. I really should have been stopped long ago. But they had no proof.

Until I told them everything.

They took me out of the farm real quick and put me back in the higher-security jail. And they called Clark.

Clark was still on the police force (he's retired now), and it was a respect thing that he'd always get the first phone call when I was arrested. Not that he did anything. He didn't come to see me or try to use his clout. And I didn't care anyway.

Chris got arrested around the same time I did. He was also in a stolen car, and he passed out—he had been up for days. He ran somebody over and was charged with vehicular manslaughter.

So we were both in jail.

I did not turn him in. I told them everything *I* did, but Chris told on *himself,* too. He even tried to say that he did *everything* to try and save me. He was already facing seven years and strikes, so he was trying to take all my stuff since he figured he was going away forever anyway.

The two of us wound up on the same bus going to the same court for the same charges. They separate you so you really can't see each other, but we saw each other anyway. He slipped me a note, trying to get me to tell my lawyer that he did everything.

But I didn't do that.

I confessed to everything.

I was hit with more charges, of course. They tried to give me eight years at first, but I didn't take it—which meant I'd have to go through a big trial and maybe lose big time. So when they offered me four years with two strikes, I took it.

They're called "silent strikes," which means I didn't hurt anybody physically; but they're serious. And because people were home during the break-in, they do consider the strikes to be violent.

So Chris got seven years and I got four.

And now we both have two strikes.

When the charges and sentencing were all over, I remember feeling relieved. I remember feeling cleansed as I told the detectives *everything.*

I think they felt bad having to charge me with all this. Those cops even came and visited me a couple times just to check on me. First of all, I was a cop's kid, and they all help each other out and all that crap; but I think they really felt sorry for me. And they knew that I was about to be sent away for quite a long time. I didn't have any resentment toward them for that. But I think they felt worse because I was forthcoming and they *had* to use that information against me. The cops actually tried to give me lesser charges because I came forward and confessed—and in the end, the charges *were* lessened.

So now I'm in prison. They sent me to Chowchilla—the state pen. You take the bus ride up there and you get out and they put you in a little room where you get naked and cough and squat over mirrors and all that fancy stuff—*that* was my welcoming committee.

I looked around and there's some fucking mean-looking women there. I'm a little white girl and I'm scared to death. I did know a couple of other prisoners who had come up with me, but nothing was going to make this a fun experience.

They put me in the receiving yard and then a holding cell by myself. That wasn't unusual, because I'm usually "red banded." That means I'm isolated from the general population because I'm a cop's kid. They did that to me in the county where Clark worked—but not where I was arrested.

Once I'm back in the receiving yard, I see a lot of fights, mostly over "girlfriends"—like, "Hey, are you looking at my girlfriend?" There's a lot of "politics."

Then I was sent to the dorm-style living, which has eight-person cells. In the room next to me, some girl was getting raped with a broomstick, so I'm hearing screams and things like that.

The guards don't care. They're having sex with the women there and bringing in drugs and lighters. There are drugs everywhere. It's a fucking mess. Disgusting. So I figure the only thing I'm going to do is read and stick to myself.

Actually, when I was at the farm, because I was a cop's kid, one of the female deputies put me in a GED class. They're supposed to be optional, but she made me do it and I ended up getting my GED. Truth be told, she was a lesbian who had a thing for me—but it worked, and I couldn't have done it without her giving me that push.

I certainly had no intention of getting that GED, but it was the first little "light" towards a brighter future. After that, I started taking all these classes in the county jail and then in prison.

I was just beginning to experience what I would hear Dave Bishop refer to years later as getting a "taste" for better things. I started seeing more that I might be able to turn this around. I didn't want to go back to what I had been doing.

I took health classes—anything I could. I went to twelve-step meetings. I was doing all I could to reach out for help, to talk to people, to figure out how—when I got out—not to go back. I was deathly afraid. I just didn't want to ever go back to prison.

I wouldn't make it again, in there.

It's hard to keep track of people once they're in "the system." The authorities don't notify family members. But somehow Larry found me, and he sent me a letter. He hadn't actually seen me in a long time. He came to visit, and later he said I was "transparent"—I was pale and looked like crap from having no exposure to the sun.

After that, I started talking regularly to my mother and Larry, and then to my sister, and to my brothers afterwards. My mom said I could come stay with her when I got out.

I even sent a letter to Clark and Carrie from jail—just a little "I'm sorry" kind of note. I didn't hear anything back.

After the dorm, I went to "D" yard—that's when you're not in receiving any more. They've *received* you now; you're an official part of the Department of Corrections and Rehabilitation. They put me in a room with this huge Samoan lady named "Insane."

I didn't get undressed. I slept outside my covers. She fought with everybody else in the room.

As soon as I could, I requested to go to fire camp, to get trained as a firefighter. You can request three places. My first choice was fire camp. I just didn't want to be in Chowchilla—that was the *worst* place you could be.

My request got granted at like four in the morning. "You're leaving!" they said.

I got a nice good-bye from Insane: "Don't let me see you back here!"

"I'm *not* coming back here!" I said, and I went off to fire camp.

The California Institute for Women has two-person rooms with a little more space and a lot more freedom, and it's not as disgusting.

And they train you to fight fires.

I damn near died. It's not easy—running up hills and lots of other challenges. But I like physical stuff.

I was there for many months, and it was like fun to me. I got to work a chain saw. I got helicoptered into flames and things like that—an amazing experience. I was in San Diego during the firestorm of 2003. We chopped down dead trees, clearing lines to stop fires.

It's dangerous, but I liked it. Some of it was the adrenaline rush, but so much of it was a focus on something positive.

In total, I was in prison for two years—half of the four-year sentence. It's automatic. If it weren't for the two strikes, I could possibly have served just a quarter of the time. I did my entire second year at fire camp. I was amazed they let me do that.

When I was released, I still had a warrant for an old ticket, so I had to go back to court that same day for the failure to appear. Of course, I'd been in prison and *couldn't* appear, so they let it go.

I was paroled and moved back into my mom's house.

While I was in prison, I had written Larry's mom a letter asking if she knew of any programs I could get involved in when I got out. I wanted to try everything I could to *not* go back to prison.

I wanted to survive.

She had sent me information about Pathways to Independence. But I was still locked up and I didn't have phones or much of anything.

When I got out, I looked at Dave's card for a week or so, but I just didn't call. *This has to be bullshit,* I thought. I started looking for a job.

But Larry's mom told Dave's then-wife about me, who immediately called Dave. Pathways had only two slots available in their new "Pathways to Freedom" program. One had just been filled, and Dave was literally in the middle of interviewing a girl for the second spot. He was ready to accept her, but his wife urged him to meet me before making his decision.

So I talked to Dave, and he told me all these great things Pathways does for women. When we hung up, I told my mom, "I think this is bullshit."

But I went to the interview. My mom drove me.

My autobiography was just one page. I didn't really know what an autobiography was to begin with, so I wrote this brief description of "where I was at." I was desperate.

At the interview, I realized that what Pathways was offering *was* true and real. And for the first time *in years*—through all of this horror—I cried.

I was accepted into Pathways on the spot.

I think they knew that if they didn't take me right away, there was *no way* I was going to make it. I didn't even have any clothes or anything. I came out in my prison jumpsuit and with a little bit of money I'd made in fire camp, and that was it. That's all I had.

Larry came and saw me, and he went to dinner with my mom and me. We ended up dating again, and I moved in with him.

I actually started *working* for Dave—for what was supposed to be a couple weeks, but ended up being about three years. He does construction and I like physical work, so I learned pretty fast. It was interesting, and we got along well. We both have good senses of humor and he was very patient with me.

I didn't really know what to think of all this.

Of course, in Pathways you have to go to school and therapy.

I took my first class at a city college; I think I got a D. I failed all my math courses. Then I took an English and math assessment test and was placed in the lowest math and a class *before* English 100—because I couldn't structure a paragraph or an essay or anything like that.

Dave helped tutor me and tried to get me to know my times tables. He tried *really* hard, but to this day I can't really do them. I can do big equations and statistics now, but I can't do my times tables!

I never took a computer class, but I can type okay now.

Because of my record, I have a lot of roadblocks against things I would *like* to do for a living. For example, I can't teach. I can't do a lot of stuff. It narrows down my options. So I settled for mechanics. I know a lot of convicts who are mechanics, so I figured I could do it, too.

I transferred to a junior college, and I took some psychology and math classes. I spent a lot of time questioning teachers; I was a good student.

I went to school with Kaysie, who was also in Pathways. She wouldn't study, but would do great on tests. *I* have to study my butt off! She's more creative, while I'm more like, "Tell me what you want. That's what you're going to get." I follow directions well.

And that worked for me. I learned what teachers wanted and I learned how to *learn well.* I earned my A.A. degree and graduated with honors.

I had that "taste."

Then some Pathways donors paid for me to get my Drug and Alcohol Certificate in seven fast-paced months at a vocational college. My teacher there was very influential and knew I had something inside me to do great things. She was the first outsider to make me start to believe I *can* do this.

I entered an internship at a rehab center, where I worked forty hours a week for free for three months; then they hired me on. I stayed on there as a drug and alcohol counselor, working with ex-convicts.

At the time, the center was for both females and males; now it's strictly male. Women are difficult to work with. They're extremely smart, so they know how to be sneakier! They would be mean and take advantage of all the men in the program, making them do whatever they wanted. Although the women parolees are much harder to work with than the men, I continue to work with both now.

Next, I was accepted to a Cal State school in the field of Human Services. I had no idea that I would do that—I had no idea I could get my bachelor's degree. I got a 4.0 GPA and I loved it. I loved all my classes and I still talk to many of the teachers.

Some of the teachers are now involved in Pathways. I have introduced them to Dave and have had him speak at the college. They have fallen in love with the program and want to get involved—it's kind of neat to be able to do that.

I worked at the rehab center for about three years. I became the senior counselor there. But I always wanted to work with mental health systems, so I got a job as a case manager in that field. My alcohol and drug counseling studies teacher—the one who had encouraged me—helped me get the opportunity and is now my supervisor. I get to evaluate facilities that house parolees to ensure that these institutions are providing the services promised for appropriate rehabilitation. I have a company car and a company phone. It really *is* my dream job!

I'm a happy person now—I'm not pissed off anymore! The years of therapy worked, although I feel bad for what Dave and Larry had to endure for the first few years. I had to change everything—I had to change from *hating* everybody! You could tell me anything, but if I didn't want to hear it, I would argue or just ignore it.

And I *did* fight a lot. Dave was very patient with me. He knew there were reasons behind why I was acting like this. He knew it before I did. Dave kept saying, "I'm going to love you so you will love yourself." It became a joke that he would try to give me a hug and I would just pat him on the back and walk away. Now I give him *great* hugs!

My mentor treats me like his own daughter. Even with my major anger issues, he never threw me away as most people did—including myself. And his wife is an ideal woman. I have never had a female role model before, and I am grateful for her.

There are so many little things that people just don't see. Dave and my therapist taught me how to be in relationships with people. I didn't know how. It was just trial and error with Larry. Even though we broke up, I love him to death and he'll always be my best friend. I talk to him at least once a week.

I'm in a great relationship now, and we're serious. I still have problems with frustration, but I am able to talk with him, and he listens and does not hold my past against me.

With him, I'm doing things I've never done. I have never cooked for anybody before. I have never really taken care of anybody before. He hurt his ankle recently, and I was *happy* to be doing things that most people do for one another. It's all new to me, but it's very important stuff.

That's one of the most important things that Pathways taught me: to be in healthy relationships. A lot of old friends found me on Facebook and saw that I'm doing well, and they all want to be part of my life again. They're very proud of me.

I have even talked to the guy whose house I broke into. He's now my friend and supports me in my efforts to change my life. It's weird: everybody who was actually *good* in my life, I have them all back.

But it's a little strange to me sometimes. It's like, *What do you want?* But I'm not detached from my feelings now. I don't have a problem trying to communicate. I don't run away from people.

And what I do for a living has taught me *a lot.* I have to practice what I preach. What I try to get *other* people to do, I have to be willing to do too.

I think of all the things that have gone on in my life. I was called an idiot and crazy all my life—and I acted on it. I acted that way, and I turned into what I was being called.

And then I turned the whole thing around. It was very extreme.

Pathways did another incredible thing for me. Seven or so years ago, I started growing a hard bump on my forehead, called an osteoma. It made me look like I got beat up—like someone gave me a *good one*! Even my clients would ask me if I'd gotten into a fight or if my boyfriend had smacked me around.

I talked to Dave about it, and he sent me to the Pathways dermatologist. I was told I needed a plastic surgeon, and the dermatologist said he would ask around for someone who would treat me.

An osteoma is essentially a bone tumor, but not cancerous. It's very rare and not a lot is known about them. We found a surgeon who would see me, and he was very excited—it was his first one! Again, Pathways came through with medical help.

I was also able to get braces because of Pathways, as well as dental implants. In prison, there's just two treatment options for teeth: fill it or pull it.

Now my self-esteem is a million times what was. I don't have the bump on my head and I can smile. *And* I have all my teeth!

I live with my cousin now. I've kind of created my own family, and it's neat how I got to do that. I don't talk to Clark and Carrie by choice. My therapist told me that was *okay*. Everyone else kept saying, "They're your family—you *need* to talk to them." But I *don't* have to. It's very freeing.

I don't talk to *most* of my family right now, actually.

My little brother, especially, has always been kind of a lost child. He's thirty-something, but because of his brain damage, he's mentally more like sixteen. It's sad.

None of my siblings have really fared well.

One of them smokes weed and steals money to buy booze. Another is HIV-positive from a brief bout as a homosexual. Another is doing okay in life, but still has emotional issues and can be mean.

I can't be a part of that right now.

My mom and I are like best friends, though. I've always been her favorite—she's always let me back. We just had a bond. She lives on the other side of the country now, and I try and go out at least once a year to visit her.

She's never actually *apologized* for all she did. Pretty much all she ever says about the past is, "You guys have been through a lot." She still drinks, and healthwise she isn't too well. I think her drinking keeps her from truly feeling emotions about what happened.

I was arrested in March of 2002. I was twenty-five years old.

My "speed years" started at age twenty-three.

I did all sorts of stuff really fast.

Usually it takes people *years* to become that extreme—and to go down that hard! I look around at these people in their fifties and sixties who are still using. I look at women who have been doing speed for ten years and who've maybe gone to jail for thirty days here and there—and I'm like, *Fuck!*

I guess if I'm going to do something, I do it big!

I've done recovery big too.

Today, I am eight years clean and sober.

I have a B.S. in Human Services from Cal State and graduated *magna cum laude*.

I have a CADAC certification to counsel people with a chemical dependency.

I'm an ex-convict who works for the government!

A few days after my Pathways graduation, I told Dave: "I'm shiny now!"

So *much* has changed since those early days. So much has changed because of Pathways.

The Good Girl

"I would do anything, including lie, cheat, and steal."

—Ashley

I was fifteen when I took my first drink of alcohol.

I was with my girlfriend, and I thought her friends were *so* cool—the way they dressed, the way they acted. The way the boys thought they were cute. The way they drank and smoked—both cigarettes and pot.

I didn't think about my alcoholic dad, or my high chances of falling into the same traps as him—all I thought about was wanting to fit in.

Almost instantly, alcohol did for me what it had taken months of extensive work in twelve-step family support meetings to do. I felt pretty, interesting, popular, and fun. I could talk to people without worrying what they were thinking of me. I didn't second-guess myself. It was as if I had found the secret potion I had been searching for my entire life.

I didn't drink *too* much that night, but it was enough to give me a good buzz. I ended up kissing my friend's boyfriend. I regretted it instantly and everything got smoothed over, but I blamed it all on the alcohol.

"I'm sorry, I was drunk, it wasn't my fault" became my tagline for years to come…

I always knew there was something wrong with my dad.

I was born into a family with generations of alcoholics on either side. This didn't give me much chance to escape the disease of alcoholism—the horror that eventually destroyed my father and nearly destroyed me as well.

My childhood is hazy. I have absolutely no memories of my parents being together, although they actually didn't divorce until I was in the third grade. My dad's job took him out of town for weeks at a time, providing the perfect stage for his drinking.

Suffering with my dad's alcoholism, my mom began attending support meetings while I was still a baby; consequently, I have been going to twelve-step meetings, on and off, *literally* my entire life. Although I didn't completely understand them as a child, I knew we went because of my dad.

After my parents divorced, I was scared to spend the night at my dad's house. I was afraid he wouldn't wake up in the morning and get me to school on time. Even at that age, I began to see the irresponsibility that accompanies alcoholism.

While I felt my dad wasn't capable of taking care of me, I was at the same time a complete Daddy's girl.

I had a fierce love for him. He was the one who organized birthday parties and fun outings, who bought me comic books and McDonald's, who let me stay up late and play video games with him.

My mom was the disciplinarian. But though she wasn't as much fun, she was the one I knew I could count on. The one I turned to when my dad passed out and wouldn't wake up; the one who came over in the middle of the night to pick me up from his house.

When my mom was away on short support group retreats, I would stay with my aunt and uncle. I remember having fun with them—until I had to go to bed. Then, I would lie in the dark and imagine my mom dying in an airplane crash or some equally horrible thing. I'd get scared I'd never see her again. These fears kept me up half the night, making my stomach ache and tears pour out of my eyes. I needed my mom; she was my rock.

As I grew older, however, I spent more time at my dad's house and became closer with him. Although he sometimes failed to pick me up from school or a friend's house—or wouldn't awake from a deep "sleep"—he had sober periods as well. Strangely, when I reflect back on those years, I cannot recall a single memory of my mother's house—it's images of my dad that fill my head.

And school. I *loved* school. It was a haven for me when things weren't going well at home, a place for me to escape to and excel in. That's one reason I'm studying to become a teacher—I want to provide that same environment to children who have less-than-stable home lives.

I remember it being extremely important to me that my classmates like me. I wanted to be the most popular. I wanted all the boys to like me. I was intimidated by people I thought were "cool" and amazed when those cool people wanted to be my friend.

These thoughts and feelings have stayed with me my entire life. Sometimes they ebb, and other times are more apparent, but they are always with me.

When I was eleven, my mom decided to move across the country to California. There was no question I was going with her. I *wanted* to go. California was a magical place: a place of movie stars, palm trees, sunshine, and new beginnings. Although I had many friends and was happy, I thought that if I moved to California, I could become a different person. I could be cool and popular and the envy of all my friends back home.

When it came time to leave, however, I rued my decision. I hadn't considered how I'd feel leaving behind my dad—as well as my sister, who was ten years my senior. I spent much of my first two years in California trying to convince my mom to move back.

It didn't help that I didn't fit in *at all* at my new school. I was different, and everyone could see that. I was made fun of for being so pale; because I didn't know how to match my clothing; because I wore shorts in winter; because I wore glasses—the list goes on.

I became friends with another California transplant and all we talked about was where we had come from. I was lonely; I wanted to be liked; and I missed my dad and sister incredibly.

Around this time is when I first *really* thought about my dad's alcoholism. When I left, I heard from him frequently, but then months would go by without a phone call or a letter. I started blaming myself—thinking that because I had moved away, my dad was drinking away his sorrows.

I blamed my mom as well. Every so often, a random child support check from my dad would show up, and when it did, I'd get mad at her. I knew my dad was spending money on alcohol, and I thought my mom taking more money from him would make him end up homeless.

I think I subconsciously knew that my mom was strong; I knew she could take care of us but that my dad didn't have that ability. All of the fear, worry, and resentment triggered by my dad was taken out on my mom—again, because I thought she could handle it better than him. My mom would love me and be there for me no matter what.

I never showed my dad these feelings at all. When he called, I was grateful to hear from him. I was grateful he was alive. Even when he called drunk—which became more and more frequent—I would talk to him. But I had to fight not to hang up on him; it hurt me so much that he had to be drunk to call me.

When I did go home to visit, I always stayed with my sister because she was more stable than my dad; my dad even lived with her occasionally. Other times, we didn't know where he was. Or his drinking caused him to stay away, even though he lived nearby.

On one of my final visits, when I was fifteen, I stayed for about two weeks but rarely saw my dad. On my last night, though, he came over for dinner. My sister told me after he left that he'd hidden alcohol in the bathroom and nipped away at it the whole night. I felt so disappointed that my dad couldn't make it through even one night with me without feeling the need to drink.

When I wouldn't hear from my dad for months, I'd imagine him dead somewhere—lying in a ditch, alone, with no one knowing that he was no longer alive.

The pain hurt me so badly that I pushed it deep down inside. There was nothing I could do about it, so I chose to ignore it, deny it. I chose to not talk about my dad, and I'd push any thoughts of him away. It was so much easier to live in denial than to live in reality. When I *did* feel pain, it fueled my anger toward my mom, for no better reason than my needing someone to take it out on.

Meanwhile, I'd finally started attending a teen program for friends and relatives of alcoholics. For years, I had resisted my mom's attempts to get me there. I didn't want people to think I had problems—that there was something wrong with me or my life. I wanted so badly to look like I had it together. And I didn't know how to talk about my feelings. I didn't think anyone could understand what I was going through.

What finally compelled me to go is that I started losing friends at school. I was in eighth grade and, as always, was desperate to be liked. I wanted it so badly, I would do *anything,* including lie, cheat, and steal.

I gossiped to my friends about each other—thinking that highlighting their defects would make *my* assets more apparent. I shoplifted stuff from stores and gave it to my friends as gifts, hoping they would like me more because of it. I would pretend to be anything, anyone, to make someone like me.

But my behavior had the opposite effect: the friends I had strived so hard to acquire stopped hanging out with me and started talking about me behind my back.

School had always been my haven. As long as I had friends, I was okay. When I started to lose them—when I started hiding in classrooms during lunchtime, faking illness to avoid school, and contemplating faking suicide so everyone would feel sorry for me and forgive me—I started to see how messed up my life really was.

I needed a change—on the inside.

Despite my low self-esteem, my lack of self-love, and my apathy about wanting to live (I didn't really want to die, either), my life still looked rather nice on paper. I was getting straight A's, I had lead roles in several plays, I was a speechwriter for our commencement, and I won first place in the honors division of a districtwide writing contest. Despite everything going on, I still *had* to keep up appearances.

After I joined the support group, my life did improve. I began to understand that my dad had a *disease*. That my dad loved me to the best of his ability and that his drinking had nothing to do with me. While this didn't lessen the pain, it helped immensely to have a place to talk about it and to see that I wasn't alone.

This was incredibly important: not having to be lonely anymore—and not having to be alone with my thoughts. There *were* people who understood, people who lived in similar—and worse—situations. While I still experienced denial, I was able to work on *myself;* I was able to examine my *own* words and actions instead of blaming everything on other people. I was able to reestablish friendships.

But at fifteen—a few months after my visit with my sister—I took my first drink of alcohol. That first drink with my girlfriend. The beginning of that worn-out rationalizing mantra: *"I'm sorry, I was drunk, it wasn't my fault."*

That night, I wound up staying at the house of a girl I'd just met while lying to my mom about it and skipping out on another friend's party.

These actions—lying, spending the night in strange places, and skipping out on commitments—became synonymous with drinking for me, for years. In fact, my entire drinking career can basically be summed up by that first night I ever drank.

Although I fell in love with alcohol at first drink, I did not have many friends able to access it, so for the next couple of years my drinking bouts were infrequent. But just about every time I drank, it was to excess. The third time I ever drank, I blacked out. This, too, became a normal condition of drinking for me.

Up until that first drink, I had been doing well in school. I was in three honors classes and on track for the International Baccalaureate Program. My mom and I were working on our relationship, and she trusted me. I was a good kid.

Then.

After my first drink, I started ditching school. Even if I wasn't drinking, I felt that other things—like my new, non-academic friends and loser boyfriends—were more important.

I got into other sorts of trouble as well.

After my first blackout, I was grounded for not coming home until six a.m. Another time, my friends had to carry me up my front steps and knock on the door until my mom answered.

Yet, somehow, these were not warning signs to me.

I still met with my teen support group and became very involved with it, serving on various committees and attending lots of events and meetings. But I truly believed it was just my *dad* who had the problem.

Having attended open twelve-step meetings, to me, an alcoholic was a person who didn't have a job and was homeless—one who lost everything, including his family. I could not identify with any of these things.

Although I had dropped out of regular high school and was attending a continuation high school, and although I was grounded more often than not and my relationship with my mom was strained, I felt like I was just having fun and doing the same things other teenagers were doing. Blacking out was not a sign of alcoholism—it just meant I shouldn't drink the beverages that put me in that state, like vodka. I should simply be more *selective.*

When I was seventeen, I started hanging out with a group of older people who partied all the time. I, of course, wanted to fit in and for my insecurities to vanish. Everything seemed more fun when I was drunk.

I started dating a guy who was, to me, the epitome of coolness. I couldn't understand why he was dating me. He was older and handsome and everything I felt I wasn't. I lost my virginity to him after a couple of months—but only because I thought he would like me more. I didn't really even know him, but I was afraid of losing him. He broke up with me soon after.

This didn't deter me from hanging out with the same crowd. While drunk, I started making out—and eventually sleeping with—any of the guys who gave me attention. For some reason, I thought their sleeping with me meant that I was pretty and interesting—that I was *somebody.* I didn't understand that they were just using me.

At times, I convinced myself that I was using them. And in a way, I was. I was using *them* to make myself feel good, to feel like people liked me. I didn't see the kind of person it was turning me into—I just thought I was having fun. In the year after I lost my virginity, I slept with eight guys, all from the same circle. And every single time, I was drunk.

And although I still thought my drinking was working *for* me, I *did* see it working against me as well.

One time, I brought a younger friend to a party. When the cops broke it up, I forgot about her and left with a guy; the police found her with her eighteen-year-old boyfriend. When the girl's mom found out, she forbade her from ever seeing me again. We were never friends after that. Still, I didn't understand why it was *such* a big deal.

Another time, I had a huge crush on a guy I'd been sleeping with for a few months. One night, he left to go to another party and I wound up sleeping with one of his friends. He found out, and that ended all chances of my ever having a relationship with him.

This time, I was *crushed* by my own actions. I didn't even *like* the guy I'd slept with—or even find him attractive. It was the attention that was so irresistible. And I lost all self-control when I was drunk.

A few months later, I slept with my best friend's ex-boyfriend while drunk. Her response to me was: "It's okay—I figured it would happen anyway." This devastated me as well. I felt like a horrible friend; one who couldn't be depended on—who couldn't be trusted.

And I *couldn't* be.

But I *still* didn't think I had a drinking problem.

On the contrary, I thought I might be a sex addict. I looked up a self-help group for people with this malady and contemplated going to a meeting. However, my feelings passed after a few days.

I only regretted actions when I *felt* the repercussions of them—and that didn't happen too often. When I *did* feel bad for hurting people, I would cover up those feelings with *more* alcohol. And I surrounded myself with people who drank like I did, so there was a sense of normalcy about it all.

At age eighteen, I went to my first rave. Up until then, I was very against using drugs. I'd never been around anything except pot. I drew the line at drugs.

Up until then...

The night of my first rave, I changed my mind. Everyone else was doing ecstasy, and I wanted to fit in. I didn't want to be the only sober person there. I convinced myself that ecstasy was a teenage drug—not a *real* drug like cocaine or speed—so there wasn't any harm in it.

Once again, I fell in love upon first use. Ecstasy made me feel beautiful and love everyone. I had peace of mind. Never mind that I threw up multiple times, made out with my friend's ex-boyfriend—*again*—and felt like crap for the entire next day. For the next year, I went to raves and used ecstasy whenever I could.

Using ecstasy spurred me to start smoking pot as well. Because while I couldn't use "E" all the time and I couldn't drink every day (I still lived with my mom), I *could* smoke pot. I'd come home from work, smoke pot behind my house, and then hang out at the nearby coffee shop until I came down from my high. I did this every day that entire summer.

Around this time, I graduated from high school. I started working at an office and entered community college. Despite my progressing drug and alcohol abuse, I was determined to make something of my life. Not many people in my family had graduated from college, and I knew I wanted to be different.

At eighteen, I had started paying rent to my mom—not much, but at least something. I paid for community college as well. While not yet completely self-sufficient, I knew I had to work for what I wanted.

I rarely heard from my dad. Even contact with my sister was infrequent. She had divorced and then had a child with a man my dad didn't like. When I did hear from her, she would cry to me about the terrible things going on in her life—about how my dad kicked her out of his house, about the horrible things he'd said to her, or about the awful way her boyfriend was treating her. I disconnected myself from this. I still couldn't bear to hear anything bad about my dad. I didn't want to believe it.

When I was nineteen and about to enter my second year of community college, I fell in love for the first time. I was one of the main speakers at a teen support group event in another state. He was in the support group but had also been sober himself for a year and a half. It amazed me that someone so young could be in recovery; it made me take a long look at myself and my life.

After the trip, I didn't think I'd ever see him again. But I decided to stop drinking and using drugs—at least for a little while. Not that I was an alcoholic, of course; I just needed *a break.* My life needed more substance. I deserved more than what I was giving myself.

I soon started dating the guy, long-distance.

I made it five months without drinking or using. Then one night I smoked pot. I felt terrible the whole time, but I remember thinking: *Don't worry about this now; it will mess up your high. Enjoy it now and worry about it later.*

I felt like I had betrayed my boyfriend and myself. But I began drinking and smoking pot occasionally anyway. Since I didn't have a "problem," I didn't see why I shouldn't be able to recreationally use substances every once in a while.

I decided to transfer to a university near my boyfriend for the fall semester. Two months before I was to leave, my sister called me. She was sobbing. She told me that my dad was in the hospital, in a coma. *Brain-dead.* She said he had been drinking with some buddies and had started choking. His "friends" thought he had passed out, and when they realized he wasn't breathing, they left him. They didn't call the police until after they'd gone. By the time the ambulance got there, he had been twenty minutes without oxygen.

She told me I needed to get there.

I didn't know what to think. It seemed impossible that my dad was going to die. During the previous year, I had started writing to him, letting him know what was going on in my life. I had finally realized that if I wanted a relationship with him, I needed to put in some effort, too. Relationships are a two-way street.

In one of my letters, I told my dad how much I loved him and how grateful I was for the time we'd spent together when I was a child. I thanked him for writing stories with me, because this inspired me to want to write books as an adult. On Valentine's Day, my dad had sent me a package—something he hadn't done in a long time. It was filled with things that he thought I would like, based upon my likes as a child.

When my sister called, I had just sent my dad a Father's Day card—the first in several years. Today, I am so grateful I did that—grateful that I was able to tell him I loved him.

My mom and I flew out the next morning. I was in complete denial of the situation; I didn't understand why we had to get there so quickly.

We went straight to the hospital, and I saw my dad lying there, bloated—so different from how he used to be. And I was scared. I didn't want to see him like that, didn't want to remember him like that—tubes crawling all over his body; his breathing sporadic; his eyes flickering occasionally, giving me hope. My entire body repulsed the experience. I wanted to throw up. I wanted to run away—to be anywhere but there, to catch the next plane home. It didn't seem real.

This was the first time I had seen my dad in four years.

My sister and I were given a few days to decide whether to keep our dad on life support or to take him off and most likely watch him die. It was a terrible choice.

Meanwhile, my mom and I, along with my aunt and uncle, were adjusting to the dysfunction that was my sister's life—a dysfunction I hadn't fully realized until then.

My sister had just had her third child, and her oldest child was living with her ex-husband. She had a boyfriend who didn't lift a finger to help us the entire time we were there, and the two of them continually fought over drugs.

My sister poured out the tragedy of her circumstances to me, including my dad's drug use and the terrible things my dad had said to her. I wanted to tell her to shut up—that I didn't want to hear those things. But I couldn't. So I put my mind elsewhere. I walked around like a zombie, smoked a lot of cigarettes, and tried not to *feel.*

Although I don't remember coming to the decision, we took my dad off life support. We gathered around his hospital bed, and I remember the rest of the family praying over him and telling him to go to the light, while I just stood there and cried. My mom tried to comfort me, but I pushed her away. I felt like she didn't understand.

I tried not to think about how my dad would never walk me down the aisle when I got married, how I would never be able to mend the relationship we used to have. That this was it.

I watched him die and I shut off my emotions. I remember smoking a cigarette with my sister afterwards and feeling nothing. I was numb.

We left a week later, after a memorial service and more of my sister's drama. The next day I got high. The rest of the summer, I got high. I don't recall anything but that. And soon, I was packing to go away to school.

I was excited to start a new life and to live near the love of my life, but I was also scared. I was afraid to leave my mom—my constant. I was afraid something would happen to her, too.

After I left, life got even more complicated. My student housing fell through, so I had to bunk on the floor of my boyfriend's parents' house. My tuition loan fell through as well, so my mom had to scrounge up all her available savings to help pay for my first semester. I had barely enough money for food, and my school schedule—along with my long-held fear of driving—made it extremely hard for me to get a job. But I tried. I went on so many interviews that ever since, I have rarely been nervous when applying for a new job.

I disliked living in someone else's house, living out of boxes, scrounging to make ends meet. Most days I would have coffee for breakfast, soda for lunch, cigarettes in between, and food when I got home around five or six. I didn't have many friends, so I was especially clingy toward my boyfriend. I was resentful whenever he left the house without me.

I was miserable.

I finally got an apartment with a friend. While this helped, it was another bill to pay. I drank a few times with my roommate, and my boyfriend saw me drunk for the first time. While I knew he didn't like it, I didn't care. I had just turned twenty-one, and I had to find release somewhere.

A month later, I was home for winter break and decided that I needed to move back. The move was just too hard on me—emotionally, spiritually, and financially. But I would stick it out for one more semester.

I told my boyfriend my plans, and a few days later he broke up with me. He told me he was no longer in love with me.

I was devastated. I did everything I could to change his mind. I didn't understand how someone could fall out of love. I didn't think it was possible. Love was supposed to be forever. We had talked about our future, and I thought we were going to get married. I thought my life was all planned out and that I knew where it was going.

Now, everything stable in my life—everything I thought I knew—was flipped upside down. The two major men in my life had both left me in a span of six months.

I got drunk a few nights later and again made out with someone I shouldn't have—a mutual friend of ours. I felt sick about it. And these actions scared me. I had thought those days were over—that falling in love had changed me and that I would never act that way again.

It was time for a major decision: Should I move back home immediately?

I weighed the pros and cons carefully.

My life at school was finally coming together—I had landed a job, I had a place to live, and I was finally taking classes for my major. But if I stayed, I would have a hard time getting over my love. Constant reminders were everywhere, especially since we had mutual friends.

In California, I would be able to move on with my life more easily. I would be around people who loved me, and I wouldn't have to worry about money as much.

But I had fears surrounding that, too.

The drunken night was a reminder of my past—a past I did not want to have turn into my present again. I was afraid that at home, I would fall back into my routine of partying and sleeping around. I was afraid I wasn't strong enough to resist.

This was the first time I ever considered that I *might* be an alcoholic. I even admitted it to a few people.

As I prayed and meditated about my choices, the answer became clear: I needed to move home now. I knew then—and I believe still—that this was the healthiest choice for me.

As for alcoholism, I put that thought on the back burner. I was still too *young* to be an alcoholic. Sure, I had made some poor decisions in the past, but I could overcome them. I was going to be *different*.

Life back home started off seminormal. I was in pain—I missed my dad and my ex-boyfriend—but I enrolled again at community college, found a job, and tried to get on with my life.

Unfortunately, I was indeed not as "strong" as I'd hoped to be. I soon fell back into my old life. They say that if you drink after you have been sober for a while, you will pick up right where you left off. This happened tenfold for me.

The ensuing years are a blur.

I could legally go to bars now, so I took advantage of this. I blacked out even more than before, and found myself sleeping with almost any guy who gave me attention. I can't even recall how I felt about this, because my feelings were drowned out by alcohol and pot.

I started getting drunk or high every day. I became anxious if I thought I wasn't going to be able to use that day.

But I was never one to drink by myself. Drinking was a social activity and drinking alone made me depressed—the exact opposite of how I wanted to feel. However, I loved smoking pot by myself; in fact, I preferred it. Again, I was numbed. It made everything—no matter how bad—okay. *I just didn't care.*

Over the years, I had occasionally ingested ecstasy, acid, mushrooms, and cocaine; but I usually stuck to alcohol and pot. Not only were they easy to get and inexpensive, but I could use while still appearing to have it together.

During the haze of that year, I managed to get my A.A. from community college. Although I ditched class frequently and was sometimes unable to purchase books because I'd spent my money on substances, somehow I pulled through.

I found a full-time job that paid well—and that had employees who liked to party as much as I did.

Throughout all this, I was still attending support meetings for families of alcoholics—which I still needed, even though my dad had passed away.

After my dad's death, my sister's life had gone downhill fast. She'd started using crack, and—like my dad—I heard from her infrequently. When I did, she was usually under the influence of something. My sister's use put me in fear not only for *her* life, but also for the lives of her children. This fear, hurt, and anxiety was yet another reason for me to ingest chemicals of my own.

While my memories from age twenty-one to twenty-three are hazy, several instances of my depravity and hopelessness stick out to me.

I remember blacking out at a male coworker's party and coming to while having sex with him. I had no idea how I'd gotten myself into this predicament, but I was so used to finding myself in situations like that anyway, that I just went with it—even though I didn't find the guy attractive in the least. I hated myself for doing these things, but I would push down my feelings of regret, of shame, of remorse, because I thought I couldn't change.

At age twenty-two, I found out I was pregnant. I had denied the signs for a while, and when I confirmed it, I cried. I knew I was not capable of raising a child. I didn't even know who the father was because I had slept with several people without using a condom.

To deal with this, I smoked pot and got drunk. *For days.* But it wasn't something I could just ignore. I didn't want anyone to know, but

I eventually confided in my mother. Because I also knew I couldn't handle this on my own.

I decided to have an abortion. I saw no alternative; I was not willing to give up the life I was leading.

Since I had waited so long to take a pregnancy test, I had to have an operation. I was petrified. That made it more real. The night before, I got high. I had to keep my emotions as numbed as possible to cope with the situation I had gotten myself into.

The next day when my mom dropped me off at the clinic, I felt so alone. During my intake, they asked if I had done any drugs in the past twenty-four hours. I had to tell the truth. And because I had, I could not be put to sleep during the procedure. Once again, my own actions had put me in a situation I did not want to be in. *It was terrible.*

I got high as soon as I got home. I could not allow myself to feel—I knew it would be too overwhelming.

It *was* terrible—but apparently not terrible enough to make me change my lifestyle. I went right back to the way I had been living. But now, I would internally beat myself up for continuing to get drunk and sleep around.

And then I would get high to forget my pain.

And then I would start the cycle all over.

My obsession with attention from men became just as bad as my obsession with alcohol. It was exciting to me. There were times I couldn't wait to see what would happen during a night of drinking—who would give me attention? Who would I hook up with? Would I meet somebody new?

For some reason, I thought that these sexual encounters would give me what I felt was missing inside. I didn't realize that they in fact did the opposite. It was a seemingly endless cycle of excitement, self-loathing, and numbness.

In the back of my mind, the word "slut" echoed around, but I pushed it aside. I thought that these people didn't know the *real* me. On the inside, I wasn't really like that; I was a good girl. I was girlfriend material. Though my actions didn't show it, I wanted a long-term boyfriend badly.

I became close with a girl I had known in my youth. She liked to party as much as I did, and she didn't make me feel bad about my encounters with men. She basically cosigned all of my bullshit. We would go to bars and I would find a guy I wanted to make out with (how I loved the thrill of the chase); then she would stand by while my craziness kicked in. Not that she didn't have her own conquests. Looking back, I see how we used each other to make our own behavior acceptable.

Right before I turned twenty-three, I started dating a guy I'd met one night partying. It was the perfect drunken relationship—for that was basically all we did. For me, it was ideal, especially since my last boyfriend had been sober. This guy would drink a beer *while* driving; and while I admonished this behavior in others, I realized that if *he* drank while driving, I could drink too. I thank God, now, that I lived through that. The relationship didn't last long though—he heard rumors about my extreme sexual behavior and broke up with me.

The next guy I dated, I met while blacked out. When he called me the next day, I thought he must really be worth keeping if he still wanted to hang out with me after seeing me so drunk. The guy lived about an hour away, so I only got to see him on weekends. I'd take the train there and we'd spend the whole weekend drinking.

I remember one time he bought a six-pack for the two of us, and I got extremely anxious because I knew it wouldn't be enough for me. At this point, I was blacking out from every kind of alcohol I drank—including beer. I never knew how alcohol was going to affect me—if a few drinks would get me drunk, or if I would be drinking all night and not feel drunk. It was always a gamble.

So I started hiding alcohol at parties so I would have enough to last me until I blacked out or passed out. I made myself throw up so I wouldn't pass out too early and could keep on drinking. If I *couldn't* continue drinking for some reason, I would agonize about my next drink—where I would get it, when I would get it—because I hated for my buzz to go away.

I despised being sober. I found it hard to cope, hard to be personable, and hard to *live*. I drank or got high at lunch just to get through the day.

And I did all of this while *still* trying to maintain the image that I wasn't an alcoholic. That was foremost in my mind—to appear like I still had it together.

I hid my extreme desire to drink from my boyfriend; if I got drunk too quickly, I'd be quiet so my drunkenness didn't show. I also tried to hide the sheer quantities I was drinking. I didn't want anyone to know how bad it was getting.

Amidst all of this, I had been accepted to a university, due to start in the spring. In anticipation, I had saved up enough money to travel through Europe for two months, by myself.

My boyfriend and I decided to stay together despite the impending separation. (Actually, I decided to stay with *him,* despite his kissing another girl while he was drunk. Instead of breaking up with him, I told him I needed more of a commitment, so he asked me to be his girlfriend.)

The weekend before I left for Europe, I invited my best friend to his house so I could celebrate with the two people I truly cared about. After hours of drinking, I passed out.

A month and a half later, when I was in a foreign country, my boyfriend told me over the phone that he'd slept with my "best friend" that night.

I was devastated. Although we'd only been dating a few months, for some reason, I had believed that he was my future. In fact, I had spent the entire month and a half abroad obsessing about our relationship, wondering why he wasn't e-mailing me more frequently, worrying about why he seemed so distant. I wasted so much of my trip on these thoughts.

Both of them betrayed me, but I wanted to think I could still be with him.

I look back on that moment as one of the lowest in my life: I was willing to accept a man who had cheated on me with my best friend while I was passed out in the next room. *He* was the one who had to break up with me. *He* was the one who told me I would find someone better. *I* was the one who said, "I don't think I will." And I believed it.

I got extremely drunk the night I found out. I drank until I could pass out without images of them running through my head. I called the ex–best friend, and she told me that he had raped her. The he-said/she-said drama of it all played havoc in my head for months.

I got as drunk as I could for days, mostly by myself, and then I decided to return home three weeks early. I knew that if I continued to travel alone, I would find myself in a worse situation than I was in already. I thank God I had the foresight to make that decision. I have never regretted it.

I got high within an hour of landing in California. Being high made me forget the betrayal and the loss of more people in my life.

In my sober moments, I began to reassess my life. Once again, the idea of my being an alcoholic flitted to the surface. But I didn't do anything about it—after all, *they* were the ones who had betrayed *me* while I was drunk. *I* hadn't done anything wrong.

But I couldn't stand the thought of *feeling* the emotions I was going through. I didn't know how to handle them—I had been stuffing my feelings with alcohol and pot for too long.

I began to see that I wanted *quality* people in my life, rather than a *quantity*. Although I had been drinking and using for years, I was still attending the support group that encouraged me to look at myself and my actions. I saw that I had surrounded myself with the wrong kinds of people. I needed a change in my life, or I was going to continue down the same road of hurt and destruction.

But this didn't mean I changed everything all at once. I still drank. But I didn't do it *as much*…

First, because I was losing all elements of control when I drank.

Secondly, I usually went straight from sober to drunk—bypassing the fun buzz I was always chasing. I would wake up in the morning after a night of drinking and barely remember any of it. But I assumed I had fun—because if I was drinking, I *must* have had fun. However, drinking was *actually* making me extremely emotional—a state I did not want to be in.

Thirdly, I had started attending a university and was trying really hard to excel in school. Going to school two days a week and working three, I tried to fill up my time and mind with responsibility.

Also during this time, my sister was losing custody of her children because of her drug use, so she and her husband fled the state with my niece and nephew. They were found a few months later, and the children were put into foster care.

My mom was asked if she wanted to be their primary caregiver. Neither she nor I could stand the thought of these children being placed in the system, so we decided to do whatever we could for them. At the time I didn't realize what a huge decision this was. I was filled with disappointment in my sister, sadness for her children, and fear—once again—that she was going to end up like my dad.

And my sister was pregnant—*again*—adding to the emotional roller coaster.

To avoid all this disappointment, sadness, and fear, I smoked as much pot as I could, whenever I could. I smoked pot before I did anything: before I went to work, to school, to a meeting. I smoked before I cleaned my room or did homework. It made everything more bearable. It made me not as lonely. It helped me live in a haze.

And it worked. *For a while.*

I still felt like something was missing. I prayed every morning as I walked, high, to the bus stop. And I wondered why I didn't feel connected to a higher power. I felt like something intrinsic was missing inside of me, but I didn't know what it was. Although I was trying to clean up my life, I knew something else had to change.

And one day, it did.

I was at a weekend retreat for family and friends of alcoholics—something I had been going to for years. After one of our nightly meetings, I went to bed and cried because I felt like I was leading a false life. I was lying to the people who truly cared about me, and I was sick of it—I was sick of myself. I prayed to God to help me, to show me what I needed to do, because I knew I couldn't live this way anymore.

And the answer came to me: *I needed to get sober. I had a problem with drugs and alcohol. I needed to start the twelve-step program.*

But I *still* had reservations. I still felt like I was too young and that maybe this wasn't as bad as it appeared.

At this gathering was a young woman who I knew was in recovery. I had never talked to her. So I prayed that if I was supposed to get sober, the next day God should have this woman approach me and I would take this as a sign from Him.

This was an extremely specific prayer. I did not expect it to be answered.

But the next day, this young woman approached me to take a walk with her. My heart pounded. I knew what I had to do, but I was so scared. I knew that once the words came out of my mouth, there was no taking them back. Although I had voiced concerns about being an alcoholic before, this was different.

I took a roundabout tactic. I asked her how old she'd been when she got sober; her answer was twenty-four—my age at the time. I asked her *why* she'd gotten sober, how she'd known she was an alcoholic.

Then I told her *my* fears: that I thought I might be an alcoholic, that I needed to get sober, and that I was scared. I poured out my heart to her, and she became one of my angels.

During our meeting that night, I finally admitted aloud—to a large group of people—that I was an alcoholic. It was one of the scariest and most liberating things I have ever done in my life. There was no going back from there.

I felt so free. I no longer had to live a double life. I no longer had to remember who I had told what to, or cover my real feelings with lies. I felt like I had torn a mask off my face and exposed my real identity.

And it felt right.

I knew, beyond a doubt, that I was doing exactly what I was supposed to do. Except for coming home from Europe early, I hadn't felt that way in a *really* long time. I knew my path wasn't going to be easy, but I also knew that I didn't have to make the journey alone.

I started attending meetings every day, and I asked that young woman to be my sponsor. She is still my sponsor to this day.

I immersed myself in the program and with the people I met there. I stopped hanging out with the people I'd used with—who I realized weren't really my friends anyway. I started changing my life, little by little.

A few weeks into my sobriety, I met another recovering alcoholic at school who was in the same major I was. She told me about a special scholarship program she was in, called Pathways to Independence. She gave me Dave Bishop's number and told me to call him immediately.

I was hesitant to do this. I didn't feel like I deserved such an amazing opportunity. I knew I had experienced some hardship in my life, but I also knew that most of it was self-inflicted. So many women out there were more deserving than me.

My classmate helped me understand that different people need help for different reasons. I needed help too.

I met with Dave and was accepted to begin the following January. I couldn't believe it—the program seemed too good to be true. And I wasn't used to people giving me things because they thought I was *deserving*—especially not people I didn't know. In the back of my mind, I kept thinking, *What do they <u>want</u> from me?* It took me a long time to realize that the only thing they wanted was for me to succeed.

Meanwhile, I kept attending school and was getting a 4.0 grade point average. I went to meetings, I worked the twelve steps of recovery, and I talked to my sponsor every day.

I had thought that all of my internal problems would go away when I got sober, because I truly believed that they were *caused* by my drinking. It took me a while to realize that the spiritual, emotional, and mental maladies I possessed were around long *before* I started drinking—alcohol was but a symptom of my disease. I had far more to work on than I had ever imagined.

To not know this when beginning my recovery was actually a blessing. If I *had* realized it, I might not have been able to make the decision to get sober.

Life started to get better. I started to gain self-esteem and confidence; I started to like myself again. It wasn't easy. I didn't know how to interact with others without having a chemical in my system. I didn't know how to have fun without being drunk or stoned. Luckily, I fell into a group of people who absolutely insisted on enjoying life. I gained a social life that surpassed any from before. I started to laugh and smile again.

Not that I didn't have my bad moments, but I didn't have to experience them alone. I would call my sponsor or a sober friend and talk to them about my anxiety, my anger, my sadness—and they would tell me that they had experienced those emotions as well. It made me feel like I was exactly where I was supposed to be, and it helped me to know that it *would* get better. That this, too, would pass.

In December, my niece and nephew came to live with my mom and me. The responsibility of caring for a four-year-old girl and an eight-year-old boy overwhelmed me. But it also made me extremely grateful for my sobriety. Not only was I able to support my mom, but I was also able to be there for the kids—to set a good example, to give them love, care, and stability.

I entered Pathways a month later and my life, *again,* changed dramatically for the better. No longer did I have to worry about finding enough money for tuition, books, and supplies; this really helped me to be a better student. And I was assigned a mentor to help guide me along my career path—a mentor who has been supportive of me every step of the way.

One condition of Pathways is that clients must attend therapy once a week. To be honest, this was the most difficult requirement for me to accept. I had been made to see several different therapists throughout my life, and my experiences had not been satisfactory. But that was prior to getting sober. *Back then,* I had not been willing to open up—nor to change my behavior.

Today, I have benefited greatly from the wisdom of my Pathways therapist. He is a gentle soul who never hesitates to point out my growth. This is so crucial when I am hard on myself.

Today, I have been sober for over five years. I have completed my college degree, and I just recently graduated from Pathways.

I can't imagine having accomplished any of these things without the support I have received. I had cheerleaders encouraging me every step of the way, telling me I could do it when I didn't have the same faith.

But the biggest change is on the inside. I am accountable for my actions today, not only to myself, but to my mom, my niece and nephews (my sister's fourth child came to live with us when he was nine months old), my therapist, my sponsor, my mentor, my twelve-step group, and to Pathways.

At times, being accountable to so many people *can* be overwhelming. But I have learned over and over again that I can do it, and that I am worth it. For an alcoholic like me, these are sometimes the hardest things to realize.

Along the way, I have struggled with my sobriety and with my feelings. For example, when my grandma died, when my sister relapsed, when I went through a breakup, and when a friend committed suicide.

But I had tools to use during these times. And I have a support group of people who love me, and who are accountable for *their own* actions as well.

There are *still* times I struggle with feeling my feelings. Times I wish I could shut off my head, times I wish I could numb the pain and sadness, times I wish I could fit into a social situation better. But I don't drink or use, no matter what.

I know now that this is not the solution for me. That it will only make me feel worse about myself. I am grateful for this knowledge. I have learned that I can do anything sober, and the leading proponent of this has been Pathways.

It is hard for me to put into words the amazing journey I have gone through. Through the help of Pathways and my twelve-step program, I have conquered many fears that had hindered me in life.

Before entering Pathways, I was afraid to drive. I feared the responsibility—both personal and financial—that came with owning a car. Pathways showed me how to tackle my fear by taking things one step at a time, to avoid being overwhelmed by thoughts of learning and doing everything at once.

I eventually got my license and Pathways gave me a donated car. They made what had seemed impossible, a tangible reality.

And the same went for all my fears—fear of going to the doctor, fear of paying bills, fear of living on my own, fear of taking a creative writing class. All of these were conquered as well, through the help and encouragement of Pathways to Independence.

The opportunities that have come my way since entering Pathways are innumerable. There are times I *still* don't believe I am worth what I have been given, but when everyone around me seems to think I am, it starts to sink in.

The women in Pathways to Independence have been given a second chance at life. In a way, we are living the Cinderella story. We have risen from the ashes, against all odds. Our fairy godfather has come in the form of a man named Dave Bishop. He is an inspiration to all of us, a wonderful human being who shows us the meaning of unconditional love. My gratitude is endless.

Pathways to Independence has given me hope—not only for myself and the life I am going to lead, but for others too. Witnessing the trials and tribulations that others have walked through has shown me that *I* can get through anything. It has opened my heart toward helping others, toward being the best person I can be.

I am now a credentialed teacher and I cannot wait to create a haven for students who do not have one at home. I cannot wait to instill the love of learning in children, to let them know they can do anything they put their minds to, to lift them up when they are down. I want them to see the many beautiful opportunities that life has to give, and I want to be a good example to them. I know that these things are possible and that I can create these opportunities. Having come from so much destruction, this is amazing knowledge.

I remember lying in bed at night, when I was using, and wondering how I had gotten myself to such a low point. I knew that I could do so much better, but I didn't know how to ever rise up from the depths.

I was shortchanging myself, but I had begun to accept that.

Today, I lie in bed and I thank God for my blessings. I think Him for the amazing love that I receive from so many different individuals; for the beauty I see in other people; for my sobriety program; for Pathways to Independence.

I thank Him for giving me a second chance at life.

I thank Him for showing me that *I am worth it.*

Four O'Clock

"My father told me he loved his dog more than me."

—Lin

I finally made the call to Dave Bishop.

I told him about my life.

Dave told me I would qualify for Pathways, but I might have to wait up to a year. So during that time, I just continued with what I was doing.

What I was doing was trying to keep myself alive. I was trying to survive. I wouldn't come home at night until my mother was there to protect me.

And when Dave told me I'd been accepted into the program, I moved all my things in one day—all before four o'clock.

Four o'clock was a really interesting time for me. It was like my life ended at four o'clock—*because that's when my dad came home…*

I'm Filipino and Chinese.

I was born in the Philippines and first came to America when I was a year and a half old. My entire family came here, except for my dad. You have to petition to come to the United States; you can't just come live here without immigration approving it. Petitioning was a long process, and my dad had some problem with his. So he stayed behind.

When I was about three, I moved back to the Philippines and attended kindergarten there. A lot of that time is a blur, partly because I was so young.

I *do* remember playing over there.

I remember *kind of* having a childhood.

I remember having a lot of cousins and a big extended family.

I don't remember my father having *too* much anger while we were in the Philippines. But I do remember him one time turning my brother upside down and dipping him into a bucket of water in the shower.

It was an omen of things to come.

There are three kids in my family. I am the oldest, born twenty-six years ago. My brother was born less than two years after me; the big gap is between my sister and us—she is ten years younger than me.

At age four, I came back to the United States with my mother and brother, and we've lived here ever since. My dad remained behind in the Philippines, *still* waiting for his petition to be approved.

I remember I would see in movies where kids were excited to talk to their dad when they were apart. But I distinctly remember my dad calling on the phone and my mom asking if I wanted to talk to him; I didn't. I didn't know him. I remember *not* knowing him. I remember being afraid of him.

My mother has five siblings. When we were new to the United States, her family all shared the same house for a few years. My mom's oldest brother and his wife owned a small three-bedroom home and we *all* stayed there: my uncle and his wife, my mom, a couple of my mom's other siblings, her parents, my brother, and me. My brother and I were the babies of the house. Almost everyone on my mother's side of the family had their hand in bringing us up.

I was already seven years old when my father finally joined us in the States. When he arrived, he was filled with *so* much anger.

When my dad got angry he got *really* angry. And he got angry *often.* You just didn't go near him; he exuded such negative energy. I remember him and my mom yelling at each other. I could feel all the tension and antagonism.

Before and after my father first arrived, we lived in the home of my Uncle Adam—my mother's oldest brother. He was a definite father figure for me. But he was also a disciplinarian; he sometimes got violent with us. His wife became a second mother figure to me. In general, she was the "good guy" of the household, though I remember her shaking me violently when I wouldn't stop crying. I don't recall *why* I was even crying, but I remember vividly the consequences.

As I was entering the third grade, my family moved in with my mom's sister Rosa and her family. It was here that the abuse by my father *really* started.

It was a four-bedroom house: one room for Rosa and her husband, Jun; one for each of their kids; and one for my family.

My entire family had one tiny room.

In fact, all the way up through nine or ten years of age, I shared a single room with my parents and my brother in other people's homes. We had no privacy. Our whole life was within the confines of four walls—that was it. It didn't seem normal, but it was all I knew for many years.

One reason I knew our lives weren't normal is that there was always someone to compare it to. My cousins were three or four years old and they had toys—they *played.* I resented that.

I also resented that they had their own rooms—*and* that they didn't even appreciate them! Granted they were just toddlers, *but still!* The younger one *always* slept with his parents, and the older one insisted on joining them.

She never used her room—a room filled with toys and stuffed animals and her own bed covered in pretty, pink flowery sheets. It was frustrating.

My uncle was in the navy, so he was gone a lot. But he was a loving father. I never saw Uncle Jun raise a hand to his kids; he spent time with them, laughed with them, played with them.

But then my dad would come home and we'd all go to our corners. *No one* wanted to be exposed to his anger.

I compared myself to other kids at school, too. That's another way I could tell our lives weren't normal. *Other* kids looked forward to summer vacation. Time off from school, no homework, lots of play. But my brother's and my summers were spent cleaning the house and learning. We always had homework. No recess. It was like a less fun version of school.

Even *having fun* wasn't fun. We were always told, "Don't have too much fun," "Don't laugh too hard." Any joy you experienced was considered an omen that something bad was going to happen. I never understood it. But to this day, I still struggle with these thoughts—I'm always waiting for the other shoe to drop.

We didn't have too much time to play anyway. My father worked nights, so he was home most of the day, and he tried to teach my brother and me our native languages. That's where a lot of my dad's anger was centered, or perhaps that's where it started.

My dad taught us two different dialects of Filipino, plus two different dialects of Chinese. He would assign us these lessons, and we had to stand there and recite them back to him.

At school, if you don't get the answers right, you get a bad grade. At home, it was a different story. If *we* didn't get it right, he would hit us or would jab his index finger into our foreheads or the back of our heads. It hurt.

My dad was constantly yelling at us. It's hard to translate because he spoke Filipino, but it would be like comparing us to stray dogs; the lowest of the low. Whatever it took to make us feel like shit, that's what he would say.

My mom was too scared to intervene, and I don't think she could have done anything anyway. She tried to talk to him, but it had no effect, other than to cause even more fighting—between *them*. This in turn caused even more anger and resentment toward my brother and me.

And it's not like my mom was perfect either—it wasn't like good guy/bad guy. It was more like bad guy/less-bad guy. She was severely codependent with my father and couldn't see *how* bad his behavior was. And when we misbehaved, *she* abused us too: she'd pull my hair, slap us, hit us with her slipper, or twist and pull us by our ears.

Still, *she* at least had a semblance of a "reason" when she punished us. Perhaps we weren't listening to her. Or we'd talked back to her. We never *dared* talk back to my father; my mother seemed like a safer bet to vent our frustrations. But my mom provoked a lot of my dad's anger too. She would say or do something that would frustrate my dad, and that would cause him to lash out at me or my brother.

Unlike my mother, my dad's abuse seemed intentionally spiteful. No matter what he was angry about, it was *our* fault. We were about seven or eight years old; what could we have possibly done to generate *that* severity of anger? Sometimes he was just in a bad mood.

I walked on eggshells. We *all* walked on eggshells. I could hear my own voice in my head telling me, *Don't make any noise.* I wanted to be invisible. I wanted to blend in with the walls—breathe so silently I didn't exist.

Everybody in the family used us kids as weapons against each other—we were caught in the middle. My mom's siblings all believed they knew what was best for us. I think they *all* knew that the way my dad treated us was wrong. Yet at the same time, everyone seemed to hold him up with some kind of high regard or respect.

Perhaps it was simply fear. We all feared what he might be capable of, but no one dared confront him about it. The big elephant in the room was that my father was explosive and abusive, and cruelly so. So they played us against my father. And all the while, all this fear was building up inside of me, and it was *constantly* emphasized and perpetuated.

My dad seemed to resent *all* of my mom's siblings, but he was particularly hostile to Uncle Adam. Neither of them liked each other very much; neither liked how the other did things.

I think the main source of all my dad's anger is that he didn't get to raise his own kids. So the person he resented most was the man who *did* raise us.

"Just go back to your mommy and daddy!" my father would shout, referring to Adam and his wife, Jan. That became the recurring theme: *"Go back to your mommy and daddy. You are not my kids! You want to spend more time with them? Go ahead! Go back to your mommy and daddy!"*

Another sore point was that my brother and I don't carry my dad's last name; because of the immigration issues, we took my mom's maiden name. Therefore, on paper, I am considered an illegitimate child!

Questions came into my head. With my dad's constant yelling about us "not being his kids," being "worthless," and his telling us to go back to our "mommy and daddy," I began to wonder if he really *was* my father. It became something that haunted me throughout childhood and into adulthood: *Is he really my dad?*

He treated us like strangers off the street—like the bad kids on the block he had to put up with. He openly despised delinquents and gangsters, calling them a "waste to society" and saying they all belonged in jail and out of his sight. He unleashed his anger on us like we were *those* kids—a waste to society.

I never heard my parents say "I love you"—not to us and not to each other. But on the outside we were the perfect family. My parents would take us everywhere. To the mall, to the grocery store, to church, everywhere—everything was done together as a family. In our culture, parents are highly praised when they've got their kids "in line"—your kids go with you all these places and they don't complain about it. You have them in check and they're well behaved. This means you are good parents.

People didn't know we would get our asses kicked if we did anything different.

Behind closed doors, my father showed my brother and me virtually no positive attention, and he never showed any remorse for his actions. The only thing I perceived as affection was this thing he did where he'd stand behind us and give us each a little bitty mini-pinch on our necks. That was his thing. I have no real idea what it meant, but it did seem to be some sort of affection. At least it didn't involve hitting or shouting at us.

My timeline of early events in my life are based on the home we were living in at any given time.

In the fourth grade, my family finally moved into our own home. My brother and I got our own room, which we shared, and we rented the third room to a friend of my father's. So again, there was a witness to all the abuse. But again, no action was taken.

And it got progressively worse.

One day, my mom and I were having a little argument. She was mad because I was running late for school. My dad overheard us and he just completely went off on me—screaming and hitting me. He would always smack me across my face with the back of his hand or jab his finger—or fingers—into my head.

When this particular attack ended, I was crying. And I was really upset—angry even. I guess I gave my dad the "evil eye" or something, so he came at me with a fist and hit me dead-on in my nose.

I was nine years old.

He'd never hit me like that before. He would kick us and hit us, but never close-fisted straight in the face before. I went into a panic, looking at my hands to see if there was blood. There wasn't; just spit.

And tears.

In our home, the punishment never matched the crime; and of course, there was seldom any "crime" at all.

If my dad caught us watching television, we would be punished. "Okay, you want to watch TV?!" he would yell. Then he would turn the TV to something like the stock channel where the ticker tape symbols keep whizzing by along the bottom of the screen, or to Channel 3 where there was just static and fuzz—and then he would force us to kneel in front of the TV with our noses pressed against the screen and our eyes wide open. He was trying to teach us a lesson; he said that if we spent too much time watching TV, it would hurt our eyes.

So he would make us stay that way for *a half hour or so.*

I can still remember the smell of the TV. I can see the condensation of my breath on the glass. My mind would tune out and I'd make a game of it: if it was on the stock channel, I'd read each ticker symbol and see how many I could catch. I would try to escape in my head to somewhere else.

I still knew this wasn't normal. I knew my classmates weren't going through this torture. *Who would do this to a child?*

My dad would hold these grudges and anything could set him off. On any given day he could just explode. We never knew what was coming.

One time, my brother and I were sitting on our beds and our grandmother was making us laugh. Of course, my father came home from work in a pissed-off mood. Hearing us laughing, he walked into the room and said something along the lines of: "What's so funny? You're being too giddy." He left and returned with two *huge* tomatoes which he stuck into our mouths—we were like pigs with apples in their mouths being readied for roasting.

I hated tomatoes growing up. I hated the taste. It tasted like blood. *Who does that to their children?*

My grandmother witnessed the whole thing, and of course *she'd* been the one making us laugh; *she* wanted us to be kids. But she feared my father as much as everyone else, so she said nothing.

Anybody who lived in close proximity to us could hear my dad's raging. They heard all the things he said to us—at least, I assume they did—but nobody ever called the police.

No one in the family would call the police either.

"If you want to call the cops, go ahead!" my dad always said. Then he would throw the phone at us. "Put me in jail," he'd say. "I don't care. When I get out, I'll come after you!"

It was fear, but I think it was also cultural. It was so dishonorable to call the cops on your own father or family member. That was so ingrained: *Blood is thicker than water.*

So I never called the cops and I learned not to ask for help.

The day my dad punched me in the nose, I still had to go to school. I missed the bus, so my dad ended up driving me there a half hour later. All he said before we went was: "Go clean up your face!"

We kids used to have to line up in the schoolyard before classes started. Ironically, I *still* got to school on time that morning, after all the mayhem and despite my mom being so frantic over my being late.

I was sitting down, and it was clear that I'd been crying. Another girl asked me, "What's the matter? What's wrong?"

I told her that my dad had hit me. This was the first time I had ever told anyone what happened.

I have resentment to this day toward the classmate I told. The way she reacted demonstrates how bad things can become normalized; she probably also came from a dysfunctional home.

"My mom hits me all the time," she said. "It's no big deal. That's the way it is—you get in trouble and you get hit."

It was like nobody grasped the concept that my dad had just *punched* me, close-fisted, directly on my nose. He punched me in the face! It was not like this was a *spanking!*

From then on, I knew to keep my mouth shut. The impression I got was that nobody was going to understand anyway. So I just continued on, and I never called the cops.

I had learned very early on how to live a different life on the outside—how important it was to my survival to live "multiple lives"—so I just kept doing it.

As my brother and I suffered through our father beating us up, we had nowhere to direct our anger and our energy. So we began taking it out on each other.

This wasn't normal sibling rivalry. We would *beat each other up*. Things my father did to us, we started doing to each other. We would throw each other against the wall. My dad used to grab us by our necks, so we would do *that* to each other too. We were around ten years old, and we were nearly murdering one another.

One time my father caught us fighting and he didn't say a word. He walked into the kitchen and pulled out two big knives. He handed us each one and said, "Go ahead—you wanna fight? Go ahead! Fight!"

That stopped us dead in our tracks.

If his goal was to end our fight, it sure worked. But there was none of that positive, loving, "you shouldn't be doing that kind of thing" feeling. He was incapable of that. He was incapable of being kind or loving to his kids.

The strange thing was, though my dad and my mom fought with each other over many things, I never once saw him lift a finger against her. Their worst fight ended with them hitting each other with pillows—or rather, my mom throwing pillows at my dad.

As I lay there witness to this in the confines of that tiny bedroom in which all four of us lived, I feared that *I* was next—and that it would be more than pillows thrown when it came my turn. Somehow, I feared, this fight was going to be *my* fault.

All the violence was directed at my brother and me. Just us.

I was ten years old when my mom was eight months pregnant with my sister. I remember all four of us sitting in the Laundromat.

My dad was beside my mom, and he put his hand on her very pregnant stomach. He looked at my brother and said, "Finally, I get a *real* child. I finally have my own."

That was probably the most painful thing my dad ever said.

For me, there was no celebrating this coming birth. Here came someone we could compare our *worth* to—I mean *really* compare it to—and we were worth nothing compared to this new life about to join us.

From the moment my sister was born, I was torn. I was torn between my love for my baby sister and knowing that *she* was what my father loved and wanted.

"This is my number one," he would say. "I love her so much."

We weren't number one—we weren't even assigned a number! We just didn't exist.

Home for me *never* felt like a safe place.

There was no sanctuary. And there was *no* privacy.

When I was about twelve years old, I invited my best friend over and somehow we locked ourselves out of my bedroom. When her dad came to pick her up, her things were still in my locked room, so I *had* to ask my dad for help.

Well, that was it.

My dad marched over and took the door off its hinges. He was *furious*, but remained silent until my friend and her dad had left.

"*This* is what happens when you close doors!" he said.

After that, it became common practice for my dad to take doors off their hinges, especially whenever he saw a bedroom door shut all the way or found it locked.

He would invade our privacy whenever and however he felt like it.

Even when my dad *wasn't* home, we weren't safe.

The relatives who raised me also had a hand in my life. And unfortunately, they were abusive too.

When I was in the fifth or sixth grade, my aunt and grandmother were at home with me and my mom. My mom and I got into an argument that escalated until we were screaming at each other. I don't know what we were fighting about, but I remember having so much anger. I was *so mad* at my mom. I think that was my way of acting out all the anger generated by my father. I'd fight back with her, because I *couldn't* fight back with him.

As the argument worsened, someone called Uncle Adam. He drove over from his house a few blocks away.

I didn't see him coming. I didn't see *it* coming.

Uncle Adam charged straight into where my mom and I were, and he dragged me out of the room by my hair. He dragged me through the hallway and across the living room, and then he beat me up near the tile kitchen floor. All while my mom and my grandma and my aunt stood back and watched—probably in horror. Their screams for him to stop were faint, muffled. It was chaos.

Times like that built a lot of distrust of women for me, I realized in therapy. It seemed like *they* were the ones who instigated so much. *They* were the ones who put me in positions with the men in my life to beat the shit out of me. Because it was *mainly* the men in my life who indeed *beat the shit out of me!*

My father didn't know about the times my uncle "reprimanded" me. I sometimes wonder what he would have done had he found out. *Secrets.* There were always secrets. No one person knew everything that was going on.

And nobody ever came out and said, point-blank: "Abusing these kids is *wrong*, you *need* to stop." They may have said or thought it privately, but no one ever stepped up.

I was probably twelve or thirteen the first time I contemplated suicide. But I never acted on it and I never told anyone. My teachers and classmates had no idea how miserable I was. My closest friends didn't even know.

That's why I always had a boyfriend. For some reason, I felt that a boyfriend was the only safe person to tell my secrets to. Only my boyfriend would have *any* idea of what was really going on.

I lived my whole life like it was fine and dandy. I was now a master at living multiple lives—a master at the art of "fronting." No one would've guessed anything was wrong.

But in high school, I started ditching classes—or missing school altogether—for days at time.

When I was younger, I had really wanted to go to USC. I was virtually a straight-A student, on the honor roll year after year.

And from the second grade on, I was really involved socially. I was always class president or in some kind of leadership position—all the teachers and administrators knew me. I probably became active in hopes of getting some positive reaction from my parents—but it never worked. Nothing was ever enough for my dad. I never got any praise.

I was in the tenth grade when my parents sat me down and told me they couldn't afford to send me to a university. They said I needed to go to a local community college, so that there would be enough money for my brother's education too. After that, they said, I needed to get a good job so that I could pay for my sister's education, because they'd be too old to work by the time she reached college age.

It seemed a long way off before my sister would be college age, and I wondered anyway why this was *my* responsibility.

All that resentment boiled up again. Why the hell had I been working so hard at school all these years? What did all my good grades count for at the end of the day? There was nothing *wrong* with community college, but it's not what I was striving for. It was like *my* dreams and goals didn't matter, but my sister's did.

My attitude about school changed.

I didn't want to be in class with everyone anymore. I resented being there. I was still doing well *scholastically*—I could do all the homework, write the essays, read the books. But I just couldn't sit in a chair in class while nobody had a fucking clue about my home life.

Then one of the teachers found out I was ditching. She discovered I was forging the notes to get back into school, and she notified all my teachers—plus, she requested that they all *fail* me! All of the grades and assignments I had earned or completed were erased from my records.

By the time my mom got wind of all this, that same teacher had written a letter to the vice principal urging her *not* to meet with my mother. I knew this because all of my teachers were given a copy of that letter, and my chemistry teacher showed it to me privately.

Perhaps if just *somebody* would have asked what was wrong, maybe I could've said something.

I think that was my biggest resentment. Here I was going to school and having all these teachers who were supposed to uphold the American institution, and they were just oblivious.

I was very much acting out. I was ditching school. I was sick all the time. I was depressed. Something was wrong! But nobody stopped to ask what was the matter. You can't see a drop from nearly straight A's to straight F's in a matter of days without questioning what's going on. You can't have an honor roll student out of school for twenty-one days and not question what's going on.

But they didn't question. And I didn't offer.

Maybe they didn't want to get involved. Maybe they figured I was just another delinquent—like my dad always said. I don't know. But I had a lot of resentment about it.

I look back and ask, *Would I have even been ready to say anything had anybody asked?* I don't know. But I wonder how many people go through life like I did. Not seen, not heard.

For two years, I struggled with being in school. I wanted to escape. I'd take my boyfriend's car and just leave.

I just couldn't sit there in that chair.

My friends joked that they'd go to class every day and I'd still end up with a better GPA than them. I brought all my fails up to C's and B's. I just forced myself to get through.

I finally managed to graduate from high school—*on time* even. My dad didn't attend.

I had applied for a Cal State school, in spite of what my parents had told me. And I got in.

My dad was up and down about enabling me to go. He seemed to be struggling, too. It appeared he might pay for it out of duty: *Okay, I'll put her through college because all the outside people will see I'm putting my daughter through a university.* It was selfish. It was self-centered. I think it was for the benefit of his image.

But he *did* pay for it.

So I continued to live at home for my first year of college. And it was still hell.

The physical abuse had tapered off when I was sixteen or seventeen. It was like, *Oh, she's getting to be a woman now.* But the mental and psychological abuse continued.

My father was still always comparing me to the dog.

"I love the dog more than I love you."

By then, my younger sister knew what was going on. The physical abuse never touched her, but she was witness to it all, which in some ways was just as bad.

It was no secret that my father loved her more than he loved us. She knew that. I think all the time about what that has done to her, how it altered who she is. Because despite the favoritism, I loved—and still love—my sister very much. I helped raise her, look after her, nurture her.

I was glad and grateful that my father didn't abuse her.

When I was nineteen—at the end of my freshman year—my dad's favorite nephew came to visit from the Philippines; he stayed with us for quite some time. He was about twenty-seven years old.

We all went to Disneyland. You take *everybody* who comes to visit to Disneyland—it's the "touristy" thing to do. Toward the end of the night, everyone was really tired and undecided about what to do next. But nobody wanted to speak up—we always followed Dad's lead. Whatever he wanted to do is what we would do.

So we kept deferring to my cousin—passing off responsibility—because the whole trip was for him. But he just kept shrugging his shoulders. Finally, I spoke up and said I had a school project due tomorrow, so I'd rather just go home because I was already tired.

My dad got angry. *Really angry.*

You always knew when my dad was furious. He wouldn't talk at all—not a word. *Not one damn word.* That's when you *knew* something was boiling inside and was going to explode. It was like the calm before the storm when my father gave me, or anyone, the silent treatment.

Well the silent treatment that began that night continued on for another *few months*. It was torture.

One night, as expected, it all boiled over.

My brother was not doing well in school. He was failing classes and was in danger of not graduating on time. My father got angry and was yelling at him.

Meanwhile, I was on the other side of the house minding my own business. I was in my own room, at my desk, writing an essay. All of a sudden, I heard my dad charging across the house. He stormed into my room yelling, and he launched himself *at me!*

Every time my dad attacked us, we had to submit to whatever punishment he decided to lash out with. It's natural to put your hands up to protect yourself when you're being hit—we couldn't do that. We weren't allowed to react. We weren't even allowed to cry. When we cried, we knew we were going to get hit even more.

"Why are you crying? Crying won't help you!"

Sometimes my brother and I would just stand there side by side while we got kicked and hit and slapped and whatever. Metaphorically speaking, we had both developed full-body "calluses" against the pain, both physical and emotional. We just had to take it.

But this time was different.

I had been in my own world. I was working on *a paper*. This latest "affront" had nothing to do with me, yet here was my dad, invading *my* room and screaming at *me* about the Disneyland incident a few months ago! He kicked me *hard,* making me fall over sideways with my desk chair onto the hardwood floor.

I lay there for a minute, still on my side, unsure of what had just happened—and then unsure of what to do next. My heart pounded and my muscles tensed in anger. But I composed myself as quickly as I had fallen to the floor. Avoiding quick movements and neutralizing my expression, I got to my feet, righted my chair, and sat back down. I kept my eyes low.

My father wasn't finished yet though. He kept right on screaming, right into my ear.

What the fuck?! I thought.

I suddenly decided that I *wasn't* going to let him do this. For the *first* time, it was clear to me that I had done *nothing* wrong.

My dad was good at psychological games. The truth never mattered—at the end of the day, you felt like it was all *your* fault that he was angry. But this time…this time, I *knew.*

My dad's words became jumbled, muffled by some surge of gumption.

I stood up.

And then I stood up *to him.*

"I haven't done *anything* to you!" I said. "I don't know why you're so angry!"

That was a big deal. I had *never* defended myself or expressed how I felt. It was an unfamiliar reaction and it startled me. I think it startled everyone.

As soon as I opened my mouth, I knew I had already gone too far. You aren't supposed to open your mouth. You're supposed to wait until given permission to speak. But there was no going back.

All the shit started to come out. My anger, my fear, my resentment, my pain—it all surfaced. There I was, finally standing up for my brother and my mom and me after all these years—*for* all these years.

We were now in the living room and my brother came out of his room.

"Shut the fuck up!" my brother yelled—*at me!* "Just shut the fuck up!"

Are you kidding?! I thought. *Here I am trying to stand up for us and you're turning against* *<u>me</u>*?! *Now* *<u>I'm</u>* *the liar?* *<u>I'm</u>* *the one in the wrong?*

And that just gave my dad more power.

My cousin was there too. It was so "dishonorable" to fight back, and here I was doing it in front of a guest from the Philippines, who was sure to take this back home and tell the rest of the family how this man's daughter yells back at him.

My dad threatened to kick me out of the house. I knew he wanted to kill me. He lurched at me and I struck a defensive stance, ready to take his next attack. But my mother screamed and held back his arms, begging.

That was painful.

How the yelling and fighting ended that night is a blur to me still. What I *do* remember is lying in bed unable to sleep, unable to stop crying. I cried as quietly as I could to avoid waking anyone.

My dad was apparently restless too, though. He came to my room and stood in the doorway.

"Hey, hey you…" he said, pointing his finger at me, his eyes piercing me with hate and fury. "I'm not done with you. I'm not finished with you yet. You better watch your back!"

My chest tightened in fear and pain.

"I'm not done with you," he repeated. Then he left.

I cried harder and quieter.

From then on I *did* watch my back.

My father's words echoed in my mind, over and over. I was scared shitless that my dad would come after me and kill me.

I had done the most dishonorable thing to him: I had humiliated him in front of his nephew. I had yelled back at him. I had stood up for myself. I had called him out on his shit—on what he had been doing all these years. And *that* was the worst thing I could possibly have done—the ultimate wrong.

All these years, my dad's rage against *other* people and *other* things had always been turned toward me and my brother. But now, I'd given him a *real* reason to turn it against me. Now, it was: *I'm going to come after you <u>because you did something wrong</u>.*

And in my mind, I did. I had knowingly wronged him in *his* mind. It didn't matter if anyone else thought I was standing up for myself and doing something good. I had put myself in danger.

I could *hope* that my dad was bluffing (there had been many threats before) but I was truly afraid—terrified—that this time he was really going to come after me.

I was going to school full-time and my mom was working nights. She wouldn't come home until almost midnight. I feared that if she—or *someone*—wasn't home when I got there, my father would kill me.

So I wouldn't come home.

For nearly a year (or what felt like a year; I truly lost track of time), that's what I did. I would take everything I needed for the whole day—and *week*—in my car. I would go to school. I would volunteer at the church; I spent a *lot* of time doing volunteer work.

I also had a boyfriend. My boyfriend knew what was going on and his family had an idea, too. So they all took me under their wing. They fed me and treated me like a normal human being. I felt safe. I felt "a part of." Their home became my haven for hours every day, as I waited for my mom to get home.

My mom would call me when she was getting off the freeway. I would time it so we arrived together. Not that I thought my mom could really protect me, but I thought that she at least provided a buffer. He might *beat* me with somebody else there, but maybe he wouldn't *kill* me.

I *truly* feared that he would do it this time. I didn't want to call his bluff.

I had already walked on eggshells most of my life—as though my next step could be an exploding mine. This was no different. Except that now it was day in and day out of sheer terror.

My anxiety was relentless. I began having panic attacks. My fingers would tingle and weaken, to where I was unable to hold the steering wheel while I was driving. My car felt unsafe. I was always afraid somebody was lurking in the backseat, ready to pop out at me. And I was constantly looking in the rearview mirror, thinking somebody was following me. It could have been anybody in the car behind me, but deep down I feared it was my father coming after me!

There was so much fear. So much anxiety. So much paranoia. In retrospect, I know it wasn't rational, but it was *so* real to me.

Depressed, anxious, and paranoid, I contemplated suicide all the time.

Who would kill me first: my father or myself?

Now I'm coming home at midnight, arriving with my mother so my father won't kill me, and I'm petrified to ask for more money for my next semester at college.

"What do I do?" I asked my mom.

She asked my father to pay my tuition.

"She's not my daughter!" he replied. "She doesn't belong in this house anymore. *Ha!* You think I'm going to keep paying for her to go to school?" My dad almost always spoke like that—in rhetorical questions. You could only guess what his true answers were. This time it was pretty clear though. "She has no gratitude," he continued. "After everything she did, you think

I'm going to pay for her tuition?" He laughed. It was a scary, eerie laugh, so scornful in nature. It held so much anger, so much hate.

By "everything she did," one thing my dad was referring to was my staying out every night.

Months and months after kicking me over in the chair and telling me to watch my back, *he still didn't get it!* It didn't click. His assumption was: *She's not coming home because she's disrespectful. She is out there prostituting herself and doing drugs.* He accused me of that all the time. He once turned my arms over to check for drug-addict needle holes. I was a lowlife in his eyes.

Here I was in fear, in hiding. And he assumed the worst. He made up a character of me in his mind. It never seemed to dawn on him that *she's not coming home because I threatened her and she's scared!*

His view of me was always the lowest of the low. And apparently, the lowest of the low didn't deserve an education. Or perhaps his decision was simply vengeance. Maybe even just a bluff. But what he said next catapulted me in a new direction, onto a different path.

"I'm not paying for college anymore," he stated definitively.

As I stood there mutely, he told my mom that I didn't deserve to go to school anymore. He told her he was getting ready to take away my car and that by the way, "She doesn't belong in my house." He spoke to her as though I didn't exist, but loud enough that I'd hear every word.

He wanted me out of the house.

This changed everything.

I got frantic. I didn't have a job. Of course, that was because *he didn't want us to work.* In fact, he made me *quit* my first job, as a consequence for ditching school. He said it was to teach me a lesson about responsibility and accountability—he told me to tell my boss that I was a bad person who didn't deserve my job and that *that* was why I had to quit.

I realize now this was probably another way for him to have power over us and control things. If our lives did not depend so much on him, if we had our *own* money, we might have left—maybe a long time ago.

So there I was: no tuition for school, no job, and at risk of losing my car and the roof over my head at any moment. I didn't have enough money to pay for another two or three years of school. I did have a one-thousand-dollar scholarship from scoring in the top tenth percentile on some high school standardized test. It would be enough to cover half the tuition due that semester. I figured I could take out a loan to pay the rest and perhaps for the following semester as well. But thereafter, I would have to drop out and work full-time to support myself. I had to find work fast.

Out of sheer desperation and fear, I finally did something that I'd so long ago resolved never to do: I opened up and talked.

Classmates and friends knew that my father was "strict," but they had no way of knowing the extreme circumstances of my home life. I was careful about what I shared for fear of police or child services getting involved, and for fear of not being understood.

But I talked to three of my closest girlfriends about what I was facing now—and *why.*

I felt ashamed to tell them about my life—I thought they would think less of me. I had been brainwashed into thinking there was something inherently wrong with me, that this was why my father treated me the way he did. I was afraid they'd think so too.

But they didn't. They were quiet and seemed saddened. They wanted to find out how they could help.

One of my friends' cousins was in Pathways. The friend had previously mentioned some sort of "scholarship program" her cousin was in, but I had *no* idea what it was about. I had never even met this cousin. But my friend told me it was very important that I contact her. So I did.

"You need to call Dave Bishop," her cousin told me, and she gave me his number.

I gathered some information about the program on my own, and then I sat on Dave's number for a week because I was terrified. I thought: *This is an American institution and the website told me it was about abuse. This might be a trick to ferret out abusers!* I was so paranoid. *What if this is a way for the government to locate perpetrators*?

I had this elaborate conspiracy paranoia, and it was ridiculous. I would sit over at my boyfriend's and just cry over it. Day in and day out, the same tape played and replayed in my mind.

If I do this, I'll have to tell my story. And if I tell my story, they might call the police on my dad. If they call the police on my dad, the whole family is going to hate me because that will pull the family apart. And then, when Dad gets out, he is going to kill me!

During that time, I went on a job interview and I was waiting on a phone call to see if I got the position. I also made the call to Dave—*finally.*

I know now that it's a major step for all Pathways clients to make that call. It's a big deal. I think I came to the realization that I really had nothing to lose. What else was I going to do?

It was so unnerving to tell my life story to another soul, much less a stranger. I felt very private all of a sudden; I asked my boyfriend to leave the room and shut the door. But I told Dave. I was trembling the whole time.

"Thank you for sharing that with me," he said. He told me I definitely sounded like I qualified.

A few days later, I interviewed with Dave and his then-wife, Joyce. I told them things that I'd never told anyone before. I cried all the way through it. And they listened and they cried and they nodded. And for the first time, I heard somebody say, "You didn't deserve that."

Nobody had *ever* told me that. It was like suddenly I wasn't crazy. This stuff really *did* happen to me, and it really *was* wrong.

After the interview, they left the room to discuss my fate. They returned to tell me that Pathways was completely full and that there was already a long waiting list. "But," they told me, "we absolutely believe you deserve to be in this program." I might have to wait up to a year to start, but I was accepted.

In that moment, Dave and Joyce affirmed me. They affirmed me as a human being. Suddenly you're human, and you're being *treated* like a human. They gave me a hug and said they'd be in touch. It was so surreal. I was still shaking all the way home. I didn't know what to make of it all.

That same day I received a call from the employer I'd applied with—I got the job! God was putting things in motion for me; I could feel it.

During my potentially yearlong wait, I shifted into "survival mode."

I had managed to enroll in the next semester of school, paying my tuition with the scholarship. I charged the rest of my expenses to my credit card. I was determined not to skip a beat.

I started my new part-time job as a recreation assistant at an elementary afterschool program. I got paid to play! This job was a godsend—not only for the obvious reason that I needed money, but also for the less obvious reason that I got to be a kid again. I got to laugh, and run, and play. This was such a blessing.

In addition to working and going to school, survival mode meant continuing to stay out of my dad's way. After working for the same company for many years, my dad no longer had to work nights. Instead, he worked "normal" hours, which got him home every day by four o'clock in the afternoon.

Therefore, *I* tried to be *gone* every day by four o'clock. I didn't want to risk triggering my dad's upset again—mainly because I still needed my car a while longer and I was afraid he might take it away. I was afraid he'd take *everything* away before Pathways was ready to help me.

In my excitement about Pathways, I began to search for my first apartment. Even if it was a year away, I wanted to be ready. I *needed* to be ready. I had to have a plan.

Thankfully, that "possibility of a year's wait" ended when Dave called just two or three months later.

"It's okay to move now," he said.

I had the place all picked out. It was finally time for that move—that move *before four o'clock.*

I was twenty when I officially started Pathways and left my parents' house.

My father had no idea I was leaving. I just left.

I emptied my room from top to bottom—making it appear as if no one had ever been there. My move was like swimming with an air tank and knowing you have to get to the top before the air runs out. I had until four o'clock. That's all I was focused on. *Just get it all out, please, because he's coming home.*

I didn't have much—just a bed, a desk, a chair, a dresser, and all my clothes. It was very little.

I remember taking one last look when everything was out. That image is so clear in my mind—I don't even have to close my eyes. I see my room completely bare; I see the gloss on the hardwood floor. If anybody walked into the house, it would be very clear that I was no longer there. It was a statement: *It's empty. She's gone. Where did she go?*

I never asked what my dad's actual reaction was; I don't think I wanted to know. That was just for me.

When I finished, I stood in the doorway and took a deep breath. "Okay," I said, and I left.

By four o'clock my life had changed.

I moved into an apartment with one of my close friends. Neither of us owned furniture, other than the few items I'd brought with me. So all the rest was stuff donated by people to Pathways.

When everything was as moved and settled as it could be, I remember sitting in the dining area. We'd been given one of those old oak dining room tables with matching chairs—the rolling kind with cushions covered in tweed. It was odd.

I rested my hands on the oak arm rests and leaned back and looked around. From where I was sitting, I could see all the way around the apartment. Looking in the kitchen and then into the living room, I smiled.

I'm safe now, I thought.

That was a very significant moment for me. I had just been going, going, going for about a week. My roommate wasn't home, and I think it just kind of clicked or something: *This is mine.*

You know when you're by yourself and no one else is looking, and you're like, *All right.* You get real giddy. Talking to yourself. Looking around. Wide-eyed. *This is all mine.* I didn't care how old and weird that table was—it one of those old-fashioned hexagon tables with chairs on wheels—it was *mine.* This old couch from a country home—I didn't care.

I don't think anybody can take a home away from you. For the first time, I felt really safe. I think about it and I still remember just how that felt. To take a deep breath and look around and realize that my life had changed.

It was different.

I still had fears and paranoia and all that—I *still* struggle with that—but in that moment, sitting in that chair, I was the happiest person on earth.

When my roommate came home, I told her, "This is my house!" I was really excited. Because I could have people over. And not be afraid of my dad lashing out. Or have to walk on eggshells. I didn't have any of that. I didn't need that here. I had my own room, and the living room, and I liked my neighbors.

That was a miracle for me.

From then on, it was miracle after miracle—I don't know what else to call it.

Miracle after miracle.

I no longer spoke to my father after that. But I would still go by the house on weekends to visit my mom and my sister. I had the same amount of fear, but I loved my sister and mom. I wasn't going to let fear stop me from seeing them.

If my dad was there, I would just stay briefly, and it was like I didn't exist. We never said a word, and he wouldn't acknowledge that I was there. He'd walk right past me as I stood there frozen. *Silent.* Of course, that's how it had been when I was living there anyway.

My grandpa called me near the end of my first year in Pathways.

"Do you know what today is?" he asked.

"Yes," I said. "It's my father's birthday."

"Did you call to wish him a happy birthday?"

I had to laugh.

"*You* know what's going on," I said. "I haven't talked to my dad in almost a year!"

"Yes, but you need to remind him that you are still his daughter," my grandpa said. "And you *are* still his daughter."

I was so angry. Why did *I* need to call my dad to say happy birthday after all the shit he'd put me through? But I said okay to be respectful to my grandfather.

That "okay" was definitely easier said than done, though.

For the rest of the day, I battled with myself. As I contemplated the possibility of calling my dad, my head reran the tape of my dad's cold and scolding voice over and over. *But I'd promised my grandfather…*

When I got off work, I sat in my car in the parking lot with a friend I'd brought with me for support. And I called my dad.

My mom answered and I asked if I could talk to him.

"Really?" she asked. It was like a verbal double take.

He got on the phone.

"Hi, Pa," I said. "Uhhhh..." I paused. "Pa, happy birthday."

When he replied, there was a tone in his voice I'd never, ever heard. It was *surreal.* The second he opened his mouth, he just sounded so completely different.

And what he said was "Thank you."

It wasn't "What are you calling for?" It was "Thank you." My dad had never said thank you to me before. Ever. *Ever!*

And it was loving. It was loving and humble.

And then he asked, so softly, so kindly, "What are you doing today? We're just here at home—we didn't plan anything—but if you have time, maybe you can come over."

I sat there in my car, astounded, thinking, *Is he really inviting me back home?*

"Uh...okay," I said. "I'm at work but I think I can come by after."

"Okay," he said.

I had never heard my dad say anything like that or talk to me in that way before.

When I hung up, my friend and I looked at each other.

"What happened?" he asked. "Is everything okay?"

"My dad said 'thank you' and asked me to visit," I answered.

My friend knew everything. He asked if I was really going.

"I'm not sure," I said. "What if he's setting me up? What if he just wants to get me to the house so he can finally kill me?"

That's how twisted all of this was!

Still, this was the most unbelievable moment in my life. If the sincerity in his voice was real, this was everything I had ever prayed for.

Are you kidding me?

I had to go for it.

I never actually hated my dad. For some reason, I have a lot of forgiveness for him and everything he did. I strangely understood that this was his upbringing and the only way he knew how to raise us. That's *all* he knew.

It was just so unfortunate that *that's* how we had to grow up. I had prayed for it to be so different. From when I was really young, I *knew* this could all be so different—it didn't have to be this way. I prayed and prayed. It's really all I ever prayed for growing up. And that day my prayer was answered.

But I was still so scared and so paranoid, thinking it was a setup; so *I* set up an emergency plan. I had my friend follow me there in his car and sit outside.

"If you hear any noise, come get me," I told him. "Or if you see me running down the driveway, start the car and we'll go." I knew it wouldn't take long. "If my dad's luring me over to kill me, it's going to happen fast. Just be ready."

And I brought a cake. We went all the way across town to get a King's Hawaiian cake. I think it was partially a peace offering—like waving a white flag—and partially to give me something to do when I got there.

So in I walked with the cake, honestly expecting to be faced with a gun. It was scary.

But there was no gun.

So I walked across the room to my dad, and I kissed him on the cheek! I had never done that before. Not ever. But I walked in and said, "Happy Birthday," and I kissed him on the cheek.

It was very awkward. We never shared. Our life had so many contradictions. We had a lot of family gatherings but we never really did anything for each other out of love. It was, "Let's have a party because that's what everybody else would be doing." There was never any real intimacy.

But this time I brought a cake and we sang "Happy Birthday" and it was so terrifying. After a while, my mom and my sister went outside and I thought, *Oh shit, it's just the two of us on the couch.* So I went to the kitchen to clean up and pretend like I was busy. I didn't know what to do with myself.

My dad called out my name and said, "Come sit next to me." He patted the couch.

Fuck, I thought. *I'm so scared.*

He sat there and as he started to speak, he began to cry. And then he did something even more shocking: *He apologized.*

Not for crying. He apologized for *everything.*

For the first time in my entire life, my father admitted to me that what he had done was *wrong* and that *he was sorry.*

This wasn't just an apology, it was an affirmation of everything I had ever prayed for. All the things I had hoped to hear when I was younger, he said to me that day.

He told me that he loved me.

He told me that he was proud of me—*most* proud of me.

He told me that he loved all of us—all of his children—dearly and equally.

The exact words that came out of his mouth were exactly what I had prayed for. No affirmation that I could get from anybody or anything could compare to *that* affirmation from my dad—just acknowledging that I was his daughter. That how he handled things was not right. *That he did care about me.*

My dad had *never* said these things.

All I had ever aimed for was my dad's approval. And for him to have freedom to express that to me—for him to bring up my being his first child, for him to bring up my being so important to his world and to my mom's world, when I was told the exact opposite for so long—that was a fantasy for me.

When I had prayed for that, I had thought it was impossible. You're literally praying for a miracle when you pray for something that you think is impossible. And this *was* a miracle.

"I stopped going to church when you left," my father told me, "and I'm sure you know your brother's not around much."

My brother still lived there, but he kept himself scarce. To this *day,* my brother lives there. But he works in the evenings and sleeps all day. He doesn't involve himself much with the family. And I don't blame him for that. He's had it rough—maybe even rougher than me, being the boy of the family. And he hasn't had the opportunities for healing that I've had with Pathways. It still makes me sad.

"I never wanted our family to be torn apart like it has been," my dad told me. "Your mom made me go to church this morning because it was my birthday. I said, *Okay, God, give me a miracle! I'll know then that you're listening. All I want is for my kids to come home.*"

I don't know what strange twist of fate brought about my grandpa's call or my agreeing to call my father, but that's what my dad needed at that moment in *his* life—and that's what I needed to do at that moment in *my* life.

I cried. My dad held me. He wrapped his arms around me. He let me rest my head against his chest. I sobbed harder. He held tighter. My broken heart began to mend.

That could never have happened if Pathways hadn't taken me out of my situation. I would still be there today—still living in fear. Still under all of my dad's rage. And my dad would never have had to stop and think about what he was doing.

It's been different ever since.

My father is a changed person. I do still have a lot of fear. I get scared sometimes that the "old father" will come back—that he'll get annoyed by something and just blow up.

But he is *so* different.

And I stand my ground now. It helps so much that I don't live in that home anymore. I can just walk away. That was one of the most freeing things—that I suddenly had this choice that if things got too dangerous or scary, I could just leave and have somewhere to go. I had *my own place* to go to.

That was never apparent to me growing up. There was never a *choice.* Not in my mind. It was like I *needed* to put up with that. I was *supposed* to be there.

For most people, home is your safe haven. If there are bad things outside in the world, you run home. For me it was the opposite—home was the most dangerous place.

My sister has had to witness a lot of abuse, but I thank God she doesn't have the same father I had. Though I do admit that I resent it sometimes. As grateful as I am for how good things are now, as I watch my sister and my dad have an amazing relationship, I think, *Why wasn't I worth that? Why didn't he do that for me?* I struggle with that still.

My sister and my dad joke around and laugh. We all had lunch together the other day and my sister and my dad came down with headaches. They wound up sitting on the couch leaning their heads together. Even today I can't imagine leaning my head on my dad's shoulder. The only time he has ever held me was the day he apologized. That was when he held me for the first time like a father would—and *should*—hold his daughter in pain.

Today I am so happy that Pathways gave me the ability to make a choice for myself—the choice to not be in that kind of environment with my family.

And Pathways did so much more.

Little did I know, I had a *long* way to go.

In Pathways, I began seeing a wonderful therapist, Sharon Dickson. And it was she who discovered that I was a sex and love addict.

I still remember my first crush. His name was Brian. He was a blond-haired, hazel-eyed boy, and I had just the biggest crush on him. I thought I was going to marry the guy. And that was *in kindergarten.*

I think that with the horror of my home life, I was seeking somewhere to escape to. And the idea of marrying somebody—the thought of this

Prince Charming sweeping me off my feet and taking me away from the danger I was in—*that* was my escape.

I didn't know it then, but what I wanted was to be rescued.

And that pattern went on and on and on. There was *always* a boy I had a crush on, and as I got older, always a boyfriend there. When one relationship ended, another was already in the wings. That was my safehold.

My boyfriends were the only ones I told the truth to. I made them my confidants. I shared my deepest secrets. And whether they—or *I*—knew it, what I subconsciously expected was for them to save me. To keep me safe.

I had one relationship after another. I was fortunate that none of them were dangerous—*until* the relationship I entered into when I was twenty-one years old and already in Pathways.

This relationship was with a man ten years my senior, who was my supervisor at work. He was the ideal person to save me.

But when that relationship started to fall apart, I started to self-destruct.

It deteriorated to the point where there was a lot of fighting; a lot of verbal abuse; there was cheating going on; there was lying. It became physically abusive and sexually abusive. Yet still, I could not walk away. I could not walk away if my life depended on it.

And it *did* depend on it. It reached the point where my life hinged on it.

The beginning of the two-year end was when my boyfriend bought a home in Mexico. He made me a lot of promises, including that he wanted us to get married and for me to move there with him.

This was a dream come true. First was the enticement of a waterfront home in Mexico. But even more so, although things *were* better at home, this was finally my chance to escape. And it was ideal that this man was going to save me. He was going to whisk me away and marry me, and we were going to live a happy life in a beachfront condo and roll around in the sand.

This was the ultimate fantasy. And I was willing to—and *did*—throw my life away to chase after that.

Things got abusive in that I became destructive to *myself* when the relationship wasn't going right. I blamed myself, so I hurt myself physically and emotionally. And I became even more depressed and anxious than when I had actually been being abused.

I would literally hit my head against the wall. In therapy, I learned there's a lot of correlation with that: My father did a lot of poking our heads, or hitting or slapping our heads. So that felt the most familiar to me.

Whenever my life felt unmanageable or chaotic, or I didn't feel like I was being heard, or I was in a fight with a boyfriend—that's what I would turn to. I would bang my head against the wall until I was too tired or too dizzy to continue.

That was the only way I felt I could contain myself: by being incapable. Just *incapable.* Not through drinking or anything else, but by being dizzy or delirious. *That* was my drug. That was my way of numbing out. It was my only way of stopping the chaos.

That same tape kept playing in my head: *I'm worthless, I'm shameful*—all the things my father used to tell me, repeated over and over. And even though things were getting patched up with my dad, the tapes kept playing and playing. It was still there.

So whenever the tape played, I would hurt myself the same as my dad hurt me. I hit myself too. I hit myself to the point where I'd try to give myself bruises, but I couldn't. I never had a bruise from my father either; there was nothing ever to show.

My lowest point came when I got into a fight with my boyfriend over the phone and banged my head against the wall so hard that I gave myself a minor concussion. That was a pretty *low* low for me: sitting in a doctor's office, trying to explain how I had injured my head.

Of course, *before* I went to the doctor, I drove two hours on the freeway in a painful daze because I *needed* to see my boyfriend. He had taken off during our fight and the fight wasn't over yet.

I chased and chased. I needed to fix us. I needed a fix.

It was destructive. I drove myself crazy. I drove him crazy. I drove *everybody* crazy!

The day my boyfriend left for Mexico, I found out he had lied to me about circumstances—including whom he was going with. A lot of things came up that didn't make sense. But I wanted it so bad that I was still so forgiving. And that was when my love addiction spiraled out of control into a sex addiction.

After my boyfriend moved, we started an ongoing long-distance relationship. So I'm living this life with him over the phone and still trying to work out our relationship, even though I'm infuriated with him for all the lies. Big lies. Little lies. Petty lies. So many lies. In the two years of our roller-coaster relationship, I visited him in Mexico three times, while he came back to California three times. Though we saw each other scarcely, our relationship was toxic.

We'd talk daily and fight daily. Fight, make up, fight, make up. He'd tell me he was going out with female coworkers. He'd tell me about drugs, women, and partying, and how good life was down there. He'd tell me things to hurt me.

How familiar.

To cope with all that, I started going out to bars and clubs and being promiscuous with people I didn't know. That became my escape from what was going on inside. And it was an even unhealthier escape than what I was already in.

My boyfriend would tell me about his escapades in Mexico, and I would turn around and re-create them here with my life. It was really my way of saying "Fuck you" without really saying it. Every person I saw after that represented my big fuck you to him, though he didn't even know it.

He would *never* have known unless I told him. But I *did* tell him, and that just fueled things. For me, it fueled my sex and love addiction, my codependency, and my alcohol addiction. I can only assume he was an addict too. I can't say for sure, but I do know we fed off each other. Our toxicity was addictive.

There was something intensely satisfying about the roller coaster of emotions we experienced daily.

I think my love addiction was prominent and my sex addiction was just a manifestation of that. I didn't *want* to be intimate with any of these people; I was just using them to numb the feelings caused by my current relationship. So it was all very chaotic.

It was all very destructive.

It was all very unhealthy.

It was all very dangerous.

It was *my* way of living on the edge. I didn't know what it meant to black out. I didn't know what it meant to get high. I didn't know what it meant to get arrested. I didn't know what it meant to do any of those things. But *this* was my edge.

And it was a silent edge. Because nobody knew what was going on behind closed doors. I knew how to live multiple lives; I *grew up* living multiple lives. So I was perfect at it.

Even my friends who went out with me—they each only went out with me once a week. I had *different* groups of friends who I went out with on different nights, so that each group wouldn't know that I was going out five nights in a row.

I involved myself with strangers. I knew their first names and that was it. You hear news stories all the time about things happening to women like that—and I was walking in there with my eyes closed.

I sought out dangerous people, because if I was in dangerous situations, then my current relationship wasn't so bad.

My last trip to Mexico was nearly four years ago. The visit began like the previous two: honeymoon-like, both of us acting oblivious to our toxicity and destructiveness. We were together and all was well.

But it wasn't long before insecurities and tempers flared. I skipped my scheduled flight home.

I was excited to spend more time with him, but by that evening, instead of lying in my bed at home, I lay in mud beside some bushes that he had flung me into during *another* fight.

That night, which I should have spent safely at home in bed, I spent in some sex motel in the middle of the city where he dropped me off to stay. I lay there in that strange, scary place, covered in mud and tears and running mascara, alone and terrified that I had been left there to be raped. I thought I had just been sold for sex.

It was four o'clock in the morning when I got ahold of a friend in California.

Four o'clock.

"Please take down this hotel name," I told him. "I am supposed to be on a plane home tonight. If I don't call you back, send help. Please."

That's where things really came to a head.

When I did make it home, my therapist said to me: "If you don't stop this, Lin, you'll end up dead, one of three ways: You'll contract something that will slowly kill you"—referring to HIV/AIDS—"you'll end up with a man who will kill you, or you'll end up killing *yourself* out of depression and from shame of how your life is going."

She was right.

Truth is, I was *already* dead inside.

My therapist's words were what brought me to the rehabilitation facility that eventually changed my entire life path. It changed everything.

Going into rehab, I was afraid.

I had an upcoming trip to the Philippines planned with my family, so I'd already negotiated a month off of work.

"How convenient is that?" said Sharon.

"But how do I tell my parents that I can't go on this trip that we've been planning for nearly a year?"

There was *no* excuse for it—other than to tell them the truth.

Sharon actually did a house call; she came with me to my parents' house. It was just too scary for me to do alone.

In my family's eyes, everything was resolved because my father and I had made up. We had at least a year under our belts already. So this came as a huge surprise for them all—my brother, my sister, and especially my parents.

They didn't know I was suicidal. My depression was something I hid very well. I was always laughing and joking.

Now, for the first time, I had to get honest with my family. At least in part. We didn't touch on the sex and love addiction; that was all extremely private. But Sharon told them I needed to go for treatment because I was severely depressed.

It was actually a blessing to see my family so concerned about me. I had never given them that opportunity. After the patch-up with my dad, I had lived as though everything was okay, because I didn't want to rock the boat anymore. Because it *was* okay—now.

But I still hadn't healed from the past. I still wasn't better. I had to come to terms with God. I had to tell the truth.

The rehabilitation facility I went to was basically a psychiatric hospital that treats people with all sorts of problems: alcohol addiction, drug addiction, eating disorders, love addiction, sex addiction, depression, post-traumatic stress disorders. It was in another state and Dave Bishop accompanied me on my flight there.

I had already done a lot of therapy with Sharon and some work with Dave, who was my mentor, so I had learned what it meant to open up and face my issues. But *this* was really intensive. It was like: *This* is your reality. *This* is where it has brought you.

I discovered I had been reenacting my childhood in an abusive relationship. But I hadn't *seen* my relationship as abusive because for such a long time I couldn't see my family situation as abusive. And as with my family, I couldn't fathom *leaving* the relationship.

I think I can finally look back on my whole life history and see it for what it was, because I was first forced to see that relationship for what it was. That's what *really* drove me into full recovery.

In rehab, I had to face my childhood trauma head-on. I finally examined all the facts realistically. Before that, I had viewed it as "not that bad." I had rationalized it. I had minimized it. I had compartmentalized different parts of my life, placing each experience in a box and tucking it away where I didn't have to look at it. But my childhood trauma was a *real* part of my life. And though my father's apology had begun the mending of my broken heart, I certainly had not yet healed *completely*. So a lot of my recovery has been trying to heal those childhood wounds.

I also had to look at my relationships. I started going to twelve-step meetings and that's where I learned to look at my pattern, to see that it started *way* back. I had such a lack of male nurturing. I had sought relationships with guys to make up for what my dad and my uncle did. I was still seeking a relationship to fix me or make me whole. Yet I sought out the type of men I thought I deserved. And in my years growing up, I'd learned that I didn't deserve much.

Twelve-step is also where I learned that my behavior was an *addiction*. It wasn't about love or sex; nor was it about wanting to be in a relationship. I was addicted in a compulsive and excessive way to something destructive. It didn't matter how many times I was asked to stop or how dangerous I *knew* someone or something was, I couldn't stop. I *wanted* it to stop and I *needed* it to stop—but I needed the numbing effect it had *more*. It was too painful to be alone, too painful to face reality, too painful to *not* be numb. It was all too painful.

Hence, sex and love addiction.

We also discovered I had post-traumatic stress disorder (PTSD). You think of PTSD arising in people who've witnessed murders or who've fought on the battlegrounds of wars and such. I didn't think of my *childhood* as being capable of causing it. But it did.

I can now see why. I can see how I was reacting like a war veteran; how everything on the outside was supposed to be nice and perfect and okay, and how everyone else seemed to be going about their life okay. But inside, my life was really messed up. The anxiety I experienced; the tingling in my fingers; the paranoia of people following me and lurking in the dark; the broken record playing over and over in my head; freezing up, unable to move, in unsafe situations—post-traumatic stress disorder.

I have been asked if I was sexually abused—I'm not sure. I do have a memory of being naked in the bathtub with my uncle at age four. I also realize that his explicitness about my womanhood and breasts, from puberty onward, was and is inappropriate. For instance, when I arrived at a party one time, he exclaimed, "Gosh, your boobs got bigger!" And this was in front of all the family and guests! I think my lack of appropriate relationship boundaries stems partly from not being shown where they *should* be.

My therapist also said I was abused in terms of the male-female factor. As a female, I was suppressed. I grew up in a home and cultural dynamic where women say nothing and the man is the head of the household. The man makes the decisions and the women are supposed to be submissive and compliant. It didn't matter how we were feeling; there was no voice. In that sense, there was sexual abuse for sure—like the time my uncle beat me and the women just stood back silently and let it happen.

I feel like I've always believed there is equality between men and women; but nothing in my life history backs that up. But today, I live by that. I don't think there is anything a man can do that I can't do. Still, things "trickle" into my mind sometimes because of all that was ingrained in me. I'll look for relationships where I can fall into that role where the woman takes care of the man—*codependent.* And mine is to the extreme!

After I was in rehab for thirty days, they recommended that I stay in aftercare for four more weeks—and after *that,* even longer. "Our clients can only stay up to twelve weeks," they told me, "and, really, even twelve weeks is not enough for you." That was very humbling.

They moved me to an aftercare facility that dealt specifically with sexual trauma and childhood trauma. I lived in a home with seven other people and we all did group therapy together and were basically roommates. It was less strict than the hospital facility, but the work was more intense.

We had freedom to use the phone there, but within the restrictions of our addiction—if this is your compulsion, you shouldn't be doing it. But I couldn't stop trying to contact my boyfriend.

Of course he was by now my *ex,* because in the thirty days at the thirty-day facility, it became clear to me and to everybody else that he was not showing up. That fantasy bubble had been popped.

But even still, I wanted to fix it. I *needed* to fix it. So I couldn't stop. Not once did I reach him or hear his voice, but I couldn't stop dialing. I couldn't stop trying to contact him.

My counselor put me on a "three-strike policy" for my compulsive behavior. I wasn't allowed to call him.

The day I broke my third strike, both of my counselors were out. A lot of things had triggered my compulsion that day, but regardless, I did it. When it was time to check in with the substitute counselor, I told her what I'd done.

I came clean because that is all I knew to do. I *had* to because that's what I was trying to recover from, and I wasn't able to stop myself.

She didn't even know about the policy on me—but I told her that too. "I think I just struck out for the third time," I said. When she asked what that meant, I explained that I would be kicked out. *I* didn't know what getting kicked out really meant, other than that I would have to leave. But what it meant was that I had to pack my things, buy a ticket, say my good-byes, and be out of the facility *within the hour.*

I was shocked and devastated. I was supposed to be there for another six or seven weeks. I was settled in. I was *living* there.

Plus, I had made friends there. I had shared deep, intimate secrets with these people—they had become my family. And now I had to suddenly leave; a driver would be here in an hour.

This is it, I thought, sitting in the counselor's office. *Nobody outside here knows that I'm headed home. No one knows I've been kicked out.* The plan in my head was: *I'm going to have the driver take me to the motel down the street, and I'm going to kill myself.*

I hit bottom.

I knew how I'd do it, too. I'd drink myself into oblivion and drown myself in the tub. This was how I planned to go. It would be my biggest "Fuck you" to everybody. Fuck you, to my counselors. Fuck you, to my parents. Fuck you, to just the whole thing, because I was done with it. I felt like a hopeless, helpless case.

Adding to my torment was that my *entire* stay at this facility had been funded by Pathways benefactors—out of their *own* pockets, not the Pathways account. My flight there. Every day there. Everything I had. My *entire* treatment. To this day, I am so grateful to the generous family who saved my life. But that was all the more reason to be ashamed. Because it was like, *I can't even get this right for these people who helped me!* It began to sink in that perhaps my dad had been right about me all along when he used to tell me I was stupid and couldn't do anything right… that I was worthless.

I was very clear on *exactly* what I was going to do when I left the facility. In my mind, it was perfect.

But I called Dave.

If he didn't pick up, I decided, that was it.

And he actually *didn't* answer—but he called back immediately.

"I have an hour to pack up and go," I told him. "Please pick me up from the airport."

Those words came out of my mouth by the grace of God. It wasn't *me.* I had *my* plan. I was *set* on what I wanted to do.

But for whatever reason, I asked Dave to come pick me up.

Getting off the plane back home was a shock. Here I had been in this safe and nurturing facility—or what had *seemed* like a safe facility—with people who were going through the same thing I was. I was having to work through some hard stuff, but as difficult as it was, you don't know what you've got till it's gone. Now I was outside in the real world. It was like, *I have to be alone again. I am alone again.*

"What are you going to do now?" Dave asked me. "What do you *want* to do?"

I didn't have an answer for him. I told him what my plan had been.

"Are you willing to make an appointment with Sharon?" he asked.

I shrugged. There was nothing I could say.

The whole thing was sort of like *actually* attempting suicide and not succeeding; it felt like that for me. It was as if I'd killed myself in that counselor's office when they told me I had an hour to pack and go. I didn't have any plans *after* that—my plan was to die.

So I think what I did is just the very next thing that I was asked to do. I don't know how I got up in the morning—how I did anything. I was just a robot for a while.

Dave took me under his wing, and for all anyone else knew I was still at the rehab center. I was too raw to be back in the world.

I stayed in my own apartment, but Sharon and Dave kept me on a regimen. "We have to replicate what you were doing there," they said. "We have to keep your schedule."

So I worked and I went to therapy.

During the day, I worked with Dave in construction, helping remodel homes. And every day I saw Sharon, who provided her services pro bono. She saw me *every* day, so that I could be alive. Not *live*, but be *alive*. Alone.

Sharon told me later there were days that I *looked* dead. My eyes were blank and you could tell I was dead inside.

When she finally saw a spark of life coming back, she said to me: "Lin, you may not have *thought* you were trying to fight for your life, but when you called Dave and you came back home and then you appeared in my office, you *chose* your life and you chose to live.

"Somewhere inside," she continued, "you must have known that there was something to live for. You must've known that there was something better for you and that you deserved more."

And it's true.

I could barely see that for what it was, until I had crossed all these barriers and gotten to the other side of it. I got back from that dark place and I was like, *Holy shit, I do have a lot to live for.*

And I *did*. But I couldn't see it. Dave and Sharon literally held my hand; I couldn't have done it without them.

This was definitely life-changing stuff.

It was a big year—a *really* big year. A lot of changes. A lot of facing reality. Everything since then has been picking up pieces and putting things together. Rebuilding my life almost from the ground up. Re-parenting myself.

Even though things are good now with my family, my head is still back there. So I have to re-parent myself. I have to learn to love myself and to remind myself that I have worth; that I deserve to *live*.

And I have. My life is different. I can't imagine banging my head against the wall anymore.

Still, letting go of my ex has been an ongoing battle. Because I am an addict. And he was my drug.

When I got kicked out of rehab, I *still* wanted to put the pieces back together. I called him from the airport before I flew home. And I tried again after I landed. I called him for a long time trying to fix something.

There is *still* something that I'm trying to fix. I think my trying to fix the relationship represents something even more that I have yet to discover. It has yet to be revealed.

But the urge, the compulsion, *has* finally dissipated.

It's now been over a year since I was in that relationship. It's been difficult to stay away from potential relationships or the whole dating thing. It's been *really* difficult. Where so many would turn to a drink, I would turn to a relationship or to a man. I still struggle in my twelve-step programs.

But I've managed to do it. I've managed to stay away from alcohol as well. Though for me, it wasn't so much the drinking, but the lifestyle that came with it. *These* people were drinking; that's the arena where I would engage with them. Drinking went hand in hand with it all. It's still easier for me to put down a drink than to walk away from a relationship—or even a *potential* relationship. It's much, much harder to do that.

Recently my ex-boyfriend tried to get in touch with me. People in my fellowship teased me, saying, "Well, we know you've made progress because you haven't packed your bags and gone to Mexico!"

Because that's what I would have done back then. I would've dropped my life—my entire world, everything I have and do here—I would have traded it all in for the possibility of that relationship. No promises, just the *possibility* of it. Or the possibility of *fixing* it. I would've dropped it all in a heartbeat.

I'm not willing to do that today. I'm not willing to throw my life away again.

I have so *many* good things worth staying for—worth *living* for.

When I went to rehab, I had just become a regular, full-time employee at my job. But they had approved my trip to the Philippines, because I had just graduated and I told them I hadn't been able to go home in years.

But even that was unconditional; it really surprised me. When I told them of my change in plan—not all the facts, but that I had childhood trauma to deal with and wasn't going to the Philippines anymore—they were fine with it. They were really supportive.

Then I had to call my boss a month later and ask him to give me four more weeks. I then had to call him back and say, "I actually need *twelve* more weeks." I told him I would understand if they had to let me go, but that this was very important to me and I needed to work on these issues, regardless.

"Take all the time you need," he replied. "Call us when you're ready."

They eventually *did* have to take me off the payroll, because it didn't make sense to keep me on it for so long. But they rehired me just as soon as I called and said I was ready.

Today I'm their human resources manager. I'm doing exactly what they promised I'd be doing.

And they have never questioned what I had to do or what it was all about. The most I've ever gotten is my boss joking around with me, saying, "So, have you been with us for as long as you've been on vacation?" For a long time I was in the negative—I was gone for five months after being officially employed by them for only two!

That's God's grace working. Working in ways I can't fathom. They are just good people.

I learned so much about relationships and about myself through my therapy at Pathways and the treatment facility. I learned so much by going to twelve-step meetings.

I had to *find* worth. I had to realize that people still love me regardless of my past, regardless of what happened, and regardless of what I did when I was acting out my addictions.

Back when I first returned from rehab, Dave set up a lunch with Debbie Bickerstaff, who gives so generously to the Pathways foundation and speaks at all the graduations. I told him I didn't know if I could face her after getting kicked out of my program.

"You're just as human as I am," Debbie said to me that day, "and I love you the same as before. People get kicked out all the time. This is just *your* process." She was just so loving about it. "What would make us happy is for you just to continue to be here and keep living and keep trying to heal."

If that doesn't prove to somebody how loved they are or how deserving a person is in spite of mistakes, I don't know what does.

I couldn't have learned to love myself if it hadn't been for the people in Pathways. That wasn't something that was taught at home. I think it's something innate that I lost because of my whole life—and Dave and Sharon and the Bickerstaffs and everyone else who followed, they restored that. They restored that by example.

The times when I didn't think I was worth it, when I didn't think I deserved it, when I didn't love myself—*they* did it for me. They believed in me. They loved me. Through all of it. All of that, for me, was an absolute miracle, the *ultimate* gift.

Today, I'm still doing the same things I was always doing. I'm still very involved in things and very active as a volunteer. Overall, I'm considered successful.

In the eyes of people on the outside, I was successful back then too. But today it's what's on the inside. Back then, it was all about trying to survive or to escape or both. Now I take action because this is what I love to do. It's really who I am.

The people I choose to have in my life—my friends, my coworkers, my fellows in recovery—are all here because they're my true friends. I'm not living multiple lives anymore. What you're seeing is pretty much what you're getting.

I'm very open today. For the most part, my story is not a secret. We don't talk about it at home, but mainly because there's no need to anymore.

Everything is just different.

Today I have that *worth*. Not for anything I *do* or that I *have*, but just for being who I *am*. Just for living and breathing. Just for existing.

I have worth!

No more than you; no more than anyone else—but no less.

Back then, I felt like I needed to have good grades or a boyfriend or the image or whatever everybody or anybody expected from me—I thought I needed to fulfill that to have my worth.

Today I have my worth—whether I have nothing or I have everything.

The Nightmare After Christmas

"My mother faced my father with a gun in her hand, her floor-length white terrycloth robe soaked in blood."

—Sara

My first memory as a child is something I hold dear. This memory has a fairy-tale quality to it. I remember it as if it were yesterday—like I've been transported back in time to that little girl. The vibrancy, excitement, and sneakiness I felt then, I can feel now. I remember what I was thinking, seeing, hearing.

This memory is the archenemy of the reality of my childhood. It shouts that everything was normal and that I was a just like any other little girl the night before Christmas.

My actual journey from childhood into adulthood was nothing short of a nightmare. There would be beatings, blood, fierce protection in the midst of abandonment, and women coming and going. Alcohol abuse, drug use, life on the run, empty fridges, and molestations from multiple offenders—these were all a part of the story as well.

Maybe that is why I choose to hold my first Christmas memory in the light of a fairy tale. Because it a story that comes alive only when read aloud from a book.

I remember waking my mother to go downstairs to get something. I can't remember what it was, but I just had to have it right away.

The Christmas tree just *happened* to be at the bottom of those stairs, and it just *happened* to be Christmas Eve. I was an innocent three-year-old, excited by the idea of Ol' Saint Nick delivering all of my hopes and dreams on one night—so apparently I just couldn't wait until the morning. (Patience is still not a virtue of mine, but it's something I try to work on every day!)

I don't remember what I expected at the bottom of those stairs—but what I saw was beyond my imagination.

My hopes and dreams weren't *that* expansive; a three-year-old didn't have the capacity to wish on a little star for anything *too* incredible—just some simple things: maybe a baby doll to call my own. What I found was a room full of presents wrapped in beautiful paper. And when I say a room, I mean the *whole* living room full.

The entire space had turned into a Candyland of sorts. Presents upon presents were piled on top of each other, creating colorful walls like some sort of festive fort. Some were wrapped and others just had a big bow on top. It was as if they were all glowing in the dark, showing me the way to them. I was in heaven and nothing existed but this moment.

Slowly but surely, my mom allowed me my sneak peak of Christmas morning. This was the nicest my mother ever was to me. Every subsequent memory of her is of total ugliness and hatred.

I no longer remembered my reason for coming downstairs. It was officially Christmas Day. But it was still dark, and I had to wait for my dad and little sister. It was my sister's first Christmas, but I knew all those presents were for me; after all, I was the *big* sister. This eventually became my curse.

I don't remember much more about that day except that it was glorious. I got a sled, Cooties, games, candy, clothes, and everything I had dreamed of. The family was together. I was in my flannel pajamas, the ones with the feet. (I still want another pair of those, but I can't quite find them anywhere!) My mother, father, and baby sister were there, and almost all of those presents really *were* mine. I felt special and alive and untouchable.

I felt *loved.*

My family loved me. I knew it in my core. I could never have imagined that this all would be a rarity instead of the norm.

I have other little memories of catching lightning bugs in Mason jars; picking out my first records, which were *Disco Duck* and *Grease;* getting my baby stroller that played "It's a Small World"; and eating French toast on my Mickey Mouse plate. I remember crawling into my mother and father's bed in the middle of the night when I had bad dreams; I remember the first time I held my baby sister the day she came home from the hospital; and I remember staring peacefully at my ceiling as I fell asleep at night.

I remember walking out my front door into the falling snow, going for a ride in my dad's sporty little MG, and playing with babysitters while my parents were gone.

However, my next *big* memory leads the way into the hideousness that defined my early life.

I was in first grade and my sister was three. Our parents had separated, and my father was taking care of my sister and me. (Of his six children from three marriages, we were the only ones he fought to hold onto.) We lived in Nevada in a one-bedroom apartment, where my dad gave us the room while he slept on the living room couch.

Throughout their separation, my parents were always "breaking up" and getting back together. They would drink and do drugs and have sex, and then fight. This was one of those nights.

My mother and father were arguing in the living room. My dad had told us to stay in our room and lock the door—probably because my mother had kidnapped us once.

It was very late, way past our bedtime.

I remember being scared, but even more so, protective of my sister. She was so young and so frightened. She was just a little girl with her soft golden blond ringlets and sweet angel face.

I could feel the anger and tension growing in my parents' voices. They were yelling and screaming with no end in sight. I heard rustling and then bodies being thrown against the wall. Things were escalating and I just wanted it to stop. Even as a young child, I knew this wasn't right.

Finally, I'd had enough.

I can't remember if I was in more fear for us or them, but I knew that I couldn't take it anymore. Somehow I got the courage to let go of my sister, unlock that door, and go out into the living room. And when I finally crossed the safety of that threshold, I was met with the most horrendous sight.

My father was in his own world, with his back to me. But I didn't really notice him because my eyes were fixated on my mother. Nothing else existed in that moment.

It was surreal. She faced him with a gun in her hand, her floor-length white terrycloth robe soaked in blood. She looked like an animal.

I didn't know what to do. This was not supposed to be happening. I remained still, so they wouldn't know I had seen them. But fear of my mother being hurt was penetrating my frozen little body.

The next thing I knew, my father was picking up my mother, throwing her outside, and locking the door. When he came back in, I saw that all of the blood on my mom's robe actually belonged to him.

After that, I don't know if the cops showed up or if we all just went to sleep; my dad didn't get medical care—we never saw a doctor unless forced to.

I *do* know that things had changed and would never be the same.

This was to set the tone for the rest of my life. My mother coming and going—sometimes absent for years at a time—and my sister and me being raised by an angry drunk. It's just who and what my father was.

But I didn't know that our family was different. How could I? I was just a little girl. A little girl with two insane alcoholic parents.

My parents were the baddest of the bad, and they would beat into submission anyone who got in their way. They fought cops, gangs, bar patrons—anyone. They thrilled in acts of violence, and in their minds it brought them status.

When my mother was pregnant with me, my parents were whooping it up at our house after a friend of my dad's wedding reception. The cops showed up, entering into an abyss of drunken fun and debauchery. It was time to wind the party down, but my parents weren't having any of that business. As the story goes, my mother ran her mouth and was thrown against the wall with a nightstick to her neck. Now, I realize she was pregnant, but knowing my mother, this was probably the force needed to restrain her—not excessive to say the least. This launched a chain of events in which the entire wedding party ended up in jail, because my father jumped the cop, which led to the other cop jumping *him,* which led the rest of the party jumping in.

Needless to say, they all considered this a fun story to tell, rather than an embarrassing night of regret.

When my parents' violence wasn't thrown towards someone else, they turned it on each other. Or on me. My father abused both my sister and me, but I usually bore the brunt of it, sometimes by choice. My mother wasn't really around to beat me, but she did try to strangle me to death once.

Despite my parents' love/hate relationship, they divorced when I was in about first grade. My father went to court to gain full custody; he showed up every day to fight for us. After what seemed like a long, drawn-out court case, he won. The last day of the hearing, my mother didn't even show up.

However, my mother *did* show up at our house; she broke in with one of her many boyfriends from a local biker gang. This was not unexpected, or the first time my mother had stolen into our lives and taken us from any kind of safety.

My father had warned us to keep the house locked and not to open it for anyone, but we'd accidentally left the sliding glass door ajar when we'd let the dog out. My mom and her boyfriend kidnapped us, dragging my elderly great aunt—who held onto my leg for dear life—across the rocks in our front yard.

This shook up the rest of the family, who feared we were gone for good. The police got involved but didn't really do anything. Finally, my uncle's wife told my father where we were.

I remember being treated okay while on the run, though my mom's boyfriend was also abusive. We stayed mostly in dumpy hotels—and we were alone when the cops finally showed up to bring us home.

Years later, my mother told me she allowed us to be found because the men she was involved with were tangled up in dirty things and she didn't want anything to happen to us. Hypocritical, if I do say so.

I really could have used a mother, growing up. Every time she disappeared, we felt abandoned by the woman who had given us life.

These stings would creep into my soul and hurt me for years to come. I could never have imagined the damage done.

From there, our lives continued on how they had been. My father was addicted to drugs and alcohol, and allergic to work. Everything was a scam and I don't remember ever feeling safe.

Throughout second grade, I shared a bed with the daughter of one of my father's many fiancées. She was in eighth grade, and somebody should have realized this was inappropriate. I have no memory of what happened, but years later, my emotional and physical trauma made sense when my father nonchalantly mentioned to me that I was molested.

I was molested again in the sixth grade—repeatedly—by the eighteen-year-old male friend of another of my father's girlfriends. My father saw how "touchy" the guy was with me, but did nothing. It only ended after one more of our many moves. (Though he visited us again four years later and molested me again.)

My sophomore year of high school, my dad was working as a manager at a local fast food joint. One night, he came home late, followed closely by one of his best friends, E-Z. The mood in the house was noticeably different that night. There was an easiness to everything. Something had happened.

After having pizza and pop, I overheard my dad and his friend talking. They had staged an armed, masked robbery, in which my dad had pretended that he was being held at gunpoint by a real robber and not his best friend. The pizza we had just eaten was bought with that money.

Unfortunately, I don't remember thinking it was a wrong or bad thing. I had food in my belly, I was being allowed to swim in our pool, and my father was in a good mood. There was nothing else I could ask for.

However, there were many more days and nights of *no* food in the fridge or pantry—except my dad's booze—and a constant hustle to get some. My nana and my great aunt (Nana's older sister) tried their best to be in our lives, but my dad would only let them in when we really needed something; many empty fridges were filled by them. My nana even drove out from Nevada to California to buy us groceries.

One day to the next was a struggle, and I never knew which way was up.

Despite all this madness, I excelled at school. I got amazing grades and was even asked to skip a grade (which my father turned down). I was on the honor roll and in the president's class. But I was not allowed to do after-school activities, be on a sports team, or for the most part, have sleepovers. A lot of nurture and love were left out and replaced with toughness and fear. I wasn't taught any of the things a little girl needed to be taught.

Being raised by my father was difficult, to say the least. His ways of rearing and punishment were anything but conventional, not to mention that he was a man raising two girls. He would make us write things over and over again. We wouldn't be given lunch money. He had a belt, which he made us bring to him—or whatever he could get his hands on, such as an ironing board or glass plates—to beat us with. My father had no shame and would hit us around my friends without a second thought.

One night in high school, my friends *truly* witnessed our lifestyle. A group of us were going to spend the night at my house—an extreme rarity in itself. As we approached my neighborhood, I heard sirens, a helicopter, and overall excitement in the area. Something big was going on, and almost instinctually—as we neared my house—I knew that they were looking for my father.

That being the case, we couldn't go through the front door, so we cut through the neighbor's yard into ours. As we all scaled the fence ever-so-quietly, we saw cops surrounding the house. I tapped gently on my dad's sliding glass door, and for whatever reason, he let us in. He instructed us to go into the living room, lie on the floor without moving, and—whatever we did—not to open the door. The cops would go away.

I learned later that my father had attended a softball game at my sister's elementary school and on his way back, he had proceeded to hit a row of cars. He had somehow made it home, leaving a trail a blind man could follow.

It boggles my mind, now, to consider how we all just dealt with this without ever thinking about it. It was just the way things were at my house. I believe I developed that mentality to protect any kind of sanity I was to hold onto.

Although *this* evening ended okay, a lot of times when my father was out of control, he would punish us for anything from leaving a fork in the sink to his TV remote being missing.

Practically the whole time I was in high school, I was grounded. On top of being grounded, my sister and I would be punished with chores.

We would be sent out into Nevada's summer sun and forced to pick weeds for hours without food or water. The temperature would be eighty degrees by eight a.m., ninety degrees by nine a.m., and so on. Our swimming pool was right next to us, but we were threatened with a beating if we put even a toe into it. Another punishment was to sit and scratch my dad's arms or legs for hours, while he watched sports.

We were never allowed to be further away than the sound of my dad's whistle, or out later than when the street lights came on. And every rule or punishment could change on a dime. I never knew anything for sure. This created such an inconsistent feeling inside of me. I learned not to trust others—and myself especially.

This trend continued until I turned sixteen. Then my life *really* took a turn for the worse.

Despite the way I was raised, I was a naïve young girl—considered even a prude amongst my friends. I got good grades, rarely did anything that would get me into trouble at school, and always achieved. But eventually, the fear I was living in and with became more than I could handle. So I started drinking.

My first time drunk was terrible and amazing at the same time. I blacked out, puked, and passed out the very first time I let go. *But,* I was handed the most incredible feeling I had ever felt. I was alive and free. I wasn't afraid of a beating or of being myself. I suddenly understood why my parents drank and did drugs. If this feeling was on the other end of it, I was going to do it too.

I immediately fell into that life. I wanted to do it every day, and I was willing to suffer any consequences that came with it.

I lost my virginity just because I could and wanted to, with a boy I didn't even like. I became very sexually active, creating a vicious cycle of destructive behavior and dysfunctional relationships. I gave up my sweet youth for the life I believed I was destined for, and it felt bad—and *that* felt good. I no longer felt powerless. *I* was in control, and I was becoming more separated from who I really was at an alarming rate.

I took pride in my new lifestyle. I knew what I had found and was unwilling to let anything or anyone come between me and my drinking and my lifestyle. I lost jobs, friends, countless relationships, family, and cars. I used people, had an abortion, got into car accidents, and physically attacked people I cared about. I even went to jail a couple of times.

The first time I was arrested was for standing up to my father. When I turned seventeen, I swore I wouldn't let him beat me anymore. So I fought back—and was sentenced to community service.

After that, I was arrested for assaulting my on-again, off-again high school "sweetheart." Our relationship had always been destructive and codependent. Lots of drinking and drugs. Emotional and mental abuse. *And* violent conflicts—a few of which had resulted in police intervention. I'd gotten a black eye on at least one occasion. After standing up to my dad, I moved in with this boyfriend, resulting in the assault, which landed me in jail for three days.

I was pissed off and scared, being in jail. I don't remember feeling any other way. But everyone close to me had been to jail, so it was just one of those things that caught up with me, too. Eventually, I wore it as some sort of badge of honor around my friends and family, even though inside it was not only something I *wasn't* proud of, but something I felt didn't portray who I really was.

I agonized over my pain and didn't have any idea how to get help. I pushed everyone away, while crying myself to sleep innumerable times.

My one saving grace was writing down my thoughts and feelings. My best solution to my torment was to kill myself, but I didn't have the guts to do it. I prayed God would just take me in the night. But I woke up every time, and every time I cursed myself. But not *too* badly. I knew what the game was and I was willing to play it.

I thought I was the tough girl, but really I had lost all hope.

Then I finally hit rock bottom.

I had been sentenced to an anger management class, which I refused to take, so I was running from an outstanding warrant. I decided to kill myself on my great aunt's gravestone (she had died a few years previously) back in California. I saw no other option.

I had drugs and paraphernalia with me on the flight, which I almost missed. When I arrived, my high school ex asked me to marry him, which I turned down. (We hadn't had *much* contact in a while, but this was apparently his last desperate act to hold onto me.) Then I got in a fight with my old best friend. After that, my ex—enraged at my refusing his proposal—drove me in the back of a pickup to the middle of some remote hills and left me there alone in the dark. Then he came back and beat the shit out of me. After *that,* the cops came out and picked me up on my warrant.

I was thoroughly beaten and lost.

I surrendered during those few months in jail. I knew to my core that I was a hopeless case, but that I was not meant to be institutionalized. I knew that I had to stop.

I found a new life via sobriety. I was alive and in love with life, and I had found something bigger than myself to help guide me in a way I never would have believed. I couldn't imagine feeling the ugliness and despair I had felt, ever again. I was happy just to work my little coffee shop gig, which I took the bus to. I lived off pennies and was the happiest I had ever been. I knew what love, trust, and honesty were. *To thine own self be true* was more than a saying; it was a way of life for me.

Until it all disappeared.

After believing that I would never put another drink or drug into my body—after almost two years of sobriety—I began smoking pot again. My twelve-step attendance had dwindled and I'd eventually stopped going. I forgot that *I* was the problem and deluded myself into thinking that the booze was what my problem was. I eventually ended up drinking, while trying to control and enjoy myself. This little balancing act didn't last too long, and I was off into another life of debauchery.

I started right back where I left off, drinking as much as I could. I was obsessed, and would do anything just to get close to some beer and pot. I hung out with people who didn't care about me, who treated me like shit, and whom I felt the same way about.

In an instant, my life of fulfillment went to one of loss and desperation. And I was in the perfect location to propel me into this darkness: I lived just three blocks from three different bars, two of which I was eighty-sixed from with a warning to never come near their doors again.

Having been in a twelve-step program, I had heard plenty of stories about how bad it could get out there. I knew that despite the amount of damage I'd already done, there was still a lot more I could do.

One thing that truly stuck in my mind was the notion of not being able to get drunk no matter how much I drank; I couldn't understand that. Needless to say, that day finally came. I sat there with six hours of drinking under my belt, an open beer in my hand, a cooler full of more beers, and a head wide awake to the fact that I was not getting drunk. This scared the shit out of me.

I couldn't get home fast enough, to pass out and sleep it off. I came to at about three a.m., out of my mind. I thought I was going to end up in a mental institution; this was one of my greatest fears and a place my alcoholism had not yet taken me.

I spent four years killing myself while trying to find a way back to the light. It was the hardest thing I have ever gone through. I became a monster inside, and I thrust it upon others. I was untrustworthy, alone, paranoid, and wild. I feared for my sanity. Everyone around me feared for themselves.

When I finally reached this state, I knew where I had to go.

I returned to my twelve-step program, this time even more desperate to make it work.

The day finally came when I woke up and didn't have to put anything into my body. When I was allowed back onto the sunny side of the street.

I have not looked back since. I have worked for everything I have. Yet I know in my heart that I cannot take credit for any of it. I, alone, am nothing.

With the support of my program, I was able to get sober through a lot of blood, sweat, and tears. This was not an easy task, and looking back on it, I must have *really* wanted it. God opened a window, and I leapt.

My first forty-five days of sobriety were filled with chronic anxiety on top of two- to three-hour panic attacks. Somehow, I was given the gift of willingness, though, which I truly believe saved my life.

Not a day goes by that I don't remember the pain I felt out there, not to mention the pain I've endured to stay sober. But I can tell you that being out there is far more difficult than this new way of life. Sometimes these powerful memories are all I need to remain grateful for today.

I have a little over four years of sobriety now, and I wouldn't have a single day without the grace of God. He is ultimately everything.

God opened my eyes and allowed me my first sober breaths in a long time. The twelve-step program has allowed me to keep my sobriety. But the real savior has been Pathways to Independence.

I found Pathways through another woman who was just like me and who was already in the program. We actually didn't take too kindly to one another at first. But after sharing about our pasts, we knew why we had been brought together. We had amazingly similar upbringings, and our fathers might as well have been the same man.

This woman mentioned this wonderful program that helped her go to school. She described it to me as "life-changing."

Of course, I felt that I didn't deserve it. But the woman was persistent and finally reached the point of telling me that Dave was *waiting* for my phone call. I followed through and was accepted into Pathways not too long after.

I've heard this phrase: "There are no words to describe..." and that is a true understatement for how I feel about Pathways—and especially Dave Bishop.

I have been allowed to go to school without any worries except what is in front of me. There is a freedom in that. The people who came into my life through Pathways have given me moral, financial, emotional, and spiritual support the whole way through. I can say emphatically that I would not be the student or the person I am without them. I believe that shows in my 4.0 grade point average on last semester's transcript.

Today, as the result of God and all the angels in my life, I stand as a sober woman who not only functions in society but gets to live in it in a myriad of ways. I live the life I could have never imagined for myself and it just keeps blossoming. I am still a work in progress, but I have the opportunity to grow on a daily basis. I find love in the purity of the simple things today: a soft extension of gratitude, a shared outlook when I thought I was alone, helping others without realizing I'm doing so, being still, having a reciprocated connection to another person, watching someone find themselves, telling the truth despite my own trepidation, and most of all seeing the light at the end of the tunnel and walking towards it. I am grateful.

If there's anything I could want from telling the story given to me, it would be to show just enough hope for someone else to take another chance on their own life and fight for what is theirs. I believe more than ever that life is a gift to be used for growth, fulfillment, selfless acts, love, and togetherness. I've been blessed to know what all of those feel like today, and I wouldn't have it any other way.

Fifty-Two Beats

"This evil man broke what was left of my already broken heart."

—Annie

Today is the day that I will end my life. I don't see any other way to end my pain. I'm so very weak and in many ways already dead. My heart—my spirit—broke so long ago, that now I am afraid I may not even have one.

I am so hungry, yet I don't allow myself to eat. Sometimes I fall down and I don't even care; there is nothing within me to sustain me.

I am empty. I am dead.

The paramedics check my pulse and find it beats so slowly—only fifty-two beats a minute.

Fifty-two beats too many.

I came into this world with my umbilical cord wrapped around my neck, born in my own mother's bed.

My mother met my father in the hippie commune that she ran. She was twenty-eight; he was seventeen. I once heard she was charged with statutory rape. She already had three children, and the oldest was just five years younger than my father. So that created a lot of weirdness.

My parents were not only hippies, but die-hard heroin addicts. They regularly held parties with alcohol and drugs at our home.

One of my first memories is of my mother collapsing from a heroin overdose. Our phone had been shut off because my parents were unable to pay the bill, so my father urged me to run to our neighbors' for help. I was only three years old.

Too young to understand what was happening, but completely aware that something was terribly wrong, I begged my neighbors for help. They showed me how to call for an ambulance. The paramedics came, and thankfully, revived my mother right before my eyes.

Amidst her addiction, my mother somehow put herself through school to become a nurse while my father drove a taxi to support us. So my brother and I were left home alone nearly every day. We learned to cook for ourselves, dress ourselves, and every now and then, get ourselves to school. The only thing we never really did was bathe; neither of our parents ever told us to, and it never seemed important growing up.

My father's true love was music. He sang, wrote music and lyrics, and played several instruments. He began to train me vocally when I was only five.

When my mother was home, she was depressed and both physically and verbally abusive. My father was constantly unfaithful to her, and without fail she would threaten to leave. So I decided it was my purpose in life to keep my family together. It was quite a burden for a six-year-old little girl.

My parents' drug addiction progressed to a point that they could barely function. One day, while under the influence, my father got into an auto accident in his cab and lost his job. My family no longer had a source of income, so we were evicted from our home of seven years—

the home I had been born in. We moved into my grandmother's, where *eight* people shared living quarters: myself, my grandmother, my mother, my father, my brother, my aunt, and my aunt's two children—all in a one-bedroom apartment.

Eventually my parents and brother and I moved into our own apartment. I started the second grade at a performing arts magnet school, where I took singing and dancing lessons. This became my outlet. Without performing, I don't know how I would have survived the heartache of my broken family—and also what was to come for me.

When I was nine years old and in the fourth grade, my family got the opportunity to move into a beautiful home with my father's best friend. I was thrilled. I was so little, and the house seemed so big I could easily get lost in it. My parents were able to have a master bedroom and my brother and I had our own rooms for the first time ever.

Best of all, we had a huge back yard to romp around in, which even had a swimming pool, and a rear guesthouse that we could turn into a playroom. Our previous apartment had been in a dangerous neighborhood, so we never got to play outside. Finally, we could run and play and ride our bikes without fear.

What we *didn't* realize was that what we needed to fear wasn't *outside,* but under our own roof.

My father's friend was loved and trusted by my brother and me. Though we'd had our hearts broken time and time again by our family, we were still innocent. We had no clue as to the true potential for human depravity. This man was involved in the child pornography industry. He turned our trust on us like a boomerang, breaking what was left of my already broken heart.

My father's friend began taking nude photographs of me for his own profit. He tortured us. He committed bestiality in front of me. He raped my brother at gunpoint, at times locked in the aviary in our backyard—like an animal in a cage. I didn't have a key, so I would stand helplessly outside, simply talking to him. There was nothing else I could do.

The torture progressed until this evil man committed the act that would destroy us: He forced my brother and me to have sex together while he filmed us. I do not know if he used the film for profit or for personal pleasure, but I do know that my brother and I were never the same.

Life, as we knew it, was over. Our innocence was gone.

My brother, who had always been the light of my life, my greatest companion and support—the one and only person I could count on without fail—was now my greatest enemy. To see him was to remember the terrible act. To see him was to relive the pain, sickness, and torture that we experienced. To see him was to suffer. I began to hate him. And he began to hate me.

My brother had been the one person I could always go to. Now, with the sickness that lay between us, I felt more alone than ever.

I became very self-conscious about how my body looked. I felt fat and started to restrict my food intake as the rest of my world spiraled out of control. I became anxiety-ridden and afraid of people.

My brother and I stopped going to school. I couldn't stand being there—and neither of my parents cared if we went or not. I could not bear to be around other kids my age. I swear no matter how clean I was on the outside, I just knew they could see how dirty I was on the inside.

Finally, late one evening, my father caught his friend in his usual attempt to molest my brother. There was a scene and my father thankfully forced this man to leave our home.

But it was too late for us. The damage had already been done.

With the man gone, both my brother and I somehow began to repress our traumatic, dark memories. To the point where we truly didn't remember what happened.

But these memories spent years haunting me from deep beneath the surface.

By age ten, I had thrown myself into performing and had landed a professional acting job. I was a successful child star and was making money.

My parents, very ill in their addictions, rarely earned money themselves, so I eventually supported our family entirely. I paid rent, bought groceries, paid utilities, and even covered the cost of our holiday gifts.

My brother had become suicidal; to the point where no one in my family felt safe to leave him alone.

At age sixteen, I enrolled in a performing arts high school, as my acting career was really taking off; people were even recognizing me on the streets. At this point in my life, even though I was so broken, I felt that I had a bright and very promising future ahead of me.

But then I found my *true* love.

Alcohol.

The first time I drank, I drank everything I could possibly get my hands on. I became violently ill and I threw up for hours. But as I was being carried home in my own vomit, all I could think about was when I was going to be able to drink again.

I drank and used drugs nonstop. My parents, my teachers, my agents, and my acting coaches all advised me to stop and rethink the path I was going down; but I did not listen. When I was sober, it hurt to breathe. So I spent every moment I could under the influence.

Sober, my fear of people became even more violent. I could no longer show up for auditions, and I eventually ruined my reputation in the entertainment business. I was given many chances at my high school, including alternate ways to earn my diploma, but I had no fight left in me. Eventually, I was expelled.

At age seventeen, I left home and got my own little apartment in the heart of Hollywood. There, I was free to drink and use as often as I wanted, without interference from adults.

After about a year, I finally tired of my lifestyle—of getting loaded every single day. All my money was gone, I could not hold a regular job, I had no real education, my dreams had been destroyed, and I was completely desperate.

I had a moment of clarity. I called my mother, who was sober at this point, and she advised me to call a twelve-step program. I did, and I started to attend young people's meetings. Slowly, I started to put sobriety together.

I moved into a sober-living facility in Orange County, where I lived for two years. I created a nice, simple sober life, completely different from the destructive fast-paced one I'd been living. In sobriety, I met a man and fell in love. We got pregnant and I gave birth to my son.

My life was good: I was stable and sober, and I had a wonderful healthy baby. It was the first time I had ever known true happiness.

But then my past came creeping up. After six years of sobriety, those buried memories began their internal haunt.

I started to hear voices. I was convinced that the devil was in my home. I would wander through my entire house looking everywhere—even behind pictures on my walls—for eyes that I knew were watching me. I spent day after day, night after night, paralyzed by terror.

My eating disorder, which had always been present in my life, took off to a new level. Everything I put into my mouth I vomited out of me. I binged and purged to push all the feelings and thoughts away, to unsuccessfully gain some type of control in the world that was spinning wild.

I left the father of my child and moved back to Hollywood with my son, where—after six years of abstinence—I started up drinking again. I drank heavily to drown out the voices and to numb the pain within me.

After two years of daily intoxication, I tried to get sober on my own, without the help or support of meetings. I made it thirty days.

The thirtieth day was the day I planned to end my life.

I could not see any way out of all the pain I was in.

I was so thin that anytime I stood up, I would nearly faint. I no longer ate anything, and if I did, I would immediately vomit it out of me. But, since I knew this day would be my last, I binged on brownies at work. (I was somehow holding down a bank job, which I'd gotten when I first returned to Hollywood.) I stole them from the front counter and hid in a bathroom stall and stuffed them down my throat. I ate and enjoyed the deliciousness of the chocolate with tears streaming down my face; I thought I might as well enjoy my last meal.

I hated my life, I hated my body, I hated the pain that lay in every inch of me, and I hated my heart that still continued to beat. After binging on those brownies in that stall, I wrote my suicide note and left it in the drawer of my desk.

Fatefully, my brother happened to be staying with me. When I returned home from work, he took one look at me and called for help. Before I knew it, I was strapped down on a stretcher and taken to the psych ward, where I was locked up and put on medication.

It was on the third day of my stay that my buried memories surfaced. Lying in bed, attempting to sleep, a sudden terror seized me: *Someone was going to enter my room!* This was an all-too-familiar feeling; memories rushed back, flooding and overpowering me.

For the first time in twenty years, I was able to link an actual event to all my overwhelming feelings of shame, guilt, self-hatred, and dirtiness.

I immediately ran to the nurses' station and demanded to talk to a counselor. That very night, I told my entire story—my entire truth—for the very first time. The very next morning, I told my mother and then my father—and then my brother.

My brother puked. It was too unbearable for him.

I believe that some people are pushed too hard by life's evils, too far past a point of return. To this day, my brother has never truly recovered from the past.

I spent many years in therapy, took several more trips to the psych ward, met with a psychiatrist on a weekly basis, and obediently took all of my prescribed psych meds. I returned to a twelve-step program and did my best to live a "normal, quiet life." I got married and settled into a quaint home in Orange County, where I landed a decent, white-collar job.

I seemed to be successfully putting the broken pieces of my life back together. I was trying desperately to heal and get better, but the pain, emotional turmoil, and fear were tremendously unbearable.

I took a weeklong business trip, during which I lost my sobriety and cheated on my husband. My husband and I separated after only one year of marriage and I found it even more difficult to stay sober.

We divorced, and shortly after, my mother died.

Several years earlier, she had met and married her third husband, who was diagnosed with lung cancer. After six years of sobriety, she began taking her husband's pain pills, which evolved into a heavy abuse of prescription meds and a return to smoking pot. Within eight months, her husband was dead.

Five years after my mother's relapse, fluid filled her lungs and she collapsed in my brother's arms. The paramedics resuscitated her, only for her to end up on complete life support, brain-dead.

The moment I saw her, I fell to my knees and screamed. Most of her veins had collapsed, so they'd had to run an IV through her leg. One tube was stuck down her throat and into her lungs for air, and more tubes ran in and out of her nose. Her entire body was swollen—even her eyes, which had been covered with Vaseline and taped shut.

My mother struggled with every breath until she took her last. I was holding her hand and kissing her forehead the moment she left.

My mother's death was horrible, traumatic, and frightening for me. Although she had failed to be the type of mother I expected her to be and our relationship had been rocky, I did love her immensely. My grief over her death provided more reasons to turn to the bottle.

Meanwhile, however, I started making good money at work—into six figures a year. I thought that materialism would bring happiness; I really became a slave to that mentality. I bought a house and two luxury cars, and I had a very damaging spending habit. I traveled all over the world, living as though the money would be there forever.

But I knew that it wouldn't.

I lived in fear of losing everything. And one day, I did. A sudden industry crash forced me out of my career. My income came to a screaming halt, and with no other job skills, I was effectively unemployable.

In every aspect of my life, I became emotionally, spiritually, and mentally absent. My fear of people returned and I became a recluse. I still had my son, but he stayed as far away from me as possible. I realized that I *had* turned into my mother.

I could no longer even go to the grocery store. I was riddled with fear and paranoia. My son lived on drive-through fast food and ramen noodles. My fear grew so bad that I could not even go outside to take out the garbage. Instead, I hid it in the house, and my cupboards filled up top to bottom with trash.

Every night when I went to bed, I prayed to God to take me in my sleep. But He never did—and every morning I woke up.

Then one night, instead of praying to God to end my life, I prayed to God for help. The next day I got sober. It was the first step toward truly rebuilding my life. I returned to my twelve-step group, and I went to three or four meetings a day. I got a sponsor and started to work the steps in the program. I made amends for my wrongdoings and came clean.

But some things I'd done, I can never make amends for.

By this point, my son and I were destitute. Facing imminent homelessness, we were rescued by my friend and spiritual advisor from my twelve-step group, who opened up her home to us. She fed and housed us, and encouraged me to go back to school. She told me I needed to start my life completely over.

I hadn't been to school since I was seventeen. At thirty-two years of age, I still did not have a high school diploma. I'd just faked my way through everything. But I knew that I would have to support my son and myself on my own. And I was willing to do whatever it took. Because of my sponsor, I was able to go school full-time, and for that I will forever be grateful.

Approximately four months into my college career, I made a new friend in my twelve-step program. She was a client in Pathways to Independence. She told me it was a scholarship program that could help me. My first reaction was that no one would ever give *me* a scholarship. I did not feel worthy of one—or even capable of completing school. But my friend encouraged me, so I filled out the application.

When I met Dave Bishop for an interview, I was well aware of what was at stake—that is, the potential that lay ahead for me if I were to get in. I was nervous, and I do not remember much of what was said—other than that I cried the entire time. Before I left, Dave handed me the Pathways coin: I was accepted!

My life changed dramatically when I entered Pathways.

I was assigned a therapist, who opened his time and expertise to both my son and me and met with us for individual sessions. In therapy, I started to open up about things that had happened to me and my brother.

In addition to the therapy, Pathways covered the cost of all my tuition, books, and school supplies; I was given a housing stipend, and my son and I were able to move into our own apartment, which Pathways helped us furnish. We were both given medical benefits and treated by doctors, dentists, and optometrists who volunteered their services; in fact, my son will have braces because of Pathways. I was also given a beautiful and reliable car, which is cared for and maintained by a Pathways mechanic.

None of these things would have been possible before.

When I celebrated one full year of sobriety, my father came to my meeting to celebrate with me and my son. My father was sixty-three days sober. It was a dream come true for me, and I knew we all had a fighting chance. I was filled with more hope than I had ever known.

That night, when my father said good-bye, I hugged him twice and I did not want to let go.

It was the last time I would ever see him.

One month later, he called to tell me that he was killing himself. His exact words were: "I'm not okay. I'm dying."

As soon as I heard that, I pulled my car over to the side of the road. I still remember the spot every time I drive by it or see it.

Was it his diabetes? Did he have cancer? "What are you telling me?" I asked. In my heart, I *knew* what he was saying.

"I am dying of a broken heart," he replied.

"Are you going to take your life?" I asked him straight-out.

"Yes," he said.

I felt totally helpless. He would not tell me where he was. My first inclination was to call him every name in the book and scream, *"How dare you call me and put this on me?"* My second was to beg him not to do it.

But I knew I could not stop him. So instead of arguing, or fighting, or pleading, I told him how much I loved him. I told him that I wished I could have been a better daughter. I told him how sorry I was that he was in so much pain, and I told him I understood.

I did. I truly understood.

I still hear his voice to this day. He said to me, "You're the best, and we did the best we could. We've both been very sick and it's been wonderful with you." And that was amazing. "I know you're going to be fine," he told me.

I was in Pathways now, so I think he felt like I would finally be okay and that my son would be okay too.

When our conversation ended, I tried desperately to have the police trace his location. I called several detectives, the suicide hotline, and any other human being who I thought could help me. Unfortunately, they were not able to trace our call, and they could not find my father.

Knowing my dad's patterns over the years, I thought, *Okay, where is there lots of liquor and gambling?* So I pulled out a map and did everything possible to guess where he was. For a twenty-four-hour period, I called detectives in a forty-mile radius to get them to help me. I tried calling my dad back all day.

Finally, at four-thirty in the afternoon, my dad answered my call. He had already started taking the pills and he'd been drinking, so he was really intoxicated. He told me he saw both of his dead brothers. "They're both here with me," he said, "and I'm going. I'm on my way out."

He was really scared. He was terrified. I remember all I wanted was to hold his hand and make him feel safe. I wanted the detectives to find him just so I could sit with him and comfort him.

The police finally used our last phone call to trace my dad's location. But by that point, I had already narrowed down my search and had called the motel. I spoke only to the front desk clerk, who told me: "I'm sorry, you need to call the coroner's office." So that's how I found out.

It was eerie, because right after I hung up, the detective called and told me my father's body had been found facedown in a cheap motel; the police also showed up to notify me in person. It was a new officer and I think he was really anticipating breaking the news to me—so it was kind of anticlimactic for him. I told him to just please leave.

To identify the body, they photographed him and e-mailed it to me. A friend of mine looked at the picture for me. I couldn't do it.

The sheriff found twenty-nine good-bye letters in my father's room. One for me, one for my brother, one for my son, one for my father's girlfriend, one for the police on the scene, and the remainder to his friends in his sobriety group. My dad wrote to me that he felt his sole purpose in life was to have me, so that I could have my son who could be the first child free from abuse. He felt his purpose had been fulfilled and that it was his time to go.

Without the support of Pathways, I do not believe I would have survived my father's suicide. Pathways paid for my father's entire funeral. Dave Bishop called me nearly every day to make sure that I was okay. My therapist saw both my son and me as often as necessary, including times we were not typically scheduled. My physician met with me on a regular basis. The other girls in Pathways supported and loved me through my grief.

When I was first accepted into Pathways to Independence, I thought that "Independence" referred to monetary gain; that the girls in Pathways earned a degree and gained independence by being able to support themselves. While this is certainly true, after being in the program for nearly three years, I realize that it is about so much more. Each step of the way, we grow stronger. Each of us has our own demons to face, our own fears to master. Every time we master one fear, another is revealed; at the same time, every time we master a fear, we grow in strength and independence. We begin to trust ourselves. We begin to realize that we can care for ourselves, stand up for ourselves, respect ourselves, love ourselves.

Today, I am not sure which is the greater gift: the education that Pathways is allowing me to earn, or the love I now have for myself.

I have been sober for over three years. I can finally say that I am free. I enjoy life as I did when I was a very little girl, because for me life is beautiful. Each day is a new beginning—a day filled with new experiences, new lessons, new emotions, and lots of love.

One of the most amazing aspects of my journey is that it has enabled me to forgive my parents. I have had immense spiritual experiences in my pursuit of education, and I discovered that I had to let go of my baggage in order to be the woman I desire to be.

The anger I had was all-consuming. It had the power to kill me. It also had the power to destroy my dreams.

For me to now be free of it is a true miracle.

But with Dave Bishop's consistent love and support, the guidance of my therapist, and my unyielding desire to get well, I *was* finally able to let go of the past, let go of my anger, and accept my parents for who they were. I now see how much they loved me and how much they suffered under the hand of their disease. I am no different from them, except that I am blessed to have a fighting chance at a real life. A chance I would not have without Pathways.

Today, the world is opening up before my eyes—a world and a path that are far beyond my wildest dreams. Pathways has given me gifts that are priceless and will last for the rest of my life, for the rest of my son's life, and for generations to come.

Today I smile because I am a free woman.
Today my heart beats strong within me.

Part 2

Outside the Cocoon

"What the caterpillar calls the end,
God calls the butterfly."

—Author Unknown

Down the Stairs

"Nobody knew about my family—
not even my close friends."

—Veronica

My dad didn't love me.

I still don't think he loves me.

He doesn't even know my birthday.

You just feel empty. You grow up feeling like you don't know what to do in any situation. You're always second-guessing yourself. And you're always looking for love. But who's there to give it to you? No one is! And those who *are* there are telling you that you're worthless.

My dad used to hit us, and he beat my mom. That's all you see and that's all you know, growing up in an alcoholic home. And what you *hear* is the yelling! Even to this day my dad can't *talk* to mom; he has to *yell* at her.

I remember when my mom was four or five months pregnant with my little sister. My dad dragged her down the stairs.

I still think of things like that.

And that wasn't so bad compared to other times, like when my dad took my brother to a bar and left him in the truck all day—*in the heat, with the windows up*. It's a miracle my brother didn't die.

And all of this was *normal*...

My parents came to the United States from Mexico about forty years ago. They were both very poor and had their upbringings on a ranch, living in cold concrete houses with flimsy construction and no plumbing—the places basically had holes in them.

After my parents married, they obviously wanted to find a better life. My dad came to America first; Mom followed.

I'm the fifth of six children—six children who all grew up with a drunk and abusive father. He's not close to us and it's a shame. He now has no family and he still lives with my mom. She's never divorced him because it's traditional: Mexican women stay with their husbands. That's a concept I don't agree with and will never understand, but I love her and I feel sorry for her.

My mother didn't even know when they married that my dad was an alcoholic. *Everyone* in his family was an alcoholic—and alcoholics don't hold jobs very well.

So my mom supported all six of us kids on her own—on a salary that was essentially nothing. I remember seeing a paycheck for, like, seven dollars. I thought, *Are you serious?*

I do admire my mom for never going on welfare. Not that there's anything wrong with welfare—some people do need it. Actually, my mom *did* need it, but she chose to work. And with six of us to raise, she worked *all* the time.

She didn't have time to hug us. There wasn't *any* family time. Mom would get home late from working and have to jump right into cooking us all something to eat. If we were lucky, we had beans; that was about it.

My dad was a screamer—always yelling. We lived upstairs in a duplex, so it was embarrassing. All of this stays with me.

My mom got the worst of the abuse. My dad would throw things at her, slap her, pull her hair—I think that's how he dragged her down the stairs when she was pregnant. She had a belly at that time and everything. Plus he'd just *hit* her. He'd hit her so hard, she'd fall.

The whole time he'd be yelling at her—belittling her. He'd always call her a *cualquiera,* which means a floozy—a whore. He'd accuse her of sleeping with people at work, because for a while they worked for the same company. A lot of times that's the reason he would hit her. He *really* just hit her because he was pissed off—but he would *say* it was because she was cheating on him. *Her* cheating on *him*? It was absurd!

And as he was insulting her and hitting her, she'd be crying. I remember her always crying. Lots of times she'd say: "Stop, stop—not in front of the kids." As if it would be okay otherwise.

But he didn't care anyway. He was just a wasted drunk.

I remember when I was little, I'd be on the sofa and whenever they were fighting, I would cover my face with a blanket.

But you still hear it. You still see it.

I think my older siblings saw a lot more than I even did, because, thankfully, by the time my brother Albert—whose a year older than me—and I started growing up, the bigger kids would defend my mom.

They'd yell at my dad and they would stand in front of him. They'd barricade him from hitting or throwing things at my mom. When they got older, they'd kick him out of the house. They'd push my dad out the door and then lock it and leave him out there.

The worst part was that my mom would *defend* him! "Stop, stop!" she would cry. "Don't hurt your dad!"

Because my oldest brother, he's a big boy. Today, he weighs about three hundred pounds; he's *always* been tall and large. And he *hates* my dad. So my brother *could* hurt him, *would* hurt him. Sometimes my brother would push my dad down the stairs. He didn't care.

But my mom did. "Please don't hurt him!" she would plead.

And it pissed me off. Because here was my dad, trying to hit my mom, or trying to hit *us*, and my mom's only worried about *him* getting hurt. What does that say to us? But that's how she was. That would always happen.

To this day, my mom still loves my dad—or at least she thinks she does.

So my mom got the most abuse. And then my older siblings.

As Albert and I grew up, my dad's main instrument of torture became *the belt*—a big, thick belt he'd worn working as a security guard in Mexico. He would grab it in the middle and whip us with the end of it.

You never knew what would incite his fury. It could be something big we did, or just whatever he was irritated about. The TV was too loud, or we didn't turn it off. Maybe we'd stayed out too late with our cousins. Just whatever pissed him off.

To this day, my dad is always mad.

So he'd pull out the belt and we would *run.* We'd try to get away from him, on the bed, or by running out of the bedroom. But he'd chase us, snapping the belt at us. We were pretty quick—but not that quick. He'd get us mostly on the butt and on the legs.

If he cornered one of us—*really* got us—we'd be huddled on the bed crying, begging him to stop. And he'd just keep hitting us. My mom would sometimes try to stop him, but what was she going to do?

I don't remember ever bleeding or having broken bones, but I know I must have had welts—that thing was *thick.*

The three older kids tried to console us: "You haven't been beaten as much as we have!" I don't think it made me feel better.

Albert finally hid the belt up in the attic and it wasn't found for years.

I may have forgotten a lot of stuff, but I will *always* remember the end of that belt.

The last time my dad got really violent with me, I was in middle school. I remember it vividly.

My dad was really wasted and had started throwing plates at my mom. This time, *I* got in the way—literally, into the middle of their argument. Mom was behind me.

It was just crazy.

My dad was wasted and he was angry and I just *knew* he was going to hit me. I could see it in his eyes.

As I got older, I learned to tell from the look on my dad's face when he was about to hit someone. So that's why I got in front of him this time.

Sure enough, he took a swing. If I hadn't ducked, I would've been hammered against the wall.

Although he didn't succeed, the idea of my own father just flat out *punching* me was a lot to absorb.

Growing up, we didn't have a lot of toys or anything so we had to get creative.

My cousins would come over and we'd make up games. We called one game *El Huevito*. I don't know why we named it that—it means "Little Egg."

Anyway, we'd all stand in a row behind these markers. You'd throw the ball and then have run to a tree down the street as fast as you could. Because whoever's marker it hit had to pick up the ball and hit someone with it!

We liked hurting each other, apparently. Beating each other up. Not to the extreme—I *think* we just fought like normal kids, but I can't be sure. Anyway, I don't remember exactly how *El Huevito* worked, but I just remember we'd make up these games.

We also had a neighbor who became our little escape. He was an older man on his own, so he was lonely. He'd have board games or let us play with his Atari. Maybe it sounds weird, but he was really nice and I'm thankful we had that.

We rarely celebrated birthdays and stuff.

We never got *gifts*.

From my dad, we never even got an acknowledgment of the day—unless, maybe, by late afternoon he figured it out. "Oh. Happy Birthday."

Thanks.

I did have one party when I was about eight. It was just our cousins and stuff, but there's a cute little Polaroid of all of us—that's how I remember it. But in general we didn't do stuff like that, because we couldn't afford it.

I *really* thank God for those Santa programs. Because without them, we wouldn't have had Christmas either.

When I was around preschool age, my sister called the fire department and they showed up in a fire truck. I remember sitting on Santa's lap and him giving me a *present*.

I was *so* excited. I don't even know what it was, maybe some sort of clothing because I can clearly remember it was a soft package.

It didn't matter. *I got a gift.*

I know there are a couple of bad apples who might take advantage of these programs, but I hope they stick around. Because to us, it meant the world.

Besides *not* making money, my dad took my mom's money—those few dollars she was earning to raise us. Plus, my mom was supporting an illegitimate child that my dad had with another woman!

I found out about *that* in middle school. I remember walking into the room where my mom was talking to my older sister. My sister has always been the one to deal with the "business" end of things—paying bills, making calls for my mom, handling government matters, and so on. I don't know what I heard them say, but somehow I knew they were talking about my dad's kid.

I asked my sister and she confirmed that I have a half-sister somewhere, a girl the same age as her.

I was shocked, of course—*not* that my dad had cheated, but that I had a sister I didn't even know. Whom I *still* don't know. I don't think my dad's ever even met her. Maybe when she was a baby, but not as an adult.

I *think* my whole family knows about her now. But to this day, we never talk about it.

But I did throw it in my dad's face a couple years ago. He was drunk and he was really pissing me off. "You know," I told him, "Mom supported this daughter you had, because you decided to cheat on her with this stupid chick! That's ridiculous—" I went on, "she should have left you a long time ago."

That was a huge outburst and shock—mainly because my dad didn't know that I knew.

It's funny, because I never really *think* about having a half-sister until I talk about it. I haven't even told my boyfriend about it. He always tells me I forget things, and I guess I do. I block a lot of things out—especially my childhood.

I don't hate my dad, but I get so angry sometimes because *all of this* is his fault.

He did this to us.

It was bad, but my brothers and sisters and I did the best we could to be really good members of society. We took the guidance of my mom. She was such a good person and we wanted to be that way as well.

My brother Albert *did* tend to misbehave, but none of us did anything really bad. We grew up on the west side of Long Beach, California, where my older siblings, especially, could have gotten into gangs. But thankfully they didn't—*we* didn't.

I went the opposite way.

Because I never spent time with my mom, I was always looking for affection—and approval.

At school, I'd stay after class being the teacher's pet. I tried to excel at everything.

I was super-outgoing and popular. I was fun-loving, just trying to find comfort in *something*.

I was a cheerleader. I was in ASB. I was doing *everything*. Our school didn't have homecoming queens, but we had "International Ambassadors"; I was the Latina Ambassador. It all seemed nice and rosy and pretty.

I faked it *so* well.

Scholastically, I was also an overachiever, somehow managing to get good grades in spite of my home life. But even trying to do homework was difficult because my dad was always drunk.

Thankfully, my upbringing and lack of self-esteem never led to rampant promiscuity. I never went down that path. In fact, I was a late bloomer as far as sexual things go.

I did have people who really liked me, but I wasn't really happy with *myself*. I just played the part. So I thought guys liked the *idea* of me, but that, ultimately, that image wasn't who I really am.

Everybody in high school *thought* I was promiscuous for some reason. Maybe I was perceived as the stereotypical cheerleader or something. When I talk to old high school friends, they all admit they didn't believe I was a virgin. They figured I was lying. In reality, I was probably the most innocent one in the school!

I took a guy to my prom who looked good in pictures. I think we kissed and that was about it.

I never really let anyone get close. I didn't bring them around my family. I *couldn't* bring them around my family.

Nobody knew about my family—even my close friends. That was a side of me I didn't want to share—it was something no one needed to know about.

I worked at not letting *anyone* in. I just kept myself really busy and I didn't get close to people. Subconsciously, I don't think I *trusted* anybody to get close. Even people I liked.

I was also quick to discard people. If someone did something wrong or made me angry, my attitude was, *Pfft, whatever. I'm not talking to* *<u>you</u>* *ever again.*

I never brought anyone over to our house. And being bused to school over ten miles away made it easier to keep my life separate from my friends.

"I never knew how *bad* it was," a friend from middle school told me recently. "I never knew what your home life was like."

"I know," I replied. "I never told you."

I just dealt with it myself—I just dealt with all the horror that was going on.

Even my siblings and I never really *talked* about the abuse. We still don't. We keep it to ourselves, just like we always have.

Growing up, I could only have one pair of shoes for the whole year. And in that year, I also got one shirt, one pair of pants, and one outfit—my *new* outfit. Everything else was hand-me-downs. Luckily, I had older brothers and sisters who could keep "handing down" to me.

When I was in middle school, I had just my one pair of shoes and the tongue was flipping out so bad I couldn't walk straight.

Not having money *really* sucked.

So I began to work just as soon as I could, at age fifteen. All my siblings did too. I got a job working nights at a burger place.

From then on, I paid for all my own expenses. I'd pay for things around the house too—groceries and stuff.

Being on the cheerleading squad, alone, cost about a thousand dollars a year! But I paid for it all, and it was fun. But I'd get so annoyed at other girls complaining: "Oh, my mom didn't give me this," "My mom won't pay for that."

"*My* mom doesn't pay for a thing!" I'd tell them. "Get a job, lazy ass!" So I guess my hardships did teach me a good work ethic.

It also taught me to be frugal—maybe to a fault.

One time a friend was going to buy several pairs of shoes.

"Why are you going to waste your money like that?" I asked. "Why do you *need* that many shoes?"

"I'm not *wasting* money," she argued. "I'm *spending* it; it's a trade-off."

It was a different mentality.

It's *still* hard for me to differentiate between spending money and wasting it.

Toward the end of high school, I was trying to study, and the house was chaotic as usual. *How the hell am I supposed to study in <u>this</u>?* I thought. *How am I supposed to function with all this going on?*

So I decided I'd had enough. I was gonna move out.

A friend of mine was living with *her* friend and the friend's father; they had an extra room, which they agreed to rent to me really cheap.

So I packed all my stuff and grabbed my boxes, ready to move. I got to the place and for some reason, the friend's father didn't like me. So I didn't get to move in.

I never heard the end of that from my family. They teased me endlessly for my failed attempt to "get out."

But that girl's father turned out to be kind of a psycho. *Thank God I didn't move in,* I thought. But that's how desperate I was. I was going to go to live with this stranger and his daughter, in this house, because I didn't want to be home anymore. I just didn't want to be a part of the physical, mental, and verbal abuse anymore!

As thrifty as I was, when I graduated from high school, I had saved up eight thousand dollars.

And with it, I bought a car and I went to Europe.

I actually didn't *want* or *plan* to go to Europe.

The trip was being organized by a teacher from our high school. "That's a great deal," my brother-in-law said. "Europe for three weeks, three thousand dollars—I want to go." And then he told me, "You should come." With him and my sister, of course.

I have to thank him for that.

But my first response was, "Three thousand dollars?!" It seemed like a *waste* of money.

"You really should consider it," they told me.

I don't even know why, but I did decide to go. And I'm *so* glad I did.

That trip opened my eyes.

Because when you grow up in a family like mine, you don't see or experience much. Having been bused into a better neighborhood for school, I knew there was *something* else out there. But, really, where did my parents take me? *Disneyland? The beach?* Nowhere. Maybe to the Payless Shoe Store down the street.

So this trip was an absolute turning point in my life.

Wow, this isn't the world.

It really did change me. It made me want so much *more* for my life than I had ever envisioned. And watching other people allowed me to realize some things about myself too.

That trip changed my whole trajectory.

Another trajectory that needed to change was my taste in men. Until my current boyfriend, I always dated losers. I dated people who weren't available—just like my dad wasn't available. I always wanted my dad to be there for me, but I had to *chase* his love, and that's what I've done in dating.

There were two guys in particular—two guys I got serious with, one after the other—after I graduated high school.

Both guys were emotionally unavailable. They didn't want a commitment or a steady girlfriend. I could chase them all I wanted, but I wasn't going to get them. I didn't like the drama, but that's what I was used to and that's what I knew.

There were other similarities as well. They were both attractive and cocky "players." And they would give me *hope*. They would do specific things to keep me there. They were both manipulative and they both cheated on me.

I thought my relationships were exclusive, but neither of *them* saw it that way.

One of them hit me.

And I left him.

The first time things got physical, we had been drinking; but I don't think I was drunk. Our relationship was already getting bad. He was very volatile. I loved him, but we had a lot of low points—things were nearing the end.

We were at a family party—his niece's baptism. There was a girl at the baptism I didn't care for. She was rude and she was hitting on my boyfriend in front of me—one of *those* kinds of things. She was quite attractive and flirty, and he was flirting back.

I was *mad*. We were dancing, and he was checking her out, not paying any attention to me. I was looking cute, and it made me feel terrible. We went outside.

I don't know exactly what happened after that. All I remember is that we got to yelling and I slapped him. I'd never done that before. And I don't believe in that.

But after I *slapped* him, he *socked* me. I don't know if he hit me once or twice, but he really swung at me and gave me a bloody nose. I was bleeding all over.

I don't know if someone saw us and pulled him away or what. What I *do* remember is going to my car—we had driven separately—and his sister being there, telling me to stay put.

I also remember my dress being bloody. It was a really nice dress that he had given me, but now it was covered with blood.

I wound up leaving.

He wound up in the psychiatric ward of some hospital. I thought he was full of crap, making a big drama about this. I knew he just wanted it to look like he actually *cared* that hit me. He told me he was really sorry, but I knew he wasn't. I later found out that he thought I deserved it.

No woman deserves that. *No one* deserves that.

The next day, he got out of the psych ward and came directly to my apartment. I didn't open the door.

I didn't talk to him for *a year* after that. He kept trying to come back to me. Every so often, I'd get a CD or something in the mail. At one point, he gave a note to his mother to give to me. *Really, guy?* I thought. *You have to get your mom involved? How pathetic.*

I never picked up the note.

A year later, he reached out to me when I was going through a breakup with the other guy. I fell for it.

Maybe I can get over this other guy with the ex, I reasoned.

That's *never* a smart move—but I figured it was just for fun and I *did* enjoy seeing him again.

Then he attacked me a *second* time.

We were at a combination of his birthday party and his friend's bachelor party. And, yes, there were strippers. One of the strippers climbed up on his lap and he was really enjoying himself. Of course, I was mad.

We went outside and, again, I don't know exactly what happened. I didn't smack him or anything, but we got into a fight. He was wasted and he tried to attack me. I fled. I ran around the back of my car, and he dented my car with his fist and broke one of the windows trying to get to me. That was scary.

Finally a mutual friend drove me away in her car. The friend was shocked. She'd lived across the street from this guy for years and had never seen him like that.

"Yeah, well it's not the first time," I told her.

But it *was* the last.

Both of those relationships left me with no self-esteem whatsoever. I wrote a letter to the second guy, which I shared with one of my best friends. After reading it, she just went quiet.

"I had no idea you were that into him," she finally said, "and that he had done that much to you." And then she added, "I can't believe you're like this; with no self-esteem."

That was a turning point for me.

Someone can't do this me, I thought. *No.*

Right then, I decided that I *was* going to get over him—no matter how hard I had to work.

And it wasn't gonna happen again.

Throughout all of this, I was attending community college and *somehow* holding everything together.

But things reached a breaking point when my mom's health went on the decline.

It had actually been declining for years. Throughout my high school years, she had dealt with arthritis and chronic pain.

Now things got worse.

She had a little vein on her ankle that popped, and for some reason, the doctors couldn't fix it—they really couldn't do *anything*. So she had this big hole that just stayed there.

And then her arthritis got *really* bad, to the point that she couldn't even walk. To the point that she got laid off from her job, with them claiming she was becoming "too slow." (She tried to get her job back, but ended up settling with them for a measly sum.)

She would crawl to bed, or she'd crawl around the house. And to see your mom on all fours…it just broke me down.

On top of it all, she got sick. Sicker than I'd ever seen her. I really thought she was going to die.

I became stressed-out and depressed.

But like my mom, I was good at putting up a front.

Sunshine and a smile on my face.

Everything is dandy.

I just try not to think about the bad stuff. I have a really bad memory and I think that's because I try not to remember all the stuff that happened when I was a kid. I think I've blocked out a lot.

But while I was doing well scholastically, I began breaking down just about every month. One time someone at school asked me if I was on my period—I wasn't. It didn't matter. Every month I would have some sort of meltdown.

I was taking a course called Interpersonal Communication. It was a small class, maybe twenty people. It was one of those classes where you just start talking to people—I guess that's what interpersonal communication is! We all got really close.

One day, I *completely* broke down. I couldn't take it anymore.

Here's my mom, out of work and on her deathbed.

Here's my dad, who's just crazy.

By now, I'm working *two* waitressing jobs to pay my tuition, plus giving my mother money for rent and other things.

I've always given back to the family. Always tried to support them. But working both jobs *and* going school full-time was just too much.

I couldn't do it.

This girl in my class pulled me aside as I was bawling. "There's a program I think you should hear about," she said. "It's called Pathways to Independence."

She tried to tell me about it.

Whatever, I thought. I didn't think they'd help *me.*

At her urging, I called Dave—*once.* But I didn't get a reply, so I just left it alone.

The following semester, I got to know two other girls very well. One of *them* was in Pathways too, which was an extremely unlikely coincidence because the program was quite small at the time. "I think you should apply," she told me.

Okay, I thought, *this is the second person who has told me about this. Maybe I should think about it.*

I called Dave again and this time I met with him. After a couple of interviews, they took my application. I was on the waiting list for about six months, and then I got in.

I learned *so* much from being in Pathways…

One thing Pathways taught me was how to *save* money. I've always been frugal in my spending, but something Pathways instilled in me was to save ten percent of every check.

And because of Pathways I *had* so much more.

Pathways gave me a monthly stipend that I didn't have to give to my mom and dad. It was a *huge* relief not to have to work two jobs.

I didn't have to worry about any illnesses or health issues; it was covered. I probably wouldn't be an avid dentist-goer today if it hadn't been for Pathways.

My car got fixed if it broke down.

I didn't have to worry about my tuition or school books.

I was able to start life afresh. I could study. I could actually begin to *learn.*

I was nineteen when I moved out of my parents' house.

Thank God, because it was driving me crazy!

But I likely *wouldn't* have moved out if it hadn't been for Pathways. Most of my siblings have never been out on their own—some of them *still* live in that prison.

My mother doesn't understand. She still asks when I'm coming back "home." She doesn't *know* anything except that environment. She doesn't know what it's like to live in a house that's calm and peaceful.

She only knows living with *him*.

When I got into Pathways, I made plans to move in with another client. She gave me the keys to her apartment so I could bring some stuff over. I went in and just sat in the living room for a few minutes.

Oh my God, I thought, *it's so quiet...*

I'd never been to a place that was *quiet*.

It was surreal. It was crazy to me. Where I grew up, my dad was always yelling and there was fighting and he was always drunk and screaming and singing or whatever. And we lived right in front of a major freeway—it was always so *loud!*

And the mess! The whole household was always a mess. No one picked up anything.

It was nice to have peace and quiet and cleanliness. Actually, I needed some noise at first to be able to sleep, but after a while it was fine!

It was better than fine—it was a miracle.

I was in Pathways for about five years. I finished my A.A. at City College and then transferred to a Cal State campus, where I graduated with a double major in International Business and Marketing. This was a great accomplishment.

But the most *priceless* reward of being in Pathways was the therapy they provided.

I met with my Pathways therapist every week—sometimes twice a week or more. I know some people think therapy is crazy, but I think it's the greatest thing. A lot of girls who enter Pathways have to be "forced" into it at first. I was all in.

Growing up with abuse and with parents who have no love or time to give you causes certain tendencies—including "second-guessing" and that constant "looking for love." One of my motives for wanting therapy was to find out other people's opinions of my thoughts: *Am I wrong or am I right? Should I have done this or should I have done that?*

That kind of self-questioning makes it hard to succeed in life. A different upbringing would have given me comfort and confidence in *knowing* someone loved me. Then I wouldn't have had to chase it. But I never had that. And that's something I've had to overcome in my career: knowing that my decisions come through the proper means.

I'm smart. I don't come to conclusions by pulling something out of the air. I come to conclusions because they make sense.

Therapy has given me the reassurance that I'm not crazy. I'm not abnormal and I'm not alone. My thoughts and feelings have been validated.

All of this is very common in people who grew up in alcoholic homes. *It's okay for me to feel this way.* That may not seem like a lot, but if you don't have reassurance growing up, that validation is everything.

Getting emotionally healthy has taken a long time. Therapy has helped me tremendously to become happy with myself.

I still second-guess myself, but I am working on it every day. I'm also trying not to be a people-pleaser—because I *am* a people-pleaser.

I've done a *lot* better at getting close to people.

One girl in college just wouldn't let me get away. "You're *going* to come and hang out with us," she told me. She called me, and kept calling me, and kept trying to meet up. She loved me. And I don't even know why. She's just such a great person, and she's become like a sister.

I finally have close friends.

I met my current boyfriend when I was twenty-seven. I thank God that I've now learned to pick better people; not go after the ones who are like my dad or crazy or just not attainable.

I've had help, but my older sisters have all married jerks. One sister is totally broken. Her husband has cheated on her and done everything in the book. In essence, she married *my dad*—though at least her husband *isn't* an alcoholic. It still just sucks.

Another "tendency" you develop in an alcoholic family is the inability to say no. You let people take advantage of you, or you just don't take care of *yourself*. You don't love yourself.

I'm very family-oriented, so it sucks to see my mom, dad, and siblings like they are. It hurts. My family and my boyfriend are everything to me.

So even though I still have a lot of work to do, I sometimes just wish I could take my years of therapy and give them to my family instead.

I actually paid for my sister to attend a few sessions when she was going through a really tough time. She couldn't afford it, but she needed it, and she went. I was very happy to be able to help. And it *did* help.

But I'd hoped that if I jump-started therapy for her, she would continue going. She didn't. And I can't make her. But if there were one thing I *could* change, it would be that my whole family could—*would*—go to therapy.

Pathways is all about second chances and I'm trying to learn that in my own life. *And* to learn acceptance.

I've accepted that my dad is not going to change. I've also accepted that my mother's not going to leave him.

My mom has never been happy. My dad always told her that there's another woman he should have married—some woman whose name I don't even remember. It was cruel.

My mom's a broken woman and it's sad. I don't know how she did it: raising six kids and putting up with him. And she still puts up a good front.

I love my mom so much, but I don't I think she made the right decision staying with my dad. I know she wanted us to have a dad, and it's probably true that if she had left him, he would be dead. She held this family together.

Of course, he doesn't realize that—he's *still* a jerk to her. It makes me so mad when I see him being such a jerk to her—and a jerk to *us*, too. I don't put up with it now. If he's drunk, I don't talk to him. If he's sober, I can at least have a semi-human conversation with him—but these days, his being sober is very, very rare.

It's sad going back and dealing with it now. I feel bad because my brothers and sisters *hate* my dad. I'm the one who's closest to him, and we're not close at all! But I haven't cut him out totally; I guess that's the "closeness."

Recently, he got laid off from his job, so every single day he's beyond wasted and is screaming and yelling at my mom. It's so upsetting. But I know I can't fix it.

What I *haven't* accepted is that I can't fix things for my sisters. That's simply where I'm at.

I still try. I still talk to them.

"You can leave your bad situations," I tell my older sisters. "You have to love yourself."

My little sister still lives *at home*. "You need to get out of there," I say. "You need to be in a healthy environment."

I sound like a broken record.

They'll leave when they're ready…

In the years I've been around Pathways, I've seen a lot of things. I've seen that Pathways is not a welfare program—you have to earn *everything* that is offered to you. I believe in this program and I believe in the girls.

I also believe in the help and guidance of a mentor.

I had a mentor named Bonnie. She was a sweetie pie—she is like a mom. But a mentor is also someone you can run things by—*anything*. Whether it's what's going on with your work, your boyfriend, school—anything.

Dave was also my mentor. He really is *everyone's* mentor. He's just a great guy. He genuinely cares about all the girls in the program. He must get fifty calls a day. From the moment he wakes up to the time he goes to bed, it's Pathways.

But he's very straightforward. If he says he only has ten minutes to talk, he'll give you the ten minutes; but if he doesn't have time, he'll tell you that, too. He calls you on your crap and he tells you just how things are. But he's very loving.

He's known for his tough love statements: "You know I love you, but if you're not committed to this, I'll love you right out the door."

I've done well in my career. But it's taken me a little longer because of my lack of confidence.

While I was still in school, I received a five-hundred-dollar scholarship from the Port of Long Beach and appeared in a news article about it. A company contacted me and interviewed me for a job doing global transportation and logistics.

It was unprecedented, but when they found out I still had a year of college to go, they allowed me to work part-time until I could come on board completely.

In my five years with the company, I've learned a lot. I've learned to negotiate salaries, interact with clients, handle customer relations, and so much more. I started in brokerage and moved into sales administration. I did a management training program, and from that point on I was a local accounts manager.

But it didn't start off easy.

I struggled with confidence, with owning my beliefs.

I was easily intimidated—especially by the boss.

I felt insecure with little things, like writing e-mails. It would take me forever!

And I didn't know how to say no. I had a lot of excess work dumped on me until I learned to set boundaries.

I wasn't even confident enough to fight on my customers' behalf. I'd take whatever lame excuse was given to me for my customer's dissatisfaction and pass it along. Now I don't accept that. I say, "No, you need to do this, and you need to give me that, and we need to track down this, and I'm not going back to the customer without these things being done."

I was just *so* uncomfortable at work—as a person. I didn't know how to act! I was always trying to be a certain way—be a certain person—because that's what I thought was expected of me. I didn't even know how to act around my own friends! It sounds strange, but that was so real for me. It took me a long time to just be myself.

Plus, I didn't know proper business etiquette. Who taught me that? *My mom? My dad?*

Having that mentor, that person to ask, "How should I address this?" was vital. Be it a career opportunity, or wanting a raise, or whatever it may have been. My parents never worked in corporate America. So who do you go to? If I didn't have Pathways, who *would* I have gone to?

I am so fortunate. I think about my siblings—they didn't have Pathways. Or other kids from poor areas. Those kids don't have a chance. And it's sad, really sad, because most of them will stay in the same thing, stay in their little neighborhoods and not go anywhere. They don't even know what's out there. And it's a shame.

The kids who *do* get out are going to face these same hurdles I did at university and in their careers. Because their parents probably didn't have these jobs either.

So, I've grown a lot. *A lot.* I still have to remind myself that my opinion matters, and that I'm smart, and that I've been with the company long enough and I *know.*

It's all about developing confidence.

And it's served me well!

I recently got *another* promotion into sales, and I'm extremely content. I am so, so grateful for all that this job has taught me.

And I am *eternally* grateful for all the ways Pathways has helped me succeed. I am now extremely involved in helping *Pathways* succeed—I participate in the Friends of Pathways fundraising efforts, I help out Dave...whatever they need. It feels so good to give back to this organization that has given me so much.

I've always been a fighter and I do think I have a good head on my shoulders, even though I was emotionally whacked for a long time.

Today, I still have my battles within myself and I'm still trying to work on self-doubts and everything. But I certainly have better self-esteem than I used to. If not for Pathways, I wouldn't be as emotionally strong. I might have done okay financially, but emotionally I'd be screwed.

In the working world, I have seen people sell their souls. I've seen people succeed financially by doing that. They're the sharks—the ones who don't care about anyone else. They live for themselves and I don't think they are very happy people. They do well because they don't care. I'm not like that and I never want to be *that person.*

If not for Pathways, I may have become really bitter and gone that route. Maybe I would have just married one of those losers. Maybe I'd be married to that loser and have a kid, but still be pursuing my career; a bitter person who did whatever she could to earn money.

I've always had a decent moral compass, but I don't think I would actually *be* as good, and I definitely wouldn't *feel* as good about myself without Pathways.

Has Pathways shaped me into the person I am today?

Yes—I'm sure. One hundred percent!

From East L.A. to Law School

"Not only was I pregnant,
but it was by a drug-dealing gang member."

—Kimberly

Since I was eight years old, I dreamed of becoming a lawyer. I told *everyone* I was going to be a lawyer. But two months after my sixteenth birthday, I found myself pregnant.

I met my son's father when I was fifteen. He was a drug dealer and a gang member. He was just seventeen years old, but he had a car and pockets full of money—and at that age, the lifestyle was alluring to me.

Plus, this was the first man who really paid attention to me—he told me he wanted to protect me.

I told him I wouldn't get married or have children until after college, but he just kept saying, "You're going to be my baby's mama…you're going to have my kids."

He got me pregnant on purpose.

I was trapped.

But it seemed okay in the beginning; we had tons of baby clothes and toys because my boyfriend had *a ton* of money.

But things changed quickly. Along with the "protection" came control and possession. My boyfriend degraded my friends and told me not to hang out with them. When we were out, I was so afraid to *look* in the direction of another man, because my boyfriend would accuse me of checking him out. Still, my boyfriend's insecurity made *me* feel secure because I thought he must *really* love me.

Soon, none of this would matter. My boyfriend was arrested and sent to prison.

I was on my own, broke, with an infant to care for. This is when reality hit me…

I was born in Utah. My mother is white and my father is black. I have a sister who is eight years older than me and full white. My father was a pretty heavy crack addict—along with coke, alcohol, or whatever he could get his hands on. He was abusive to my mom when I was younger, though I never witnessed this because I was just two years old when my mother uprooted me and my sister to Southern California.

We moved in the middle of the night. We moved without telling my father. However, I *thought* the man we moved with—my mother's boyfriend—*was* my father. I had been told that my real dad was my *uncle.*

My life was also moving—moving into being surrounded by family dysfunction, substance abuse, physical abuse, constant uprooting, and eventually, the shock of having a baby at sixteen.

We wound up in one of the roughest parts of Southern California—East L.A.—where we lived until I was ten.

During that time, my "uncle" moved from Utah back to his home state of Oklahoma. He would occasionally call me, but I was very young and I had no idea he was my biological father. My mom had convinced him it was best to continue the lie, since I considered Charles (her boyfriend) my "dad."

But then, the situation changed.

Charles came to be a severe drug addict and alcoholic. So my mom told him he had to leave. She didn't want my sister and me exposed to his substance abuse problems.

I don't know what ever happened to him after he left—this man I *thought* was my father. He just kind of fell off into drugs. He called me once when I was around twelve; I could tell he was on something. He didn't really know how old I was or anything—it was a very sad conversation.

I've never heard from him since.

It hurt me because he really *was* like my dad. He treated me like his daughter, and I know he loved me. I wish I could reunite with him, but I don't even know if he's still alive.

I will never forget the day I found out the truth about the whole situation.

I was eight.

"Your *'dad'* is moving in with us," my mother suddenly said.

"What?!"

And she had much more to say.

I cried as my mother told me that this estranged man—allegedly my father, *not* my uncle—was coming to live with us!?!

When my father moved into our house, I felt really uncomfortable about the whole thing—especially them sleeping together in the same bed.

I couldn't call him Dad; I called him Gary. He really despised that.

He also returned to drugs.

My mom must have thought he was clean, but he wasn't—and it got worse. My sister was sixteen, and my father would take her out and do drugs with her.

My sister and I have an "interesting" relationship. Besides the eight-year age gap, there's that difference in race. We *look* so different. She's five-foot-nine and has a large build; I'm kind of petite with curly hair, and I'm racially mixed. When I was younger, I was really cute! I probably got too much attention, and I imagine she felt like the focus was being taken away from her because her mom decided to have this new baby.

She has always had a lot of emotional issues—many of them based on the abuse and neglect she suffered as a child from her own father.

Before my dad came to live with us, my sister started hanging out with a rough crowd in East L.A. So my mom sent her back to Utah to live with my mom's parents for a while. But my sister ran away from them and ended up staying with James.

James was my mother's boyfriend between my sister's dad and my dad, before I was born. Just as I always considered Charles to be *my* dad, my sister's father figure was James.

James was black and terribly abusive—he beat my mother badly. But despite that, and even with their race difference, James loved my sister like his own daughter and she loved him back. He was murdered about fifteen years ago, and she was heartbroken.

Just before my dad arrived, my sister returned to California to live with my mom and me. I can only imagine the effect my dad moving in with us had on my sister. Unlike me, my sister could remember the old times when my dad physically abused my mom. My sister's experimenting with drugs was probably her way of getting attention and acting out the discomfort she felt about the two of them reuniting.

It was an awkward family dynamic, to say the least.

And it added to the already strained dynamic between me and my sister. Perhaps due to our age gap, she and I always lacked a true sisterly connection. I didn't feel she loved me like a little sister should be loved. She wasn't protective of me, even though she was older and a large girl who got the best of others in fights at school. You'd think that she'd be my big, bad sister, protecting me when I got into trouble—but no.

When I had problems, it was almost like she got off on it. She seemed to enjoy seeing me struggle with relationships or have trouble with my friends. If I was upset, she would never step in and console me. She would make fun of me. When my friends came over, she would try to work them against me and tell them embarrassing things about me. It was a very weird sisterhood.

When I was younger, my sister tortured me a lot—she even tried to strangle me a couple of times. It would make my mom so mad. My mother made efforts not to leave me alone with her. She would have my cousin babysit me, even when my sister was home.

There was a time when my sister would sneak into my room and steal my babysitting money. I caught on to what she was doing, so I began to mark the bills. I put little stars in the corners.

And I told my mother.

One night, a short time later, my mother confronted her. It was one o'clock in the morning and my sister had just arrived home.

"Let me see your cash!" my mother demanded.

There were my marks.

I guess that was the beginning of my becoming a lawyer!

When I was ten, my mom got rid of Gary—*again*. And we moved *again*—back to Utah.

We had lived in tough neighborhoods in Southern California—and had moved quite a few times while we were there—but my mother had worked hard to put herself through an RN program at an L.A. trade school. That was quite an admirable accomplishment for a single mom with two daughters and no child support whatsoever. At times, she had to use the public system to help her out, but for the most part she was self-sufficient. But since we couldn't afford a home in California, it was back to Utah.

We lived a fairly decent middle-class lifestyle in Utah, but my mom worked two jobs and I remember barely seeing her. And with her not around, I became pretty self-sufficient. It kind of shocks me now how my son is so dependent on me; when *I* was his age, I was cooking, cleaning, setting my own schedule, making sure I got myself to school and sporting events, and everything else.

When I was twelve, my mother met another man.

My mother has a tendency to get into relationships with people who are needy; people who need help or people she feels she can "fix." She didn't come from a single-parent or dysfunctional household—in fact, my grandparents are still married after fifty-five years. But for some reason, she wound up with a string of men who had serious issues: substance abuse, emotional problems, financial instability, and family troubles.

First, she married my sister's dad, who was also abusive and an alcoholic. Then there was James. Next, she was engaged to *my* dad—a hard worker, but a man who came from a difficult childhood and was a drug addict. Then there was Charles, and then my dad again, and so on.

This *new* man—the man she met when I was twelve—had just gone through a divorce, and his wife was fighting him for custody of his kids. Of course, my mother helped him fight that battle, too.

From the time I was twelve—and on through when I became pregnant—she was fighting this court battle. In addition to frequently testifying and going to court, she spent time attending counseling sessions in order to demonstrate to the court that she would be a good role model and guardian for her boyfriend's kids.

I felt neglected. It was a very serious time in my life—a time when I was ultimately going to be making some poor choices—and it didn't feel like she was there for me.

Her boyfriend eventually *did* win custody—because his wife was a psycho; definitely crazy. Now she can't even *see* the kids; she's allowed nothing to do with them.

But I felt like that was my mom's new family. I still feel like that's a separate family. And my mom is still taking care of them, even though one "kid" is now in college.

My mom is always giving her time and energy to other people. I don't feel like she ever takes care of *herself.* Though she's been involved with many addicts, my mother's never been on drugs. *Her* drug is helping people.

As I entered my teenage years, I spent a lot more time with my friends and boys than I did with my mom. Perhaps that contributed to my becoming pregnant at a young age.

My son's father was the first guy I was in a sexual relationship with. I tried to get on birth control through Planned Parenthood, but they didn't really discuss options with me. They'd simply say: "Here's your pills," and I would leave. Unfortunately, I found out that I am very sensitive to hormones; the pills caused me to throw up constantly. So I stopped taking them.

Ultimately, I was just being irresponsible. But my mother never talked to me about sex or birth control. If you ask her, she'll tell you we had all these conversations about sex and things. It's very weird. And we've since had several disagreements about things that occurred—and didn't occur—during my childhood.

One time my mother caught my boyfriend in our house at two o'clock in the morning. I was only *fifteen,* but she just told him to go home.

Maybe she was just too tired to really do anything—or at least anything big enough to get my attention.

The "shock" of getting pregnant affected me on so many levels.

My drug-dealing, gang member boyfriend really wanted me to have the baby; my mother was telling me I needed to get an abortion. Ultimately, I felt like *I* had made my choices and *I* would have to take responsibility.

Before getting pregnant, I was a high school track star. I got a letterman's jacket my freshman year. I dreamt of going to the Olympics.

I also had dreams of one day becoming a lawyer. Ever since I was little, I liked to debate; I enjoyed heated discussions. I was very competitive, and I loved legal shows. I was addicted to *Law and Order, Ally McBeal,* and Court TV! Everyone told me that I'd make a great attorney!

But all those dreams seemed to fade away.

I broke my mother's heart. I quit track and field. My dreams of becoming a lawyer seemed out of reach.

So many people were disappointed in me—they had expected so much more. It was really a sad time for me. I was so disappointed in *myself.*

But I made the choice to have my son.

It turns out I suffer from hyperemesis, which caused me to throw up all nine months of my pregnancy—especially the first three. I was in and out of the hospital the whole time. I would frequently go to the hospital to get IVs to keep me hydrated. I couldn't keep anything down. When I got pregnant I was ninety-eight pounds; in three months, I went *down* to ninety-two pounds. I was severely ill, and without modern technology I definitely would have died.

I could no longer go to high school, so they allowed me to do home study. They had a teacher bring me my assignments—I was literally doing my homework from my deathbed. Surprisingly, I was still able to achieve good grades and eventually graduate with a 3.4 GPA.

A month before the end of my junior year, I was well enough to go back to classes—with a big stomach. *And I wasn't the only one.* It seemed like an epidemic; there were like six or seven of us pregnant at the high school. All during our junior year! More shock.

My son was born in August, the summer before my senior year.

After having a child, my whole concept of life—and what I needed to do and take care of—changed.

I'd taken extension courses over the summer by watching videoed lectures at home and then doing my work. I continued these when school started again in September.

And I was working.

Also, my son's father and I moved in together. A friend of my mother's rented us an apartment in my mother's name, because I wasn't legally old enough.

I was experiencing a lot of "life" for someone so young.

I was now seventeen and my son's father was nineteen. He was still a gang member and still dealing drugs. I tried to get him to earn a real living; he tried some temporary day labor, but that just wasn't working for him. There wasn't enough money in it.

He eventually got caught in a drug-dealing case and was sent to prison.

A lot was over and done with by then, so we broke things off. We had a baby together, but there's no way I was going to let my son's father hold me back.

I decided not to let anyone or anything hold me back.

I knew what I wanted to do with my life.

My son was eight months old when I graduated from high school. I had returned to school full-time for my final semester, while continuing to work part-time.

After graduation, I enrolled in phlebotomy school—a six-week course that certifies you to draw blood. Other members of my family had done that to help themselves through college, so I followed suit. I took the course, got a job at a hospital making decent money, and enrolled in community college.

My son's father was released from prison after serving about a year, and he wanted to see his son. He was still controlling and possessive of us, even though we'd broken up, but we finally worked out some custody arrangements. He got visitations and paid me two hundred dollars a month in child support.

Things were fairly okay.

But I always missed Southern California. I missed the diversity. Although I was young when we lived there, I always enjoyed the faster-paced lifestyle.

With my California friends—even when I was little—we talked about becoming doctors and lawyers and professionals. In Utah, it's just not like that. The people I grew up with didn't aspire to many dreams, and the opportunity just didn't seem to be there.

Before coming to Southern California, I'd never even seen a black police officer. And in L.A., I saw people of color with nice cars and houses. Where I'm from you don't see that. I'd never seen a black doctor or lawyer in Utah, either.

Two of my cousins had moved to Long Beach. They offered to let me stay with them for a couple months, until I got settled.

I eagerly accepted.

I didn't bring my son with me at first. I had him stay with my mom in Utah until I found an apartment for us. I really wanted to get on my feet—to start a solid life for my son and me in Southern Cal.

After my mother had kicked out Gary—*again*—I'd had an "occasional relationship" with him in Utah. Every two or three years, he would suddenly give me a call that he was in town and we would go out to lunch. It was never anything more than that.

My dad knows every nook and cranny in "the system." He would be collecting social security because of his back, but at the same time working out and lifting weights. When I had the baby, he soundly advised me to apply for Section 8—the federal housing voucher program. I applied when I was eighteen.

Some people are on the list for three or four years, but for some reason they called me after just six months. I was accepted and they told me the program was good anywhere in the United States. I was good to move wherever I wanted.

It was scary moving to California. At times, I didn't know how I would make ends meet, and I didn't have anybody to watch my son. But I clung to my determination to "not let anything hold me back."

I enrolled in Long Beach City College and transferred my course credits from Utah. I was taking my son everywhere with me, which often meant to campus.

The teachers would say, "You can't bring him to class."

"I have no choice," I would tell them.

It was difficult finding a job, too, but things began to work out. I started to meet people. I met a lady who is a great care provider for kids, and she began helping me with my son.

I met a really nice girl named Michelle in my Spanish class. We became friends and began talking about our lives—including how difficult it was for me, being a single parent and living here with no family. She shared the difficulties that she had.

When I asked her how she was able to pay for all of her classes and survive, she told me about Pathways.

Michelle brought me an application to apply for the Pathways scholarship program.

I sat on it for a couple of months, because I guess I didn't understand everything that it could offer me—plus I was younger and a bit of a procrastinator.

When I finally sent in the application, Dave got right back to me and we had an interview at his home. I brought my son with me because, as usual, I had no one to watch him.

I was asked a series of questions, like what I wanted to do with my future.

"I want to be an attorney," I said.

They asked about my schooling and my grades. Dave explained that they only accept women into the program who are already doing what they need to be doing: working part-time, going to school full-time, and achieving a respectable academic record. It wasn't like they were taking people who were just *trying* to set goals and *think* about achieving things; they wanted people who already had the ambition and drive to "do it."

Dave told me that I fit all their criteria.

"I have no reason *not* to take you," he said. "You're doing everything we want our candidates to do!"

Pathways informed me of all of their expectations of me as a client. They set me up with a mentor and a therapist.

My schedule was already pretty hectic, working thirty hours a week, going to school full-time, and keeping up with my son's schedule. At the time, I was also managing a soul food restaurant in the evening. I don't think I was actually mature enough to be the manager, but the owner liked my work ethic.

With all of these responsibilities, I had a little trouble keeping in contact with my Pathways mentor at first; but we got things on track.

It was such a godsend just to know that when my car broke down or I got a flat tire or something, all I had to do was pick up the phone and someone would help me.

And there was so much help in so many ways.

My son had a couple of really bad teeth; they were breaking off and he needed oral surgery.

Pathways took care of that, too.

I'd had a *severe* acne problem for a long time. It was big barrier in communicating with people and had a negative impact on my self-confidence. I often felt uncomfortable approaching others or getting up in front of a class. I felt like everybody was staring at my face.

Pathways' dermatologist, Dr. King, fixed that. I gained a whole new sense of confidence. It was great to go through the rest of my schooling and the entire law school application process without having to be self-conscious about my appearance.

All my books were paid for. I was given a stipend to help with my rent, and money to help with miscellaneous expenses.

Before Pathways, I remember times that were so hard and so depressing—when I felt like I'd never get to be who I really wanted to be. I was never financially able to get the things I needed to be successful; things like a computer.

I began seeing my Pathways therapist. She was amazing, too. Even if I was just having "a moment"—or if I was having a complete breakdown—I could call her and she would see me right away. She would make time for me.

I found, also, that it was very beneficial to be able to talk about my mom. In so many ways, my mom is an amazing woman. But—like with my sister—I felt as though we were missing a certain connection. I know she loves me, but I didn't feel a bond like I see with other mothers and daughters.

In therapy, I talked a lot about my relationship with her. How I wished it was stronger. How I wished my mom could have been there more. I know she was working hard to provide for me and my sister, but she just wasn't present. No one was at my sports events or other important moments in my life growing up.

Although I didn't require the intense therapy some of the girls do—I hadn't suffered any sexual abuse and I didn't have any substance abuse issues—therapy was so, so helpful.

Thankfully, I've *never* been involved with drugs myself. Although my dad was a crack addict, he wasn't a pivotal person in my life. He was negligent and absent, and my mom worked hard not to let his substance abuse issues impact my life.

Conversely, I've always loved sports and keeping myself in shape.

I actually had one professional fight as a boxer when I first moved back to So Cal, before being accepted into Pathways. I was introduced to a boxing trainer, who told me I could make some money. I was young and broke, so the idea sounded good to me.

I trained for six to eight months. I had no amateur fights. *Nobody* goes pro without any amateur fights. But I did. I went in there, made thirteen hundred bucks, and was really in the best shape of my life. But I felt exploited. I just didn't feel like this trainer had my back. And while the workouts were great, the whole thing just wasn't for me—I'm not a boxer.

Sadly, I never got back into track and field after high school, either; I just couldn't put it back into my schedule. I did take jazz and ballet dancing though, which I would love to start doing again!

My college career and the pursuit of my dream to become a lawyer became intermeshed with my life in Pathways.

I received my A.A. degree from Long Beach City College in 2002 and I began applying to undergraduate schools. Eventually I was accepted at California State University, Long Beach. I knew I wanted to study business law—or at least have a business background as a backup plan in case I didn't get accepted to law school.

At this point there was more "shock." But this time it was a good one: my mom became my backbone.

During my last year of undergrad, she moved in with me. She had gotten a job as a travel nurse and was working a few different assignments in various hospitals in Southern California.

My mom did all she could to help me. She became the primary caregiver for my son on her days off. And his taxicab—carting him around to all his sports and activities while I studied. Then she got her own place and brought her fiancé and his two kids over from Utah so she could continue to be here for me.

"Nothing will hold me back..."

I graduated from Cal State Long Beach with my business degree and a 3.1 GPA. I wasn't exactly at the top of my class, but I was right there! Still, there were no guarantees that I would actually make it into law school. I needed to do well on the Law School Admission Test (LSAT).

I had graduated from Pathways as I neared my graduation from Long Beach State. I told Dave I wanted to study for the LSAT right after graduation, rather than looking for a job in the business field. Those childhood dreams remained so strong.

I *knew* I wanted to go to law school.

Dave knew it, too.

He *personally* gave me the money to pay for my LSAT course. This was a lifesaver, because I was no longer getting Pathways money and I wasn't exactly making a fortune working in my current job as a bank teller.

But then I won the lottery—literally. I was selected to work as a longshoreman at the port of Long Beach, unloading cargo that comes in from overseas. It is primarily a male vocation, but it pays good money and is highly sought after. You put your name on a postcard and send it in to this lottery system. Half a million people apply, and they pick only eight thousand people, every ten years! I was one of the eight thousand chosen, as was another Pathways graduate. Boy, were we blessed!

Everything seemed to be falling into place. I studied for my LSAT while working at the docks.

And law school remained my goal.

"I just wanted to go to school..."

No one in my family has a graduate degree.

My dad has a fourth-grade education. One of eleven children, he was born in his home and didn't even have a birth certificate until he was six years old. He came from a time when many kids worked in the fields and education just wasn't that important. The importance was helping the family survive.

I wanted to become a lawyer because *I* had a passion for helping people who are facing life's challenges. I want to help *them* survive.

When I received my LSAT score, I was disappointed. I had hoped to do better. But I was not going to let that setback stop me. I enrolled in a community college writing clinic to get assistance with drafting my personal statement, in hopes that a great statement would offset my low LSAT score. And I believe it did.

I sent out my law school applications.

I didn't get into the more prestigious schools like UCLA or USC, but I did get accepted into *three* Orange County law schools: Chapman, Whittier, and Western.

The first acceptance was amazing.

I had scheduled an appointment with an admissions counselor at Western. The woman seemed to really like me. She called me the *next day* to tell me I was accepted! More amazingly, she said they could offer me a full diversity scholarship, effectively paying my way through law school.

I'll never forget that day. I was ecstatic. I started crying. Everyone was so proud of me. I think part of my entire education process was to disprove anyone who doubted I would make it. *I'm so going to succeed! I'm so going to make this happen! I may have made some bad choices as an adolescent, but things have changed!*

Another thing I will never forget is the pivotal role that Pathways and Dave Bishop played in my success.

When I first began applying to law schools, Dave Bishop introduced me to a real estate attorney he knew named Samuel. After I got to know Samuel a bit, I asked him to write me a letter of recommendation for my law school applications. It was kind of bold of me, but he did it.

I guess I have learned to be pretty good at asking for what I want. I've had to. I try to encourage my friends to do the same. The worst anyone can say is no.

I have a friend who wants to go to law school, and I tell her you have to be assertive. That is the only way you are going to get what you want in life.

I have been so fortunate to have so many people extend their help to me. Not everyone has said yes, but when they *have*, it has made a pivotal difference in my life. I've sure been turned down many times too, but you just have to take those times in stride.

It turned out that Samuel was a graduate of Western, and he certainly knew what I was going through with the law school application process. He told me that if I *was* accepted to law school and wanted some law clerking experience to let him know.

I later took him up on his offer, and I worked for him the entire summer after my first year of law school. I gained valuable experience working for Samuel. Before then, I had *no* clue how a law firm operated.

Once again, the connection made by Dave was extremely valuable.

When I began at Western in 2006, I had some immediate setbacks. My first semester was extremely challenging. And it didn't help that I got the flu and couldn't attend classes for nearly a week. In your first year of law school you simply *cannot* miss a week. That will put you out the door.

I couldn't keep up.

I was drowning.

So here I am, sick and getting depressed. I can barely get up and shower in the morning. I'm neglecting my son. I can barely have a conversation with him, because I can barely take care of myself.

It was extremely frightening. I was telling my mother, "I can't do this…"

So, my mother once again rose to the occasion. First, she grabbed her best friend and they cleaned up my whole house. Then she said she would do whatever else it took to help me. And she did. She did my laundry; she brought in groceries. She took care of my every need.

She told me that she believed in me and knew that I could do it. She said to me: "Completing law school has always been your dream; just take things one day at a time."

I don't think I would have been able to pick myself back up without her words of encouragement and motivation. One day I was going to drop out, the next day I was continuing on.

That semester—my first semester—I got a 2.6. I was disappointed, but I had to be thankful that I was not on probation, like some of my fellow classmates. Still, if I had anything below a 3.0 average after my first year, I would lose my full scholarship. That was another thing that scared me.

Before my second semester came around, I sat down and spoke to the law school dean. I was having trouble paying for child care and had only my law school loans to live off of. I needed to go to school part-time. The stress level was just too much to bear.

Normally, law schools don't allow students to switch from full-time to part-time programs or vice versa. It just doesn't happen.

I was crying in the dean's office. Finally, he was like, "Okay, okay, okay!" I think he just didn't want to hear what I was going through.

My second semester, I took three classes. I was on top of the world. I had juggled so much during that first semester; now it was smooth sailing. I met a great study partner, who is a close friend of mine to this day, and I was able to complete my second semester with a 3.3 GPA. That moved my overall GPA up to a 2.9, but not quite to the 3.0 I needed to keep my full scholarship. However, I was so close that the school decided they would allow me to keep fifty percent of my scholarship.

When I applied to law school, I wasn't quite sure what I was looking for in a school; I just knew I wanted to be an attorney. After completing my first year, I decided to transfer to Chapman, due to Western's low bar passage rate and ranking compared with other U.S. law schools. I wanted to put myself in a position to succeed.

There were other benefits of transferring as well.

All throughout my undergraduate work and my first year of law school, I lived in Section 8 housing in a really rough, gang-controlled apartment complex. I knew it was low income when I moved there, but I didn't realize how bad it was going to be.

There were shootings going on, and my neighbor wound up slashing my tires. Her boyfriend would sexually harass me. I had never felt so degraded in my life.

Of course, when the neighbor slashed my tires, Pathways replaced them immediately. That woman didn't slow me down. I had heard on the street that "she had people that had her back." Well, I had people that had *my* back, too!

Still, I had to get out of there.

My son was now nine, approaching the age where he would be influenced by different groups he was exposed to. So when I transferred to Chapman, I took my Section 8 to Orange County.

It was a real culture shock, living in the OC. It was a much nicer area, but I still felt guilty about moving my son around like that. My son was mad at me, so I talked to a Pathways-referred therapist about it.

Pathways really taught me the value of therapy. Having graduated the program, I paid to see her with my own money. And it was so valuable.

The therapist asked if my son had made any friends. I told her he hadn't.

"Well," she told me, "when you see other boys around, go ask them if they'd like to meet your son—if he could join them in sports and things like that."

It was a great idea.

That same day, four boys were playing outside our apartment. I asked if my son could join them and they said yes. That really helped to make the transition.

Now my son also plays sports in school. It's clean and quiet where we live, and there are no gangs.

My second year of law school was very different from my first.

In the first year of law school, people are crying in the hallways! In the second year, things tone down.

But that year, too, was difficult.

First, I went back to law school full-time.

Second, I didn't have my study partner or many friends at Chapman; just one who reached out to me and who I've been friends with ever since. It was difficult for me to identify with the student body there.

Most students who attend Chapman seem to be from either Orange County or other nice areas of Southern California. At Western, people were from Minnesota to New York and all over the United States. I wasn't raised in Orange County or accustomed to that lifestyle, so it was really hard for me to connect.

Also, there really aren't many people of color who go to law school. There were probably fifteen to twenty blacks at Western; at Chapman there were two. And Chapman didn't have a Black Law Students Association like Western did.

It was a difficult time, without anyone to study with or to get notes from when I didn't catch something in class or was absent.

But I kept pushing through.

After my second year in law school, my aunt called me from Oklahoma.

"Your dad is dying," she said. "He's in the hospital, overdosed on drugs. You need to get out here now. Make arrangements!"

Gary had had a stroke and was in full kidney failure. I hadn't spoken to him in four or five years—all the time I was in law school.

He had not attended my graduation when I received my A.A. degree. He didn't even know about it.

When I got my bachelor's degree he wasn't there.

He didn't even know about it.

And now I'm in my second year of law school, and I get the call that he is dying.

I called my aunt back. She told me the whole story—about the crack houses he haunted, about the bad drugs that had caused him to seize up.

He was a diabetic. After tainted drugs gave him seizures, he laid in a crack house for two days before some people in the house decided to carry him out to his car. The neighbors saw it. They opened the car door after the others left and called the last number dialed on my dad's cell phone. It was his girlfriend. She came right away.

She thought he was just in diabetic shock. So they got him back to their house and shot him up with insulin—but it did no good, of course; he remained unconscious.

They called 911.

I flew out there a day after it happened. I had tried talking to him on the phone, but he was totally hallucinating.

His kidneys had failed and his entire system was being poisoned, which was affecting his brain. The nurses told me that they couldn't keep him in his bed; he kept trying to get up.

But he couldn't walk because the right side of his body was paralyzed. He couldn't go to the bathroom on his own. He was coherent, but he was stuttering because of the stroke. He was getting dialysis for his kidneys.

I didn't really know how to react to this. But at least I was there. I even said, "I'm here for you."

Gary has two other daughters, both younger than me. They are my sisters, but I'm not close to them at all. And I was the only one who was there for him.

I brought my son with me. My father hadn't seen him since he was about two years old. We stayed for a few days. I tried to bring him whatever he wanted to the hospital. I tried to help his girlfriend. She was there from morning until night.

But I had to leave. I was in the middle of a summer class in law school, as I was trying to get caught up after going part-time my first year.

By the time I left though, my dad was actually recovering pretty nicely. The doctors said he was going to heal. *But*, they warned, if he does drugs again, he's dead. No question. He's going to die if he even *thinks* about doing any type of drugs.

Stroke, kidney failure, and he gets out of the hospital in three weeks! That's my dad...

My third year of law school came with its own lessons.

My ultimate goal was—and is—to be a judge. I had expressed this to Dave during my second year, and he put me in contact with a judge he knew in the superior court, so I could ask him some questions. It was a tremendous opportunity.

At the time, I was working in the public defender's office for course credit. It was right across the street from the courthouse, so the judge and I agreed to meet for lunch.

I'll never forget the day I met Judge Taylor—it was the day of a big earthquake! But we had a great conversation.

His journey was interesting. He had suffered from substance abuse. At one point he was homeless. He had graduated from high school with just a 1.9 GPA and wound up going to a community college. But when he recovered from the substance abuse issues, he graduated from the community college and got accepted to Northwestern because he'd gotten such good grades. He went from Northwestern to USC, and from USC to a very prestigious law firm. He had now been a judge on the felony panel for about eight years.

Judge Taylor told me his whole story. At the end, I handed him my résumé and my cover letter and told him that if he ever needed an intern, I would love to learn from him. That same day he sent me an e-mail asking when I could start.

Another valuable connection Dave made for me.

I worked for Judge Taylor the entire fall semester of my third year, as a judicial intern in his courtroom. He's a really good guy. He made me think about the death penalty and other controversial issues I was indecisive about.

Judge Taylor will *always* be a very inspirational person in my life, given where he came from and what his life was like. He made me think, *What am I complaining about?* I didn't have a lot of the challenges he had.

But even after seeing all kinds of trials in Judge Taylor's courtroom, I still never saw better attorneys than those in the public defender's office. I know defense attorneys get a bad rap because of the people they represent, but they really *are* enforcing the rights of the accused and our Constitution. PDs are so passionate about the work they do and such zealous advocates for the people they represent. They demonstrate immense dedication to their clients.

My experience with both the public defender's office *and* Judge Taylor was so influential. It really taught me what the justice system was all about. It just put things so much more into perspective for me and stoked my passion for criminal law.

In a total of three years, I graduated from law school.

I wouldn't have been able to make this happen without the support of my mother. She made sure my son was well cared for while I was studying, and she again helped me chauffeur him around to his various activities.

At my graduation I was surrounded by close friends and family. Dave Bishop was there; my son was there. Even my dad came! He was so proud of me.

I was proud of *myself* too. But I was also focused on the even larger challenge that I knew lay ahead: Passing the California State Bar Exam.

Hurdling the bar...

During my final year of law school, I connected with the John M. Langston Bar Association—the oldest and largest Black Bar Association in California. I went to some networking events and I applied for their prestigious academic scholarship. And I got it! It was awarded to me at their very formal installation dinner, where I was given five thousand dollars to help pay for my prep course for the California Bar Exam.

I also connected with the Black Women Lawyers Association of Los Angeles. I attended some of their events and I applied for *their* bar scholarship. At first I thought they wouldn't consider me because I had just received the Langston scholarship, but they said they didn't care; they wanted to hear my story. They also had me write a sample bar exam essay to see my writing skills before making their decision.

They gave me another three thousand dollars!

I now had eight thousand dollars to study for the bar and to help support myself during the process. What a blessing! Those types of things make you not want to disappoint!

My motivation moved to a whole new level. There was *no* way that after these two associations had given me this much money and believed in me, I wasn't going to succeed.

It was the summer of 2009.

I was studying twelve hours a day.

I was doing everything I could to prepare myself.

But the week before the test, I became extremely depressed and couldn't stop crying. I knew I had so many people counting on me, including my son. And I thought there was *no* way I was going to be able to put all of this information into my head and pass the exam. I'd worked *so* hard and it still didn't seem like enough.

When it came time to actually take the bar, though, I went into it feeling like *I just knew it*. I didn't know why I had doubted myself. The multiple-choice questions, the essay questions—I really felt like I nailed it. I walked out of there feeling really confident.

But the week before I got my results, I again felt like crap. I didn't even want to get out of bed.

I kept having nightmares of failing the exam. It was really bad. I kept thinking the whole law school thing was difficult enough and now the bar exam was like a subsequent "hazing process" to become an attorney.

I took the exam administered at the end of July and results weren't due out until November. So for four entire months, everyone kept preparing me to fail the first time around.

When my results finally came, I was terrified.

I opened them.

I passed.

When I told Judge Taylor I had passed the bar, he asked if I would like him to swear me in.

A one-on-one swearing in is an honor. Most attorneys are sworn in by their law school with their classmates.

"That sounds great," I said. "Will we do it in your chambers?"

"No," he said. "This is a monumental time in your life. You need to invite your family. We need to go to someplace nice." I really felt special.

So I set up a restaurant banquet room, invited some of the attorneys I'd worked for at the public defender's office, my boyfriend, my close friends, one of my former professors, and—of course—Dave Bishop. I was sworn in personally by the judge I worked for and whom Dave had introduced me to.

The judge was right: This *was* a monumental time in my life, and now it was accompanied by a very special memory with friends and loved ones present.

Thank you, Dave. And thank you, Judge Taylor.

While awaiting my results of the bar exam, I had begun seeking another law clerk position. My job search was difficult. Even after my test results came in, I wasn't hearing back from firms I had interviewed with.

It was a difficult time. I was broke. I was unemployed. But I was an attorney!

My mother is a member of a union that represents California state employees in disciplinary matters before administrative law boards. She introduced me to a supervisor of this union, who explained the intricacies of labor and employment law. Having developed an interest in that aspect of law during law school, this introduction sparked my interest.

When a position in that office became available, the supervisor told my mother I should apply. I did, and I got the job. I now work for Service Employees International Union; it's the largest union in the United States, representing 2.2 million employees.

I feel new to being a career woman. I feel like I'm starting all over in a new place in my life.

Most people don't come right out of law school loving what they're doing at their first job. I *love* what I'm doing right now.

I would still love to one day become a judge, but it's a long-term goal. Law school teaches you to think like a lawyer, but it doesn't necessarily teach you how to *be* a lawyer. I'm in that process now.

I feel that I'm one of Pathways' successes and I know that I'm on my way to even more achievements.

Another kind of "success" Pathways has given me is the ability to accept my family and move forward positively into the future.

My mother…

My therapist at Pathways told me about my mother's "drug": her need to help people. And how, with my being so independent and strong willed, my mother's "attention" isn't always needed. But when I *was* needy, she stepped right in. She is the reason I finished law school.

Even so, I feel we still have areas where we can improve our relationship. Her bond with my son is stronger than it is with me; she does so much stuff for him. She has more time now to be grandma, I suppose, but I sometimes wish she had been able to do all that for *me* as I was growing up.

Still, I now realize the positive influence my mother had on me in so many ways.

My mother is very strong. And even though she wasn't there a lot of the time, she always made me feel protected. If she thought I was being treated unfairly, she would call my school, the parents of my childhood friends, or even my employer, and set them straight. *She* is the person who taught me to stand up for what is right.

My mother is a very caring individual; she lives her life to help others. This may not have always been the best thing for her children—

or herself—but it did teach us not to be selfish and to do what we can to help those in need.

As a single parent, my mother struggled and overcame many difficult obstacles. She provided a powerful role model of someone driven to succeed. She never demonstrated weakness, and she raised my sister and me the best she knew how in an effort to provide us with a good life.

Today, I wholeheartedly believe that I have been able to be so strong and driven because of the example my mother set and the sacrifices she made.

My father...

When my dad got out of the hospital, he couldn't walk without a walker. Now, a year and a half later, he's walking, running, lifting weights, and is *not* doing drugs. And he's sort of "harassing" me! He calls me all the time. All of a sudden, he'll say, "I just want to talk to my baby girl!"

I just have to let my childhood go—bygones need to be bygones. I can't force myself to have the bond he wants to have with me now, but he *is* a part of my life and my son's life, too.

And he does say, "I'm sorry..." He makes a conscious effort.

"I have a few good years left," he says, "and I want to be a part of my daughter's life."

And he does support me. In addition to attending my law school graduation, he paid for my bar license when I passed the bar. He'd gotten money from a settlement for sustaining a back injury while at work. Typical Dad!

Of course, I still never *call* him Dad—just Gary. But when he was in the hospital, I thought, *He's on his deathbed; I'm going to call him Dad.* And I did.

Thankfully my *dad* lived.

My sisters…

Regretfully, I sometimes feel like I don't have sisters. My father's other daughters have never been a part of my life, but I grew up with my older sister. She and I *should be* close.

But that just hasn't happened.

Then or now.

We don't really communicate. We don't call each other on birthdays. She didn't come to any of my graduations. We just don't really talk.

I have to accept that we will never have that closeness. There's just too much history. And my mother has never really helped bridge that connection.

But with our kids it's a different story.

My sister has four kids, all by the same man she's been married to, though they're going through a divorce now. She has two "sets" of kids—one "pair" is twelve and fourteen, the other is three and five. The older pair loves my son to death—they're like the Three Musketeers.

A lot of people—even those I've known for many years—have been surprised when they've found out I have an older sister.

They never knew.

It's sad, but that's how it is.

And her relationship with *her* father is about like my relationship with my dad. She hadn't talked to him in many years but recently he's been sick so she does visit him every once in a while.

That, too, is sad.

But that, too, is how it is.

My son's father…

My son's father is pretty much a deadbeat dad. He paid some child support when we were in Utah, but since we've been in California, nothing. He'll call my son and maybe send a video game now and then, for his birthday or for Christmas. But he is not consistent.

It's never really been *good*, but it's become really *bad*.

I know he loves his son, but he doesn't know how to be a father or how to be responsible. He still doesn't work a real job—I don't know *what* he does. As long as he's not trying to fight me for custody, I don't have a problem with him being in our lives. Every summer we go to Utah, and I make sure my son sees him for a couple days. But not for any long period. I don't feel comfortable with that and I don't think my son would like it either.

I feel bad; this is the person I *chose*—although I was really young and wouldn't make that same choice today.

And I never "chose" that type of man again.

I'm so glad I experienced that at a young age so I didn't have to do it as an adult. I think that since then I've made pretty good choices with the guys I've dated. No gang members—*that* won't happen again!

My son doesn't know his father is a drug dealer and was in prison. He sees the tattoos up and down his arms and neck, and when he is old enough, he will figure it out. But it's not a conversation I want to have right now.

Of course, then I think of how I upset *I* was with *my* mother for not telling *me* the truth about *my* father. And my son is getting to the age where I *should* talk to him about it. I'm scared, though, because my son wears his emotions on his face like I do—when he gets *that face,* I know he is really sad and that breaks my heart. I don't want him to be sad.

In the end, it's just about me and my son—about us having a good life. My son is my investment. I'm trying to make sure he's a good person, a good citizen, and successful. That's what my focus is.

I have a determination "not to let anything hold *him* back" either.

Once life becomes overwhelming—like it did for me—so many people feel like they're going to give up on themselves.

I know *I* did.

But Pathways changed all that—from my financial problems to my family issues, from my confidence to my continual stress, from my self-image to my severe acne. Would I still have pursued my dreams without Pathways? I think so—but it would've taken so much longer to get there because I had some serious things *holding me back.*

I've seen so many people drop out of school with the thought that "I'll come back later…I just need to live my life and provide for my family for a while…" but quite often they just don't return to school.

But that was never a concern for me because of Pathways. I was financially stable and was able to dedicate myself to school. And on top of that, my confidence was being built because I was able to get industry-leading medical care and talk to a therapist regularly who would help me work through life's stresses.

I'm thirty years old and I'm an attorney—and a single mom of a thirteen-year-old son. Most people never imagined I could succeed like this in *this* short of time.

But Dave Bishop was there for me all the way—even taking money out of his own pocket to help me with the LSAT. Pathways pushed me, and having that accountability factor was huge—I feel guilty very easily. If I feel I've disappointed someone, it really weighs on my heart.

Failure was not an option in Pathways. I had too many people behind me, supporting me and making me accountable. Up until then, the only person I felt accountable to was my son. And that *includes* my mom. She wanted great things for me, but she never checked my grades, or helped with my homework, or made me feel accountable to her when I was growing up.

Pathways wanted great things for me, too; but there, I had to meet people and call people all the time. I was constantly accountable and that gave me just that much more drive.

It's not a welfare system.

I was talking to somebody about welfare recently. Welfare should be run like Pathways—you need to be accountable, to call in, to "turn in your grades." That isn't an insult or an invasion of privacy; if I'm asking for help and you're giving it to me, I *am* accountable to you.

I would like to have a kind of Pathways of my own and be able to help other young women facing similar challenges; particularly single mothers who have had their children at a young age. People don't expect women in these situations to succeed or get their education.

Eventually, I'd like to mentor a young woman and encourage her to pursue her career. I'd like to show her that it *can* be done—especially if she feels like it can't.

I was actually part of a program called A Woman Like Me at a nearby community college. It was an eight-month commitment in which we mentored seventh-grade girls who were at high risk of drugs or pregnancy and who were not succeeding in school.

My mentee and her family moved from hotel room to hotel room throughout the week. Even though she had no home, she had a 3.8 GPA. But she wasn't planning to go to college—she just wanted to get a job and make some money. After I spent time with her, she began to consider pursuing a higher education. Unfortunately, I lost contact with my mentee when the program ended; we never had consistent contact information for her. It was sad.

She's the kind of girl who should be helped—and saved—through Pathways. And, unfortunately, there are so many more.

I want to give back. I've been given so many blessings in life. Everything seems to have fallen into place for me, but I do realize it's because *people helped me.* It's because people gave me a chance and believed in me. People like Dave Bishop and all the volunteers at Pathways.

I officially graduated from Pathways five years ago, but the help has been everlasting. Pathways inspires me. Now I want to do the same for someone else. To teach them:

Never let anything or anyone hold you back.

No More Safe Havens

"My mother said I should have been one of her six abortions."

—PepperFanne

My mother was a drug addict.

She was a full-functioning drug addict her entire life. But as a kid I didn't know what kinds of drugs she used.

My father was an alcoholic. He was a drink-'til-he-passed-out-and-urinated-on-himself alcoholic. But I loved him; he was my heart.

I have an older sister, Jody, and a younger sister, Jade. As we grew up, my mom yelled at all of us continuously—but my sisters never got hit.

That kind of abuse was reserved for me.

I didn't know if it was the "middle child syndrome" or what, but I was always the target.

Along with the physical abuse came the mental assaults.

I was always "stupid."

I was "dumb."

I was "ugly."

Of the three kids, I was the "ugliest." The baby was the prettiest, then my older sister, then me. I don't look like my sisters. *I look like my mother.*

My mother is a five-foot-two little Mexican woman and she's a rager. My father was the defender. He was a big, tall man, but she would hit him, too! She would kick and punch my father when he was drunk and passed out.

She would kick and punch and hit *me* in the face, head, and everywhere, and she'd use anything—her fists, her purse, extension cords...things like that.

I always had bruises. One time, I went to school after being beaten by my mother the night before. I was really hurting, so I pretended to fall off the monkey bars so someone would take me to the hospital. It turned out that I had bruised ribs. My mother *never* took me to the hospital for stuff like that.

My family moved around a lot—I believe due to the family violence. And usually we weren't in great neighborhoods. I don't even know *how* many different elementary schools I attended. I think it was around six.

I was in about the fourth grade when I started to run away from home.

For a child to run away from home at that age, there's something very, very wrong. But no one tried to make it right.

When I ran away, my mother wouldn't look for me. But my father would. So I'd go away for the night, and then I'd be found and brought back by the police—and then I'd get beat again for running away. It was literally a *vicious* cycle.

My father was my biggest ally at the time. I was very close to him. I often wonder why he had to die first, instead of my mother. I used to pray to God to kill either me or her—one of us had to go.

Even though my father was a drunk—and he was *always* a drunk—he didn't treat me like my mother did. He treated me like I was a diamond. But he used to make me cry when he'd tell me, "You're acting like your mother."

And I guess there *were* times I acted like her. No matter how badly I didn't want to. In fact, it seemed the more I tried *not* to be like her, the more I felt and acted *just* like her.

So throughout my childhood, my father continued to drink and argue with my mom, and I ran away even more. I don't remember how many times I ran away. My mother eventually started officially reporting it so they'd have a record of my "escapes."

One time when I'd stayed away for a couple of days, my mother filed a missing person report. Eventually, a female police officer—who was a complete bitch—found me and brought me back home.

I told her what was happening at home and begged her, "Don't leave me here! She's going to beat me again." I even showed her the bruises. She said it was "unfounded child abuse" because the bruises were "too old" or "could have been self-inflicted." But she gave me her card and told me to call if it happened again.

It wasn't *if,* it was *when.*

As soon as she left, my mother started in. She threw chicken noodle soup at me and began yelling.

I took off with the card and called the female cop. She came back and talked to my mother.

But my mother lied, of course, and my sister Jody lied for her too. It appeared that *I* was the problem child. So, as always, I wound up staying.

And, of course, I got beat.

One Easter, my mother and I got into an argument. For the first and last time in my life, my older sister defended me.

When my mother started hitting me, I did what I usually did: I fell into a ball on the ground. This time, Jody tried to pull my mom off me, and somehow in the tussle my mom ended up biting my arm. I had a *huge* bite mark.

"You bitch!" I remember screaming. That was the first time I cussed at my mother to her face.

So my mother kicked *both* my sister and me out—on Easter. Jody took off, and I walked along the train tracks over to my best friend Samantha's house.

Samantha's family does not like my mother to this day. They never called social services, but they took me in all the time. Samantha's mother and father loved me. I practically lived there.

Sometimes when my mother came to pick me up, we would all hide from her and not answer the door.

But eventually, I *always* had to go home.

Somewhere along the line, with all my running away and getting beaten, my mother doing drugs, my father's alcoholism, and all the rest, I wound up staying at my grandparents' house for weeks or months at a time.

Also living at my grandparents' house was my cousin. He was probably fifteen or sixteen. I was nine or ten.

He started molesting me.

I can't remember exactly when or how it started. Even as it was happening, I blocked it out.

But I do remember making it end.

I was twelve or thirteen, and I was watching a movie at Samantha's house. Suddenly, I got a sort of flashback—my mind was flooded with images of my cousin touching me. I began crying uncontrollably. I told Samantha the memories that had just hit me. She started crying too.

I was supposed to return to my house that night, so of course I decided to run away again. After being gone for a couple of days, I decided to call home to let them know I was okay. My sister Jody was the one who answered the phone.

Jody asked me if my cousin had done it to me, *too.* I was surprised and relieved by her revelation. I told her yes. My sister promised that if

I came home, she would tell my mother what my cousin had done—to *both* of us. I said okay.

When I came home, my sister *did* tell about what had happened to me—but not to her. I felt betrayed and angry.

After that, it came down to a sort of intervention.

With my traditional Mexican family values, we couldn't tell my grandfather about this, because he would've *killed* my cousin; plus, it would just not be proper. So my mother, my grandmother, my uncle, me, and my cousin all gathered in the living room. My uncle—my cousin's father—asked my cousin if he had really done this. Of course, he said no.

And that's all that was said.

The abuse *did* end. But the whole horrible mess was looked on as *my* fault, and I was never allowed to go to my grandparents' house again.

So now, when my mother started in on me, I could no longer head to my grandparents' place for sanctuary, and I knew my parents would find me at Samantha's. So I began to hit the streets more and more.

I had no more safe havens left to run away to.

This was all especially sad because my grandfather and my uncle—my cousin's father—were my favorite family members.

My grandfather was my heart and my soul. We talked about *everything*. Except, of course, my molestation. I *couldn't* tell him that.

My uncle—who was also my godfather—was my protector. He defended me once when my mother let another cousin—another drug addict—move into our apartment with us. This cousin was a short little Mexican guy who thought he could talk shit to me and tried to beat me up. I called my uncle—my savior—and he came over and kicked the guy out.

But my uncle was also an alcoholic. I guess I was attracted to all the alcoholic men in the family.

And *because* I was so close to my grandfather, my uncle, and my father, my mother would tell me the most horrible stories about all of them.

At one point after the "intervention," my mother told me that my uncle had molested *her.* Yeah, *okay*. My mother has a habit of turning everything around to make it about her. I believe she told me that to take the "spotlight" off of me and back onto my poor mother. To this day, whatever happens—I mean *any* problem—it's all about how it will affect her, not us girls.

She did ask if my uncle ever tried to do anything to *me*. I said no.

In therapy, I learned that what my cousin did to me is actually not called molestation; it's called *incest* because it involved a family member. Incest is still a very hard word for me to say. How do you say you were "incested"? It just sounds so bad.

And it *was* so bad. It was horrible.

Yet, of all the horrible things I *do* remember, there's still a whole lot that I've blocked out. Even with therapy, a lot of painful stuff remains locked inside. Things I don't *want* to remember. Things that got blocked out by that incest.

And as I grew up, it became hard for me to look at myself in the mirror or wear nice clothes. I *still* don't like anyone looking at me in a sexual manner. And I don't like smells now—the smells related to sex. I have a very hard problem with that. I have a very hard problem with my whole *self* because of what happened.

The thoughts of the past, my home life, the attacks on my self-esteem—all of it was eating me alive. When I was in eighth grade, I told a friend of mine at school that I wanted to die. She told the teacher and the teacher called my mom.

My mom came to school and picked me up.

I got yelled and screamed at all the way home in the car. *How dare I say anything bad about her family? How dare I tell people I want to kill myself? How dare I present this bad image of our family?*

I was in the backseat, but I couldn't get far enough away from her; she could still reach back and pinch me with her damn long-ass nails!

When we got to the house, my mother took me into the bathroom, threw me in the bathtub, got a bunch of pills, and pulled my hair. She threw the pills at me and said, "Yeah, you want to die *now*?"

Then she walked out of the bathroom and left me there.

One time my mother was looking for some shirt of hers. She couldn't find it, so she freaked out and started searching my room. She pulled all my clothes out of the drawers and threw them on the floor. "I know you have it!" she said.

I said nothing.

A little while later, after she calmed down, my mother was able to find her shirt. "I found it!" she yelled.

Of course me and my mouth, I said, "Yeah, after you go and throw apart my room!"

Well she did *not* like that at all. She came into my room, and I again rolled into a ball to protect myself. This time, she pulled me all through the house by my hair! She pulled me down this long hallway and then she kicked me. Then she ran to the kitchen and grabbed one those little plastic honey bear containers, which was filled with dish soap, and squirted it into my mouth. She was yelling at me: "You're not going to talk to me like that!"

When she left the room, I instigated a lot of self-inflicted pain. I started banging my head into the wall. I'd rather feel my own pain than what she'd just given me.

After that incident, I did a lot of hitting of myself. I'd rip out my hair and punch myself. This began to be my only way of dealing with her abuse.

And the abuse continued and continued…

There was the videocassette incident. That one was *really* bad.

My mom couldn't find the videotape she was looking for. So me with my mouth—I don't know why I had such a big mouth; you'd think I'd keep it shut, but I didn't—I said something like, "Hey, it's here. Here it is. It's over here!"

So, naturally, she hits me with it! I bled and bled.

The phone cords were the worst, though.

There was also the belt, the belt buckle, a shoe, a hairbrush—whatever she had, she'd hit me with it.

I got hit so much it became ridiculous.

I especially hated the mornings because of my mother. She'd get up, and she's just a nasty person in the morning. If she couldn't find her hairbrush or something, she would scream and yell at everybody, and of course *my* mouth was open, so I would always say something and I would get it.

So I'd get slapped getting ready for school and wind up with big red marks on my face.

That's why I began to ditch school—*all* the time. And I was never *told* to go. Nobody checked my homework. It was just not the thing to do.

I hated my life and I hated going to school.

I started using drugs at age thirteen or fourteen. In my house, it wasn't: "Let's *not* do drugs"; it was that everybody *was* either on drugs or drunk. Drugs were always around.

I learned real quickly that instead of turning me off, drugs turned me on. I'd found my escape. I started with my mother's weed and then I got into meth. That was my saving grace. I'd found something that made me feel comfortable with who I was and helped me stay skinny.

So now I'm thirteen, and I'm using drugs, and I've also developed an eating disorder.

I simply stopped eating.

I was a very late bloomer to start with. I didn't even weigh 117 pounds until the ninth grade. I was really more like a little boy, not a little girl.

Everybody else was bigger, with big boobs. I never had that look. And especially after what had happened to me, I made *sure* I never would have that look.

I liked it like that. It was safer.

So I starved myself. I was really good at that. With drugs, I got down to about ninety pounds. I thought I looked good, but really I didn't.

The beatings from my mother continued.

At sixteen, I tried to kill myself.

I don't remember the exact situation, but I know I needed drugs and my mom wouldn't let me go out and get them. And she hit me.

I decided that would be the *last* time she hit me.

My sister had some prescription pills—left over from her own trauma she had been dealing with. I decided to take them all.

Good, you're going to die was my only thought.

So I took a shower, because I didn't want them to find me dirty, and then I lay down, figuring it would all be over soon.

But I didn't die.

What happened was, I lost feeling in my legs and I started throwing up.

I threw up for days and days. I started throwing up my stomach lining. But—as always—my mother wouldn't take me to the doctor. Instead, as I'm dying and throwing up, my mother decides to make me chicken soup. This was a Mexican chicken soup, the kind with big chunks of chicken, potatoes, and corn.

And when I couldn't eat it, she smacked me.

Then my mother took Jody and Jade to visit my grandparents. Jody must have realized something was terribly wrong, so she told my grandfather how sick I was. My grandfather called and asked me if I was okay. I told him no.

He said he would be right over.

My grandfather is a proud Mexican man—we always had to be well kempt around him. So when I learned he was coming, I took a shower and tried to get dressed. I was so sick from the pills that I had soiled myself all over.

When my grandfather and Jody arrived, I could not even walk down the stairs. They took me to the emergency room, where I was admitted immediately. They stuck IVs in my arms and I heard the nurse tell my grandfather I was dying of dehydration.

The next thing I remember is a doctor coming in the room and asking me all sorts of questions: *How often did I think about dying? How many times a day did I think about death?*

I guess I answered correctly, because they strapped me to a hospital gurney and transported me to a mental hospital for a seventy-two-hour evaluation.

So now I'm sixteen and I'm in the hospital for trying to kill myself.

I was put into a padded cell because I was angry, violent, and hostile; I was cussing at the staff. All I did was fight back. That's how I coped: I fought.

I stayed there for a while. I don't even know how long. I think about a month.

They had family groups there, to try and help patients like me with severe family problems. My mother never showed up for any of them.

But during my stay was one of the first times I got honest and told the hospital about the abuse I was receiving at home.

When I was released, Child Protective Services was called. They interviewed my mother and Jody, who both told them I was lying—nothing like that *ever* happened at our house. So again, nothing was done.

I *really* hated my life.

My mom finally divorced my father, mainly because of his drinking. Although they both had serious addictions, they were *so* different. He was a sad drunk who would cry. She was this crazy psychotic drug addict who would hit me and call me names.

She told me I should have been one of her six abortions.

Somewhere along the way, we moved back to Boyle Heights—to the ghetto.

It was a perfect ghetto life. My neighborhood was gang infested, filled with *cholos* and their girlfriends. I decided I wanted that lifestyle.

Maybe I realized I could get out of my house if I went that way. I don't know if it was a conscious idea, but I do know that's what happened.

I really liked being in the gang situation. I had backup. I felt protected. They cared about me. I couldn't be any worse than they were, because they were pretty fucked up. So that lifestyle became my niche and I took it all the way.

We shot guns.

We stole cars.

We ran drugs.

I used to hang out with the cooks—the ones who *made* the drugs. They'd be cooking, and I couldn't even wait for the drugs to dry out before I "sampled" them. Many times I would burn the inside of my nose.

I don't know how we didn't get caught for any of this.

Along with the lifestyle came my boyfriend—a gangster who would be the father of my first child: my daughter, Melody.

My backup increased. My protection was strengthened.

Often there'd be rival gangs in the apartment houses where I lived. I'd call my big homeboys and tell them that these people upstairs were messing with me. I'd pass the phone to my "neighbors" so that they and my homies could *talk.*

Those people wouldn't touch me.

Some other gangs tried to make me run drugs for them. My boyfriend would *make a call* and somebody would be sent down to take care of it. All I had to do was call my homeboys and they would take care of everything.

The gang lifestyle became very much what I liked. I used it as a catalyst to keep me into drugs.

Things were happening fast.

I got pregnant not long after I tried to commit suicide.

My boyfriend and I were really kids when we got together. We didn't know what we were doing. My mother had never talked to me about sex, so I had no idea about birth control or anything. When she finally *did* talk to me about condoms and so forth, I already thought I was pregnant.

So now I'm in this gangster relationship with this cholo who beats me—he started beating me when I was five months pregnant.

We didn't have sex that often, and he started cheating on me early in the relationship too.

I stayed with him off and on for five years.

When I started seeing my boyfriend, he wasn't hard-core. Over the years, this guy *grew* into his gang stuff.

When we met, he was just one of the little gangsters hanging around, waiting to get into the big leagues. He had hair back then; later he shaved his head. And he had no tattoos. He was just a skinny, dorky kid. I don't even know why I liked him.

Now he's this big-time gang member. That's his lifestyle.

The first tattoo he gave *me* was three dots—the Latino gang sign for *La Vida Loca* ("The Crazy Life"). *He* was the one who did that. I remember thinking how tough I was—but also telling him how much it hurt.

So much about all of this has *hurt.*

I know, however, that I wasn't *totally* a victim in all this. I do have a mouth. I'm this big ball of fire. I hated everybody and I fought all the time. I got into so many fights, it was insane. That's all I did: fight.

And I got more and more tattoos.

My baby's daddy moved into my mom's apartment with me when I was about five months along, so I would not be alone during my pregnancy. My mother didn't mind because he was selling her crack.

Our apartment got raided twice by the police. Somebody ratted out my baby's daddy for being the local drug dealer. In the apartment, we had crack, PCP, and weed. Most of it was hidden, but they did find nine "dimes" of weed and pot plants.

I told the cops it was mine, because I thought they would give me mercy because I was pregnant. They did—but they also took all the weed.

Living there all together was tough, so my boyfriend and I decided to try to distract my mother so we could have more time to hang out alone. So we hooked her up with *his* father. It was a perfect match—they were both crackheads. We figured they would leave us alone once we got them together.

But the plan backfired.

My mother started losing our apartment—I assume because she was spending her money on drugs instead of rent. So I moved into my boyfriend's house. But since my mother was now dating my boyfriend's father, she ended up moving into his house, too!

It was horrible.

When I was about nine months pregnant, my boyfriend got jumped in front of our apartment in Boyle Heights. I remember seeing the car roll up filled with rival gang members. They came up on us yelling stuff, and my boyfriend turned and told me to run.

I'm *nine* months pregnant; how the heck am I going to run?

But I ran. I remember my friend pushing me up the stairs, as we saw the rival gang members pulling out pipes and wrenches to beat my baby's daddy and his friends with. We finally made it up to the apartment.

Later, my boyfriend and his homeboys all came in. They had their heads all wrapped up with tank tops and T-shirts to soak up the blood. They all gathered around each other to plan their revenge. I just sat there cleaning up blood.

I actually *did* stop using drugs for all nine months of my pregnancy. I ended up delivering a healthy baby girl named Melody—whom I was not ready to have.

As soon as I was out of the hospital, I was back on drugs.

By now, I've dropped out of regular high school and am attending a continuation school. I have a baby, and I am not even eighteen years old.

Here's this girl who can't even *look* at herself in the mirror, let alone take care of a baby. I was a very, very, very bad parent; not to where I abused my daughter, but I wouldn't play with her and I couldn't even hug her.

So I would leave my baby with my crackhead mother. It was sad: my mom was actually better at taking care of her than I was.

I was a tweaker, and that's all I cared about.

By age nineteen, I was in county jail.

I'd been living in my own apartment, which I paid for with welfare money. My place was where people came to buy drugs or just hang out. I was always completely loaded.

After all the partying we did, the managers finally decided to kick me out. Well, that did not sit right with me. So my friends and I destroyed the place. I mean, we broke *everything.* We punched holes in the walls and broke the windows. You name it, we did it.

So I got arrested for felony vandalism—plus, since the cops could never catch me selling drugs, they busted me for possession with intent to distribute/sell.

But I was *excited*, because I thought that now I had finally "arrived." The L.A. County bus would come to take me to court and I'd see my baby's daddy's gang name scrawled on the ceiling.

I thought I was going to go to Sybil Brand—the notorious women's detention facility in East Los Angeles, just east of downtown—but Sybil Brand had just closed. So I went to the Twin Towers, the main correctional facility in the heart of L.A. I got to wear the county blues. On the street, that was a *fashion statement*.

I was there for four months.

That was the only time I ever went to jail, though; the only time I actually got busted. But along with the arrest, I got *banned* from the city where my apartment was!

It's funny—I was recently driving through that city with my husband, and he wanted to stop at a store for water.

"No!" I told him.

I know no one remembers me anymore, but I just didn't want to stop. It brought back all the nightmares I had back in my gang days—terrifying dreams about getting shot. After I got out of that lifestyle, the nightmares stopped.

I won't go back to Boyle Heights, either. There are certain cities I just can't bring myself to go to.

When I got out of jail, I had to move back in with my mother. She had gotten tired of being abused by her boyfriend (my now *ex*-boyfriend's father/my daughter's grandfather), so she had gotten her own new place at the other end of Boyle Heights.

Although I was no longer in a relationship with my baby's daddy, I still had protection from the neighborhood.

And I went back to doing all the same things.

I continued with the drugs and the gangs. I did a lot of bad stuff. I spent a lot of time with a lot of bad and shady people in a lot of scary situations.

I hated myself.

Of course, at the time I didn't realize that—I didn't know *anything* was wrong with me.

I continued to do drugs and drink. I started drinking because I got too skinny on meth. I would drink, get fat, and then go back to the meth. I got alcohol poisoning twice.

And all the while, I had this *baby*.

Melody was one or two, and I was there *but not there*. I was full-blown into drugs. So I would give my mother the baby and I'd hit the streets. I was running drugs and involved in a lot of stuff. But on the weekends, my crackhead mother would get tired of taking care of my baby and she'd give her to me.

By that time, I was basically living in a crack house. In that neighborhood, people would do "walk-bys." These were *shootings*—shootings that took place on foot, as opposed to "drive-bys" that happen in a car.

And I was part of all that.

When I knew my mother was bringing the baby over, I'd put mattresses over the windows to protect against bullets. That was my bright idea. *Not so bright.*

One time when I had Melody there, we decided to go to the store and buy some liquor. On the way to the store, we shot up some people. The helicopters came quickly, so we ran back to the house. The helicopter was hovering, cops were everywhere, and we were being told: "The residents of the house must come out with their hands up!"

We all came out. I remember having my daughter wrap her arms around me as I walked out with my hands up. They questioned us, but we all told a consistent cover story, so they let us go.

I'm amazed that I lived through all that.

After shooting up those people and the house getting raided, I somehow got this new boyfriend.

He was actually a good guy.

He didn't beat me.

He was my first sign of getting better, I thought.

I stopped using *as many* drugs. And I started trying to be a parent—at least a *little* bit.

But I still lived with my mom, and I had nothing. I didn't even know how to drive a car. That's just something we didn't learn to do there. In my neighborhood, it was just up one hill and down the next. You didn't use anything except a five-dollar taxi. That was my lifestyle.

I really liked my new boyfriend, but I was hard-core and in deep with the gang while he was like a wannabe—from a little gang in a smaller neighborhood. I was harder than him. In our circles, I made him look *good*.

My baby's daddy is a *real* gangster.

Another of those places I still can't go is the pier.

That's where my new boyfriend got killed.

Shot in the head—a gang hit.

I was about twenty and my daughter was three or four.

My mother got the call right after I left the house that day. She called me at a friend's house and told me the news.

How do you get that call? All I could think was, *He is gone and my baby's daddy is still alive. How is that fair? How is that possible?*

Melody's daddy called to make sure I was okay. I asked him how he knew and why he couldn't have warned us this was going to happen. He said he just couldn't tell me. He also said, "I told you not to hang out with those losers…"

During this time, my mother's drug addiction was coming to a head. All my life she'd been a "functioning crackhead," working in the medical field as a receptionist. I don't know how she did it. I was *never* a functioning drug addict. I just *didn't* function.

My *hobby* was pimping out girls to get the drugs they earned. *I* wasn't going to be the one to sleep with the guys; I just couldn't do that. I still had serious sexual problems due to my molestation/incest.

My mother kept her job, but again lost her apartment and was reduced to renting a room from a family member. The family she moved in with hated me, so I wasn't allowed at their house. I now had *nowhere* left to go. So I lived in the streets.

I just left and let my mother take care of Melody.

Eventually I lost my daughter. Truth be told, I gave her away—at least temporarily. I signed over custody of Melody to my mother, with papers stating this would only be until I got my life straightened out. It sure seemed odd to me that my daughter's care could be entrusted to a crackhead, but my mom *was* more capable than I was, and she had my younger sister's help.

Plus, my mother was good at hiding her drug use. Every drug test she took at work was tainted by the excuse that she was constantly on some prescription medication for something. So she would always play it off that way. And she did that for a very long time.

I was now in my twenties, but still, whenever I saw my mom, we'd fight. We'd get into an argument and *she'd still try to hit me!*

One time, my mother came over to visit me where I was staying—probably to drop off Melody. She was always trying to drop her off with me so she could go out and do her *own* drugs; but I couldn't take care of Melody either.

This day, I was coming down from drugs and I told my mom to give me some weed so I could calm down. She wouldn't. And as I turned to walk away from her, she kicked me.

So I attacked her. Physically. My own mother.

This was the first time in my life that I hit her back. I punched her in the face.

"Help me!" my mother was screaming at the homeboy.

"He's not going to do anything!" I told her.

I remember busting the glasses right off her face.

You'd think that kind of retaliation after all those years of abuse would have given me some kind of relief—but it didn't. It was the worst pain I ever felt. You just don't hit your parents.

And I beat her up pretty bad. It was mortifying.

I was *not* a nice person. I was a fighter. And I was coming down from drugs. And my mom's kicking me just triggered so many thoughts: *Why does she think she can still hit me? Why would she kick me?* My mind went back to when I was sixteen and tried to kill myself and all my mom did was hit me. I didn't understand.

So at twenty-something, I beat up my mother. For not giving me drugs.

I had no idea how messed up I was.

I tried to go back and see my mother, but of course I still wasn't allowed in there because of the family hating me and all. My mother told me to get out—*leave!* I had my hand between the wrought-iron door and the jamb, and *she slammed it shut!*

My hand was swelling up quickly as I left. *I need to get help,* I thought. *I'll go to the homeboy's house. My baby's daddy will know what to do.* So that's where I went. But for the first time, no one was hanging around there. I thought, *What the fuck?*

I had nowhere to go.

I headed back to my mom's with my hand all swollen, and she told me, "I can't help you; you need to call your father."

At this time, my father was in a recovery home. My little sister, Jade, still kept in contact with him.

"You need to come help your daughter," my mother apparently told him.

So my father called and asked me if I wanted to get sober. By that point, I didn't know what *sober* was; I didn't remember sober. And I definitely didn't *want* to get sober.

But I didn't know *what* I wanted, so I said yes.

My father found me a recovery home in Orange County—a different one from his, since his was all male. I thought I was coming up; I thought going to Orange County would be nice and all. But *my* facility turned out to be an indigent recovery home. That means they take patients who have no money, no anything. It wasn't the best.

Of course, by the time I made it there, I *was* pretty much indigent. I didn't have my own clothes; I didn't even have a pair of shoes. I'd been living on the street.

Jody gave me some of her shoes, which were too big, and she drove me to the facility.

And boy, did I hate it!

I didn't *want* to get sober. But I just did it. Maybe all this happened because the homeboys weren't home—I don't know. But I had no conscious thought that I was going to get sober. Sober and me didn't go together. It wasn't the thing to do. *Nobody* in my family was sober.

So here I am: without my daughter—I don't really know how old she was by now, maybe four or five—and I'm in this recovery home getting sober and trying to get my life together. My mother, the crackhead, still works as a receptionist and is still taking care of my baby.

So I began working the twelve-step program. *And I just did it.*

I began to get Melody every now and then. I got to see her on weekends. I started to think that maybe I could actually be a mother.

But really, at that time, there was no way in hell.

I did all that for a while. I stayed at the facility, attending a dozen twelve-step meetings a week. I got a sponsor, worked the steps, started sponsoring other ladies, and even became the house manager.

It turned out that my sponsor knew Dave Bishop. My sponsor always liked me and she told Dave about me, thinking Pathways would be good for me.

After interviewing me, Dave said no. It felt to me like he said, "*Hell*, no!"

I scared everybody.

They didn't want me around.

I was in this recovery place for a year. I got my first job at age twenty-two, while I was still living there. When I got out, I learned how to drive a car at age twenty-four.

Again, my sponsor introduced me to Dave. This time, Dave said, "Have her write her life story."

I did.

Again, Pathways interviewed me.

But again, they said no.

"If you want to show us you can do something," they said, "go to college and take a couple of classes."

I went to one class and I got an A.

I showed them the grade and they still didn't want me.

So I took another class and I got another A.

This time they said, "*Maybe* we'll help you." I went directly back to Dave with that second A and I was allowed into the program.

I remember when I met my Pathways mentor, she was scared of me. *Everyone* was scared of me!

And I was scared of *them*! Sure, these were nice white people—but where I came from, we had blacks, crack kids, and Mexicans. There were no *white* people.

So here I am with these people, thinking, *Oh my God, what am I doing?!*

I really didn't have much hope. I didn't even know if I wanted to be in this program. Pathways requires that you to go to counseling, meet regularly with your mentor, *and* go to school.

So I got out of the recovery program, entered Pathways, moved in with my sponsor, and got my daughter back. I think Melody was around six because she was just starting second grade.

I remember taking pictures on her first day of school. This is my daughter, who I didn't even teach how to tie her shoes. I didn't teach her how to ride a bike. None of that stuff. And here I am taking her to her first day of school at age six.

I was so happy and excited to have Melody back, but I still didn't know how to be a parent. It's not like I had a good role model. So to be honest, it was *really* hard. All she did was cry. She cried *all* the time, and I didn't know what was wrong with her. She just cried.

I remember my sponsor having to teach me how to parent, and it was just so difficult. I felt so guilty that I hadn't been there for her when she was little. I felt like she deserved a better mother than me.

Plus, now that I'd been sober for a year, a lot of stuff started coming back into my mind, my thoughts, and my memory.

Again, I realized that I didn't like myself.

I still had a severe eating disorder. I was five foot five and down to a hundred and ten pounds. I was a size one. I don't look good as a size one.

I wasn't really doing okay, but I was still doing.

I was going to therapy. I was working with a man at first, but I couldn't talk to him about the sexual stuff. So I got this great woman, Sharon. She's the one who explained to me about "incest."

I don't like that word.

I had a lot of stuff going on and I was still full of hate and anger at everything. I think I liked being a hater because it kept people from getting too close to me.

In the course of our activities, Pathways would take me places with all these girls and I just didn't fit in. They're all pretty and beautiful and have nice bodies, and here I am, this girl who hates everybody and feels ugly and fat. I was forced to sit there, and I'd think, *What the hell am I doing here?* I bucked everything.

And they *made* you go on these stupid retreats. I had to go for a whole weekend and be with all these *girls*. I had to be *frilly*! No! I hated it!

I discovered one thing at these gatherings: it's a bad thing when a nun remembers your name. Sister "B" remembered mine well, so it was hard for me to hide.

Sister B has this thick Irish accent. She taught us about self-esteem and looks and things like that. I wasn't ready for it. All these girls were gorgeous—I didn't look like any of them. So I would sit there very uncomfortably.

So I really didn't reap enough benefits from these gatherings at first. I was too busy being a hater.

I never thought Dave liked me and I never came to Pathways for anything.

"You never *ask* for things," Dave finally said. "Our girls *need* things." I guess other clients would tell Dave what they needed and Pathways would give it to them. *I* thought Pathways was doing the biggest deal of all by giving me therapy and paying for my schooling.

"What do I have to *ask* you for?" I'd say. "I'm happy just to be a part of this program!"

And I *was* so happy to be a part of it. But I can't tell you that I got better right away. I didn't.

When I got sober, my father ironically relapsed and drank himself to death at age fifty-one.

It was devastating.

I was in Pathways when I got the phone call that my father was in the hospital, on life support. I was just *about* to finish up my associate's degree and was preparing to transfer to Cal State University.

I stopped everything to be with my father. I didn't even call Dave. I didn't ask for help.

After my dad's funeral, I finally called Dave and said, "I'm not going to make it back to school." When I told him the reason, he of course asked me *why* I hadn't asked for help or money or *something?*

I told him, "This is not me. I'm not there yet."

When I returned to school, I had failed a couple of classes. I thought I would get into trouble and be kicked out of Pathways.

That didn't happen.

They said all was fine, but I still had a long way to go.

Right after my father died, the Pathways girls went on another retreat. One girl there was this amazingly beautiful blue-eyed, blond-haired girl. She was just so perfect. I couldn't stand her.

I felt like she was stuck-up. She was so cute and she'd look at you like *that.* Maybe it was her eyes that bothered me. I felt like saying, *What are you looking at me for? Cause I'm not a pretty white girl like you?*

But during this retreat, we were sitting in a group and she started playing with my hair. I found it really strange. I remember asking her why she was even bothering with me. She looked shocked.

Then she said: "I like weirdos."

I started laughing, and so did the other girls. They *all* liked me. I had been so busy hating myself, I couldn't see anyone every really liking me. I actually opened up more on that retreat with her and all the other girls.

Today, I love that girl more than ever. People see these pretty girls like her and they don't realize all the heart-wrenching stories that are in their lives. She has struggled a lot in the program; she's doing well now, but it *is* a struggle.

Dave helps us all immensely.

And I just kept *doing it*. The more therapy I got, the more I began to like the other girls.

But I still didn't trust them and I didn't feel safe with them.

The same year that I buried my father, some other big things happened.

My uncle—who is my godfather *and* the father of the cousin who abused me—also passed away.

That *same* year, my cousin came into town to visit my mother.

And he apologized to me.

My cousin's a born-again Christian now. He came over and apologized for what he did to me, and he said it just like that.

And he hugged me.

I took the hug and I cried and cried.

He said he was sorry for what he had done to me and how it affected me. I cried as I told him that this was the first time anybody had really *acknowledged* what happened to me. I told him how throughout my whole life I haven't been able to look in the mirror, or wear dresses, or wear makeup. I told him how I can't trust people because of this, and how much I've hated myself because of this. I told him there are *so many* things I can't do because of what he did to me—that he basically destroyed me.

Even though *he* is the one who did this to me, my cousin was the one who gave me relief. Because for over twenty years, I had been waiting for *someone* to acknowledge that *something happened to me!*

Yes, he apologized.

It was a big year.

Of course, my mother, who witnessed all this, just said, "Well, at least *you* got an apology."

I looked at her like, *Are you serious?*

"Well, my brother did it to *me*," she said, "and nobody ever apologized to *me*!"

It's *always* about her. I looked at her and thought, *God, I hate you!*

Around that time is when I had the epiphany with my therapist that I *look* like my mother. We thought about my mother *never* telling me I was pretty. We thought about her *always* saying I was the stupidest. We realized I must have reminded my mother of herself. And she *hates* herself. *That's* why I was the target of her abuse.

Ironically, as *I* got sober, my mother got worse. She lost her job, finally. She continued further down her drug-induced road. Her addiction took over her life. And here I was, the "*bad* one" from the family, turning *my* life around. They didn't like that.

There is so much conflict in my family.

Surprisingly, I fit very well back into college when I resumed my education.

It took me five years to graduate college—and Pathways—because going in, I had a really minimal high school education. In fact, when I took the English placement exam, I placed just one level above *English as a second language*. I had to work my way up from there.

And I *did*.

With my remedial English, I didn't think I could put two words together. But when I graduated, I had an overall grade point average of 3.8. I made the dean's list all the time!

I had tutors for math and I also had to pass statistics. That was hard, but it just turned out that *I did school well*. I liked it. I liked the environment. I liked challenging the teachers. I liked people telling me, "No, you can't" and then proving to them: "Yes, I can!"

When I received my bachelor's degree, Dave Bishop was at my graduation. Dave was one of the only men who'd ever cared for me without it being a sexual thing. And that was hard for me to understand. I always thought that men wouldn't do these kinds of things for you unless they wanted something.

That was not David.

He just loved me and supported me.

In fact, I don't know how he even put up with me for so long. I would call and leave messages like, "I can't fucking take this anymore... *blah, blah, blah!*"

It was a long process.

Some things have taken even longer...

We had just barely started working on my eating disorder when I left Pathways. I just couldn't deal with that while I was in the program.

I couldn't even talk to my therapist about what happened to me.

And I never developed a relationship with God because I felt that He had punished me. Even in the twelve-step program, you're supposed to have a "higher power" and stuff, but I struggled with that. I didn't think God ever heard me. I didn't think He heard my innermost thoughts:

I'm abused.

I'm ugly.

I'm stupid.

I can't even look at myself in the mirror.

I have this eating disorder.

I don't like myself.

I don't know how to have a healthy relationship with a man.

Some of the girls who come out of molestation or incest become hypersexual. Not me. No one could touch me. No one could look at me. I've had a lot of problems with that.

I still struggle with dressing up and making myself look nice—things that make people look at me. I don't like people to be attracted to me.

I've now gained a little weight, so I've put on curves and I don't like people noticing that. I don't want them to like me for that. *You need to know who I am; don't like me for my body.* I hate it.

But I've kept trying in therapy—still.

My therapist had to teach me *how* to eat. She showed me a video on eating and how it how bad it is to *not* eat and how your body thinks you're starving. Watching the video, I could see that it was true, but it still doesn't make me want to eat more.

And I *still* have so much I've blocked out since I was eleven. I *still* don't remember how the molestation (sorry, incest) started.

There are so many things I can't remember.

But so many things *are* different. And better.

After graduating from Pathways, I married a man whom I'd met through a twelve-step program. He wasn't in recovery or anything; he was a blind date! One of the crackhead girls there said, "Hey, my husband has a cute friend I'd like you to meet!"

He was my first white guy! I had a bit of a white hang-up. It was horrible, but it turned out really funny. I wind up with a white guy with blue eyes; my sponsor is a white lady; and I have a white baby! I love white people now. I've got one for a husband! (Plus, my father was actually part English and part Native American, so I guess I do have *some* white in me.)

When we decided to have a baby, it wasn't working because of my eating disorder. My body was not okay. But I *really* wanted to be a parent, so I gained thirty-two pounds. I was able to get healthy, get pregnant, and have a beautiful baby girl.

Learning how to be my new daughter's mother is *way* different. My goal is to do things with her that I should have done with Melody. Things like playing together and going to the park.

I have a new opportunity to be a mom.

But I know that sucks for Melody and I wish I could somehow make it up to her.

My family shows me photos of when Melody was a baby, and they're such sweet pictures. I do remember her being cute, but I don't remember enjoying her.

I remember leaving her.

I remember her tears.

I remember being tweaked out and trying to put her to bed real early so that I could go out.

I know things like that have hurt Melody so deep inside and that there is nothing I can do to change them. I know she will need therapy to help her deal with the trauma of not having her mother around for those precious formative years of her life.

She, too, went through a lot.

I had her *so* young that we really look *alike*—everyone calls her my "sidekick." And something in her makes her try to emulate the *angry* me. She definitely has that *mouth*.

She says a lot of stuff when she gets angry. Things like, "My Nana says you weren't there for me."

She's been in three fights in school; she's been an angry kid.

I hope someday she will understand that I was a sick little girl trying to raise a little girl. I hope she'll understand that I didn't play with her because I didn't know *how* to play. I didn't know how to do any of that.

I know it won't fix things—but I also know that I can't live in past regrets.

All I can do *now* is show Melody the tremendous love I have for her. Today and every day of my life in recovery, I enjoy every minute I have with Melody. She is so beautiful. She is the reason I am alive.

Melody is now fifteen, and I finally know how to be a parent to her.

I don't have to hit my kids. I've learned that.

We were taught to hit. And if I get angry, my first instinct is *still* to hit—but I've learned to walk away. I've learned to leave the room. I do not want to be *that* parent. The cycle of violence stops here. We're not going to continue this.

But although there is no hitting, things from the past still need to be worked out for Melody.

But now that I'm sober and healthier, I have a new opportunity with her too.

Of course, we still have her father to deal with.

He is still around.

He only calls when he is on the run, or is getting out of prison or something, and he wants his daughter.

I've learned that I have to let them talk. I didn't let him communicate with her at all for a while, because I was afraid he would hurt her, emotionally. But now I let her talk with him. If I try to keep them apart, I know she'll hate me for it.

But unfortunately my daughter has to deal with his not being there. He'll call her and then he won't call her. He'll call…and then he won't. He is the epitome of "typical nothingness" that I've seen way too often. But I know I can't protect her from this; she has to learn and see for herself.

Melody's father can't even get a driver's license. Before Pathways, when I was on welfare, I reported him for refusing to pay child support and they took away his license. So he has no license, he goes to jail all the time, he's a drug dealer, and he never graduated from high school.

When he calls and talks to Melody or me, I don't even understand his speech. He still talks like a gangster. I used to talk like that too, but now I can't even understand him with all his *yo's* and *eh's*. *What is he saying?!* I wonder.

But the gang roots run deep—some are indelible.

During my time at Pathways, we actually looked into getting my tattoos removed. They did "patch tests" to see if there would be procedural side effects—but the tests hurt worse than the tattoos!

"No, that's enough!" I said.

The tattoos are still there.

I have *Smile Now, Cry Later* on my upper back.

I have my stomach tattooed with *Troublemaker.* I don't want that one, but they're all there.

I think I would like a Japanese cherry blossom tree to somehow cover up the ones on my back. And I know this is kind of morbid, but—since my father died, I've been contemplating a broken Jack Daniels bottle with his name in the spilled alcohol.

I just got my new daughter's footprints inked on my back with her name on it.

I have Melody's name on my ankle.

And I still have those stupid three dots on my fingers.

La Vida Loca…

It may be hard to believe, but after *everything* that's happened, I'm now back living with my mother at my grandfather's house. It's only because my grandfather's kidneys are failing and, sadly, he is dying. I am here because I love him *so* much. I'm the one who's closest to him and I want to spend as much time with him as I possibly can.

I'm in that house to take care of *him.*

My mother takes care of him too, though. Which means, of course, that I have to deal with her on a daily basis.

It wasn't until last year that my mother said something nice to me, like, "You're so pretty!"

She said that at my wedding.

"You're so pretty. You've always been so pretty…"

I got really nasty.

"You never told me I was pretty!"

"I never told you that you were pretty because everybody liked you," she said. "Don't you remember growing up with everybody liking you? You just never liked yourself."

Wow, I remember realizing, *since everyone liked me, you had to put me down.*

I didn't even bother to continue that conversation. I wondered why we even *had* these conversations. She never remembers *anything.*

My mother will never admit that she hit me. She's apologized for some words now, but she won't acknowledge that she hit me. She thinks she was just disciplining me.

It's *not* discipline when your kid comes out with bruises.

It's *not* discipline when your kid goes to the emergency room because her ribs are seriously damaged.

That's *not* discipline.

But that's my mother's warped thought, and it has generated so much anger in me. That anger is something I have fought hard to get over as I have learned to take control of my life.

Growing up in my dysfunctional home, I spent all my time *blaming* my mother for the neglect and abuse. With the help of Pathways and my twelve-step program, I learned that she is a sick person. She did not know *how* to love me. Understanding that softens the pain—but she is still the only woman who can destroy my heart.

I don't talk to my mother about the past much now. There's no point. There's no point expecting that she'll ever admit that she beat me. And while she apologized for not telling me I was pretty, I don't need that from her anymore.

My mother is a *little* better now as far as drugs go; she doesn't do crack anymore. But she does smoke marijuana. My grandfather doesn't like her behavior, but he lets her live with us because deep down, he loves her, and she has nowhere else to go. Since getting fired from her job, she has nothing.

My mother actually loves her father too, but she tells me he has never shown his love for her. Not even as a child. "It was always my brother he loved," she says. "And since you were born, it's you."

And I guess it's true. My grandfather is my biggest fan. He is my confidant. And he confides to *me* that he doesn't trust my mother to take care of him.

But in his last year of life, all she's *done* is take care of him. Mostly she does the cooking and cleaning. *I* am the one who helps pay for my grandfather's medication. *I* am the one who takes him to the doctor.

My grandfather still does not know about the incest. My therapist and I decided that we could either tell him or just let him die happy. I decided on the latter.

My cousin comes down to visit every now and then. I am really uncomfortable having my girls near him, so I keep them away when he's here. It's a very awkward situation. It's sick.

My cousin's wife actually knows about what happened. She says I'm the one who told her, back when they were dating. I guess I liked her and didn't want her to get hurt.

But *I just don't remember.*

Both she and my cousin are born-again Christians. She has always told him he needs to make amends.

But nothing really makes it better.

I'm haunted by this.

Both my sisters are around, but they don't live with us at my grandfather's.

While I became anorexic, my older sister went "the other way." She never got hit, but she did live at my grandparents' house—*with my cousin.* Just two years older than me, Jody is close to me in age but not close in any other way. Most of our lives, she has acted like she hates me. Just recently, she was diagnosed as bipolar. Today, I am able to love Jody for who she is, and she says she loves me.

My little sister, Jade, got involved with a man who is eight years older than her. They have a beautiful little boy who is my godson. But her relationship is tumultuous.

And Jade and my mother are *enmeshed*.

As the baby of the family, Jade became the *parentified* child. She takes care of my mother, but their relationship is one of complete enablement. It's weird and sad at the same time.

They talk about things I can't even fathom. Everything from men to sex to money to petty dramas, and just everything. They are completely dependent on one another for emotional support at all times. Maybe a part of me is jealous of the love my mother has always shown my sisters and not me. But their relationship *truly* is not healthy.

Although Jade and I are eight years apart, she is the other part of my soul. During my "loady" years, Jade stood by my side. She was with me through everything, and never once did she think she was better than me. She loved me no matter what.

Sometimes I blame myself for Jade not being more independent. What could she do? I was the drug addict running wild while she stayed home and picked up the pieces of my mess. Now she does the same with my mother. She wasn't taught the life skills necessary to be productive and self-sufficient.

I wasn't taught those things either, but I had Pathways and the twelve-step program to help me grow into a mature woman.

I've actually encouraged Jade to apply to Pathways, but she's not ready to make that change. She has learned too much from me and my mother. I love my little sister to pieces. She is such an intelligent, loving young woman. So it's hard for me to see her not moving forward in her life.

I haven't done drugs or alcohol in almost ten years.

During that time, I've been through a lot and conquered a lot. I still have a lot of issues, and more will be revealed and dealt with the longer I stay sober.

Therapy has been so helpful. Somewhere, somehow, something just clicked with all the therapy.

It changed me.

Thankfully, I'm able to still continue therapy—*and* pay for it. I'm able to pay for my own school now, too. I'm a big girl!

Everybody has bills for their education, but I'm privileged not to have that. However, I *will* be in debt for my master's degree work. I *get* to do that.

Those are things I never did before. Maybe that's why Dave says I was one of his "hardest."

With all of my survival skills and fighting, I built walls. I pushed people away. When I got into Pathways, I learned that those survival skills would be the ones that killed me. That if I didn't ask for help, I wasn't going to be okay.

And I haven't *slipped* in my recovery process, even though everyone was scared of me and nobody thought I could do it. Maybe I did it just *because* of that—just to show everyone that I could!

I'm able to do other things now that I've never done before.

I go places and speak on behalf of Pathways. I don't know if I've told Dave enough how much I appreciate him; so the way I do it is to keep giving back. There's nothing I will not do for this program. I've spoken in front of some really rich people, and I try not to cuss too much!

This is really good for me!

Pathways is my biggest ally. Dave and Pathways provided all the support that I never really realized I needed.

But at first I didn't think I was *smart enough* to do it.

All my life, my mother told me I was stupid. After hearing those things over and over, you believe it. No matter what Dave Bishop and my teachers would tell me, I still felt stupid. It's like your mother is your God. And if your God is hard on you, you carry it with you forever.

It's taken me a long time to realize that I'm not stupid.

I still think I'm ugly.

When I was really anorexic, I was told to go to Overeaters Anonymous. They always say you have to start there, but I don't know why. *Oh great, I'm going to go get jumped by fat girls!* I thought.

But now I'm thinking *I'm* one of the fat girls! It's a distorted view called *body dysmorphic disorder.*

To this day, I can't look in the mirror.

I have no mirrors in my bedroom. When I go to the gym and work out, I can't look in the mirrors. When I was really anorexic, I went to the gym a lot, but now I really don't want to because of how I look.

And I'm still very careful about what I consume. I recently ate a burger, and that was a big step for me—but I took off half the meat!

That's *one* of the things I'm still dealing with, but it *is* a big improvement from where I was before.

At least I'm not starving!

I now have a job in the adult mental health field. That's what my degree is in—I have a B.S. in Human Services with an emphasis in mental health. I am uniquely qualified and I understand the patients' problems.

I'm also a Certified Addictions Treatment Counselor (CATC) and certified to assist women in domestic abuse situations.

During the course of training, our class was taken on a tour of this huge foster care center that protects children. When they showed us the examination room for the kids who were molested, it hurt me so much.

I just couldn't do it. It hurt me so bad. I may work in the mental health field, but I know there are certain people I just can't work with. I can work with women who are victims of domestic violence, but I can't work with predators. I'm not okay with that.

I haven't conquered that yet.

But I will.

When my grandfather passes and I get through this, I'm going to start my master's program.

I know the family is going to fight for the house when my grandfather is gone because that's what they do, but I don't want anything. Maybe just a few pictures.

My long-term goal is to be a licensed social worker. That's what I want. I want to be able to give back completely. Helping others is what I'm best at.

And that, too, is a very big deal.

I couldn't have gone through everything I went through for no reason; even if it's just to help the kid down the street. I went through all that crap to overcome and to get *here*—to where I am and where I want to be.

I don't make much money working in mental health, but the benefit for me is helping people get to where they need to be—giving them hope.

If *I* can do it, anyone can do it.

It's especially important for me to help young women. I'm now mentoring a girl in Pathways—and she just happens to be my niece. My husband and I have been together since his niece was ten. She comes from a pretty bad place.

So it's come full circle for me. It's a huge deal for me to be able to help her. All these Pathways events keep coming up, and we'll be attending them soon together. I now *volunteer* for these events—events I would only go to before because I *had* to.

This next event is a run, *and I can run!*

No wonder God put my niece in my life. As I said before, helping people is *now* what I do best.

I will do whatever Pathways asks of me. Dave says I could have asked for anything of Pathways and they would've done it, but I didn't think I was *worth* asking. But now I tell my niece that she needs to ask for help if she needs it. I tell her they don't *just know* when you need help. Being her mentor has allowed *me* to understand about asking for help.

I wouldn't be anywhere without this program.

It gave me *me*.

I didn't have a sense of *anything* before Pathways.

I had no sense of being—no sense of who I was.

I thought I was this gang member girl, but that's so *not* me. I am not a gangster. Anyone I allow to get close to me *knows* that is not me at all.

I like the *real* me better.

And God isn't done with me yet. I am still growing.

The most important thing of all is that I'm no longer a victim.

My mother claims she got beat by my grandfather as she was growing up, back when he was an alcoholic. So she sits and she talks about these things and she cries. I look at her at fifty-seven years old, *still hating her father*.

I said to her, "If I were to blame *you* for the way I turned out growing up, I wouldn't get better! You hurt me, but it's my choice to continue to feel hurt or not!"

I'm not a victim anymore. I can talk about all I've been through and not cry. And I am able to *not* blame my mother. *She* didn't make me an addict or alcoholic; those were my choices and I take full responsibility for them.

As I have continued to stay sober and attend therapy, I have even been able to forgive my mother for the past. We have begun rebuilding our relationship and it gets better all the time.

I would still like to improve my self-esteem and to deal with the incest, but I know that everything happened for a reason. It's made me stronger.

It didn't kill me. *It made me stronger.*

Epilogue: *My grandfather passed away on September 14, 2010. I am now working towards my master's degree. I miss him dearly.*

Part 3

Wind Beneath Their Wings

"The task ahead of us is never as great as the power behind us."

—Ralph Waldo Emerson

Six Seminal Steps

The powerful story of Pathways founder Dave Bishop.

My life's journey has been shaped by six significant events. Six things that all had to happen for me to become who I am. Six impactful events that wove together to make a single quilt: Me.

Of these six things, five were good. One was not.

The "bad" thing was alcoholism. It was a dark road. Ultimately, though, it was a vital step along my journey—a journey whose last major step was the formation of Pathways to Independence.

I guess this irony validates what a famous man in recovery once said about God's grace: that we get to enjoy "the happiest kind of usefulness" by His ability to transform us—through a "divine alchemy"—from being a taker to a giver; from somebody who's self-centered to somebody who can benefit others.

The Journey Begins…

I had a rough childhood; but, again, it taught me many things. One of the most important was how to relate to the girls we now mentor.

I grew up in a working-class family shortly after World War II. And my mother was a very tough disciplinarian. She told me that when I was a baby, she experienced a terrible bout of depression and didn't leave the house for several months. She said that the house was often kept in darkness as she battled that. So I suspect I didn't get much nurturing.

My mom's father was about as mean an alcoholic as you could come across. When he drank, he became vicious. That's where my mom learned her parenting skills. So she hit me. A lot. Harshly.

The harshness of my childhood greatly affected my self-esteem. It was a shame, because as I got older, I had the potential to be a really great student and a talented athlete, but I would back off because I didn't think I could accomplish anything. It's kind of like Henry Ford's philosophy: Whether you believe you *can* do something or *can't* do something, you are right.

But when I turned fifteen, my mother changed incredibly. My brother was experiencing a lot of emotional problems, so she went with him to therapy—something unheard of back in the '60s. And she became a really nice, good person.

I honestly don't resent my mother for my severe upbringing. That's all she knew to do. All any of us have are the tools we are given. As new coping skills fell into my mother's path, she began to change.

Similar opportunities for growth and change were to happen along *my* path; I just needed to be willing to pick up the tools and put them to use.

Step 1: Seminary

At the onset of high school, I enrolled in a Roman Catholic seminary to study to be a priest. Looking back, I probably took this step to please my mother—as well as to run away from my fear of competing in normal society.

I lived there in seclusion for three and a half years.

My experience at seminary taught me many things. It provided the underlying backing of the quilt that is now me.

First off, it taught me to be a bit neurotic, because it was extremely difficult. But that aside, it taught me self-discipline. And it exposed me to things I would never have been exposed to otherwise.

But it was a very different kind of life.

There was no television to watch, and if you wanted to listen to music, you didn't listen to rock and roll—you listened to classical, or the soundtracks from shows like *My Fair Lady.* That was it: Mozart, Beethoven, Chopin, or musicals.

At seminary, they pressed you to expand your mind; to go further and further beyond whatever you could have imagined or done on your own. We took Greek and Latin concurrently, along with all the traditionally required high school subjects.

And you *had* to play sports. Even if you were a nerd or a geek, you were out there every day, playing and competing. I already loved sports, but my time in seminary made me love them even more.

And it made me want to compete—a lot.

At seminary, there were always chess tournaments going on. Everywhere! So as silly as it sounds, I learned to play chess so I could compete. And I liked it!

Chess is a game where you have to be thinking of twenty things at once and then make it all come together to defeat your opponent. It just stretches your mind to its maximum ability.

I learned a lot in that regard. It shaped me.

Seminary also taught me the value of quiet time. There were times when we weren't allowed to talk for days! At first, I learned just to cope with it; later I became at peace with it.

Seminary definitely impacted my life.

Eventually though, I wanted out. My original class at seminary had a hundred twenty boys. By the time I left, only thirty-eight remained. Ultimately, only two completed the full twelve-year course.

The reason *I* left seminary is that it became more and more difficult to compete with my classmates, many of whom were brilliant. It wasn't that I *couldn't* complete, it was that I didn't *believe* I could. I wasn't enjoying it, and my anxiety was sky-high. So I finished my final semester at a regular high school.

Step 2: Alcoholism

After high school, I made a failed attempt at college, which resulted in my being drafted for Vietnam. I spent three years assigned to a naval air patrol squadron, where I was trained as an aviation electrician.

This is when I found the ease and comfort of alcohol and alcoholism, which runs rampant in my family genes.

I vividly remember my first drink. I was just out of seminary, and three other ex-seminarians and I went up to the Russian River in Northern California, where all the young people were. I took my first drink (a fifth of vodka) and went into a complete blackout.

I remember my friends staring at me the next morning.

"My God, it was like we saw an alien take over your body last night," they said. "You are *really* different when you drink. You were outgoing, confident, aggressive."

I listened to that and thought, *Oh, yeah! Alcohol made me everything I wanted to be but never was.*

At that point, I knew this could be something really good if I could control it. So it became my life's work to control it; to harness these feelings of self-worth through drinking.

But how do you harvest such an ability? In the beginning it worked—for the most part. And then it stopped working. I would drink excessively and I would black out, again and again. I thought, *What am I doing?*

In the military, we drank really, really heavily and did drugs. This experience added to my journey down that "dark road." Yet it, too, helped shape who I was to become.

When I was discharged from the military, I had to be a responsible individual. No more drinking, no more drugs. But the problem was, I couldn't stop. That's when I realized I *truly* had a problem.

After my discharge, employment was difficult, due to all the other Vietnam vets coming home. The only job I could get was as a part-time school janitor, which paid four cents over minimum wage. But while I hated it, I liked the kids.

With the principal's encouragement, I enrolled in school to become a teacher. After a few years, I got a credential and began teaching history, math, and physical education—though I'd majored in English.

What came next was a life-changing experience that I would not fully understand until twenty-five years later.

Step 3: Girls Softball

My principal asked me to coach the girls softball team.

Now, I wanted nothing to do with coaching girls. It just seemed foreign to me. I love sports, and I thought it was a travesty that girls couldn't play to my expectations. I thought, *Oh my gosh, and you want me to coach them?! It's going to be embarrassing!* I just wanted no part of it.

The principal said if I didn't do it, the team wouldn't get to play. So out of guilt, I did it.

And, boy, was I wrong!

Thirteen girls tried out for a twelve-girl roster. One girl, Cindy, had poor skills; but I didn't want to humiliate her and cut her, so I reluctantly took all thirteen.

Now, we were the smallest middle school program in the district, with some schools four or five times our size. And the other schools had two teams: one for seventh-graders, the other for eighth-graders. We had just one team, composed of eleven seventh-graders and just two eighth-graders. But having those two older kids meant we had to compete with the eighth-grade teams. The odds were overwhelmingly against us.

I remember asking my mentor, Nick Madrid, a well-seasoned coach at a competing school, who managed all their boys teams, as well as girls softball: "How do you coach girls?"

He looked at me in disbelief.

"They are *people,* Dave," he said, furrowing his brow. "You coach them just the same as boys."

My beliefs and expectations about coaching girls turned out to be completely erroneous. These girls were incredible and they gelled so well. We bonded right from the beginning.

And they were talented. Even Cindy ended up playing.

In spite of seemingly insurmountable odds, we went on to win the district championship—beating Nick's team in the finals.

At the awards ceremony, Nick shook my hand and said, "There is no greater honor than when the student beats the teacher." It is so true.

This coaching experience taught me to truly value and appreciate women. It became embedded in the very fiber of my being, woven right into the fabric of my quilt.

It made me believe in women and want to champion women's rights. I'm probably more of a women's rights advocate than most *women* are—and that's the truth. It's also a sad truth that women in our society are abused much more than men, *by* men, and are sometimes given almost no chance for a decent life.

I still see some women from that softball team—all these years later. They are all mature women now. (I recently received a flier for Cindy's *fiftieth* birthday party!) But little did I know, back then, that what we were doing would have such a huge impact on me.

That impact was revealed to me much later, at the twenty-five-year wedding anniversary of a good friend, Mike, whose best man I'd been. I had taught both of Mike's sisters, Michelle and Marlene, and Marlene had been on that softball team. I sat with them all at the anniversary party.

"So, Dave," said Michelle, "I heard about this foundation and the work you do. How long have you been doing it?"

It had been fifteen years at that time.

"Really?" she said. "What is it all about?"

I explained to them all about the Pathways mission and the girls we help.

"Wow. What prompted you to want to work with women?" they asked.

I looked at Marlene and suddenly a light went on. *"You!"* I blurted out.

And it was true. I certainly wasn't aware of it back when we were playing softball. But *now* I knew it.

"How was it *me*?" Marlene asked. "You haven't seen us in a long time."

I smiled and began to explain...

Step 4: Recovery

I continued my education and got a counseling credential and then an administrative services credential. I went on to become the principal of an elementary school for three years, and then the principal of a middle school for seven years, and was then promoted to assistant superintendent.

It was a week before that promotion that I stopped drinking.

From the beginning, I knew I had a problem. That first time I drank—back at the Russian River—I was extremely hung over the next day, so I waded into the river, seeking relief in the soothing warm water. I remember seeing my breath on the water, like gasoline fumes. At that moment, I realized something was amiss. *You must have overshot the mark here, pal,* I thought. *Normal people don't have this experience.*

Still, I continued drinking and was able control my problem—on an intermittent basis.

I remember the day I decided to get sober.

My wife was a runner, and I hate running. But alcoholics will go to any lengths to prove to themselves that they are not alcoholic. So I went with her every morning in the summer and jogged along the beach.

One day, we had just finished our run. The sun was coming up, and my head was throbbing like a jackhammer.

"How many drinks did you have last night?" my wife asked.

"Two," I replied—which was true. I had bought 16-ounce glasses, which I filled almost entirely with alcohol. "Why do ask?" I said.

"Because," she replied, "I can see your breath on the horizon."

I exhaled, and I saw it too. My mind shot back to 1965 on the Russian River.

That had been an omen.

And that's when it became very apparent to me: *Alcohol owns you. It owns you, and you know it, and you have to do something about it.* That scared the hell out of me. I don't want anything to own me.

So that's when I quit.

I joined a twelve-step program to aid in my recovery. It, too, was very frightening, and this is why:

Until I took that first drink, I had the worst self-esteem imaginable. In fact, I still don't think I've met *anybody* whose inner self-esteem is lower than mine was. That's how bad it was. It was terrible. And when I drank, it all went away.

So being newly sober, I found myself—at age thirty-eight—feeling deep inside like I was fifteen all over again. Sobriety took away what made me feel confident. And that was extremely frightening. I felt utterly incapable.

I was in the midst of dealing with these feelings, yet I was promoted at work. I even told my boss, "Are you out of your mind? I'm about to enter an outpatient rehab and you're going to promote me? Take someone else."

He didn't listen to me; he insisted on his decision to promote me.

I was upside down during all of this. But what helped me succeed is my work ethic. Because of my low self-esteem, one of the ways I've always compensated is I'll outwork anybody. I don't care what it takes. I'll sleep two hours a night, but I'll come back tomorrow and I'll outdo you at whatever it is we're doing. So my boss always got what he needed and then some.

In recovery, little by little, day by day, things got easier. I realize now that if I had never become an alcoholic, I could never have become a *recovering* alcoholic; so I would never have been able to experience the twelve steps that gave me a spiritual awakening and allowed me to enjoy the fruits of recovery.

Through the twelve steps, I have learned to live with unresolved problems peacefully—*almost* all the time—and to trust in a higher power. I don't have to run the world; I just have to do what's logical for me to do.

Step 5: A Life-Changing Revelation

I suffered from depression off and on for my entire teen and early adult life. As a result, I attended therapy off and on throughout much of that time. It was mid-December, and I had just concluded a session. I was writing out a check, and my therapist, John, was writing me a receipt.

"So, Dave," he asked me casually, "what are your plans for Christmas?"

"Well," I replied, "my boys and I will drive up to Northern California to see my family. It's a seven-hour drive, and we'll no sooner get in the car and the boys will ask if we are there yet. We will have to stop constantly for bathroom breaks and boredom breaks, which will make a long drive *very* long. When we get there, I'll sleep on a pull-out bed with that bar down the middle; I won't get much rest and my back will be killing me by the time we leave. But…it's good to see my family, and you've gotta do what you gotta do! So, what are your plans?"

"I don't know yet," John replied. "My partner and I will create Christmas the way we want to."

I thought for a moment. "*Create* Christmas? You can create Christmas the way you want it to be?"

John stopped writing and looked at me, as if peering deep inside my soul. Then he said to me words that I will never forget: "Dave, you can create *life* the way you want it to be. You just don't know it yet."

From that moment in time, I *did* know it. And I have never stopped knowing it since.

Step 6: The Formation of Pathways

My favorite job was serving as the principal of a continuation high school, where the majority of the students were kids who had lost their way for one reason or another. I found that being a recovering alcoholic served me well in my ability to relate to and help a number of young men and women at the school.

At the end of my first year there, we graduated a nineteen-year-old girl from our teen parent program. After graduation, she found a job in a restaurant and attempted to support herself and her daughter.

When she periodically came back to the school to visit, she would report how she was sinking financially. She moved from a one-bedroom apartment to renting a room. She gave up her health insurance and soon after, her auto insurance. She was welfare waiting to happen.

Other things were about to happen as well.

My wife and I had just completed our taxes, and our tax preparer had encouraged us to buy a condo to offset our tax liability.

I told my wife about my former student, and I said, "One day, perhaps when we retire, we should help people like her."

My wife replied, "Why don't we just help her *now*?"

I could not see how at the time, but my wife just said, "Let's do it anyhow."

So we bought a condo and put her up in it for forty-five dollars a month, on the condition that she would complete an educational program that would soon make her self-sufficient.

Soon came four more girls and *another* condo. And before we knew it, the program had grown to twelve. We sold our home, along with both of the condos we had purchased, and bought a five-unit apartment complex.

We were into this. This program was real, and we knew it would grow.

We knew we needed to start working out some business structure—and part of that structure was a name. We were driving home from Arizona, where we had been discussing our new venture with our tax accountant. We spent our time in the car talking about this "foundation" and how we were going to start it.

Everything was cooking now.

We were trying to decide what to call it, and we just kept trading names; back and forth, back and forth—for hours. Writing them all down, over a hundred of them.

And I kept thinking, *Just what IS it about this program? We're giving these young women a road to go down…a road where we supply different forms of support along the way.*

Of the original five girls we'd helped, two were now on welfare and one was rapidly headed in that direction. It was just a done deal. It was pathetic.

Our goal was to make them independent.

"But *how* do we make them independent?" we asked ourselves.

Our answer: Education. And we knew we'd have to forge a way to get there.

And all of a sudden, I just said: "What about 'Pathways to Independence'?"

That felt really good.

And things only got better.

I began to *learn* many things—things one must know to make a program like Pathways to Independence a success.

And I learned even more about myself.

The irony of it all is, here I am, doing this Pathways thing and helping these young women…and I'm watching these girls change before my eyes—so incredibly, beyond belief. But *I'm* changing as well. Little did I know that working on behalf of *their* transformations would result in my own.

"Coinci-Gods"

I went from being in a seminary to coming out and becoming as close to an atheist as you could find. And I pretty much stayed like that until age thirty-eight, when I got sober and began trying to believe in a higher power.

Many things have helped galvanize my belief in God—and so many are directly related to Pathways.

We were going along with our twelve girls, and then I took in more than I should have, and we had to borrow money to make it fly—quite a bit of money.

So I began talking to an expert in nonprofits, and he said, "Dave, you need to do a fundraiser." So we attempted to do that. We tried it twice.

The first year we made $11,000. The second year, we made less: $8,500. But the problem wasn't what we were doing—it's who we were inviting. My wife and I both worked in education; we didn't know anyone who was going to be throwing money around.

"There's somebody I'm going to call," said our then-treasurer. "She likes stuff like this; she's philanthropic. Her name is Gayle."

So she called Gayle repeatedly, but she never got ahold of her. So that was the end of that.

Almost.

Eventually I said, "Do you mind if *I* call her? We're desperate..."

I've now known Gayle for fifteen years. And in that time, I've called her probably a hundred times. But only *once* has she ever picked up the phone. The other times it goes to a machine, and it seems like she never listens to her messages. *Ever.*

But the *one time* she answered her phone was the first time.

When she picked up, I told her about our situation. She said, "Let me come to a board meeting."

She did and she brought a friend, Cathy. They whispered to each other during the meeting, and before it was even over, Gayle interjected that they would do a fundraiser. Within a very short period of time, she and Cathy founded a group called Friends of Pathways, and they raised $38,000. Soon it was $138,000. At their most recent event, Friends of Pathways brought in $270,000. Over the course of fourteen years, the group has raised over 1.7 million dollars!

Gayle answering my call was an awfully big coincidence.

There have been other big "coincidences."

Like when Julie came into our program, and she had one eye turned inward. It was very apparent. However, since she wore glasses, you wouldn't necessarily see it unless you were quite close to her.

But it haunted her. Her self-esteem was nil, and she never, ever looked right at you. She always looked at your feet.

We were at the Friends of Pathways fundraiser, and Julie and I spoke together on stage. It was a large assembly, and the people in the front row were about twenty feet away.

When we were done, this man seated up front came up and said, "My name is Carl, and I can change that girl's life forever."

I was suspicious; I tend to be suspicious towards men who say they're going to do these kinds of things for our girls.

"What are you talking about?" I asked.

He said, "I'm an eye surgeon."

Two months later, he operated on Julie at no charge. And it *did* change her life. She was so happy, and suddenly she looked people right in the eye. Today, Julie is a teacher and a happily married mom.

Another coincidence? I don't know—there were four hundred people in that audience!

Another time, we had just gotten a bunch of new clients and none of them had cars. Generally, we get about two or three cars donated per year. But I said, "You know what, God? I need five cars and I need them now."

Within six weeks we got five.

There's more...

Before we built our "healthcare army," our one dentist, David, had taken on eighteen of our girls as patients.

"I'm retiring," he announced one day. "I bought a place in Oregon, and I'm leaving in two weeks."

So now I had all these girls he'd been working with, and no dentist; what was I going to do?

As before, I said, "God, I need nine dentists and I need them in a hurry."

In two and a half months, I had nine dentists.

And again, call it a coincidence—*you* can call it whatever you want. But so many of these things have happened that *I* just don't buy the "coincidence" tag anymore.

If you're still not convinced, try this one:

I was planning to attend a men's retreat for alcoholics.

Just prior to the retreat, one of our girls, Kimberly, graduated from the Pathways program. At her graduation, she said to me, "I want to be a lawyer. Do you know anybody who's into real estate law?"

"No, I don't," I said, "but I'll keep my eye out for you."

So I went on the retreat, and at the end of the weekend as my son and I were leaving, I realized I had left something in the coffee room. When I went back, a man named Samuel was sitting in there.

I picked up what I had forgotten and said, "See you next year, Samuel!"

"Okay, Dave," he answered.

I was halfway down the hall, when—*and I don't know why*—I went back and asked Samuel what he did for a living.

"I'm a lawyer," he said.

"What *kind* of lawyer?"

"A good one!" he joked.

I laughed. "What kind, really?"

"Real estate," he answered.

My gosh, I thought. *What a big "coincidence"!*

I told Samuel about our graduate, and he said, "Send her to my South Central office; that's where I do most of my pro bono work."

So she became a clerk for him, and he helped her to get into law school with a big scholarship. Today, Kimberly is a practicing attorney.

Since starting Pathways, I have seen so many *coincidences*—way more than I have ever seen before in my life (or in anybody else's life)—that I can only conclude that they aren't *coincidences.*

They are "coinci-Gods"!

It's through seeing all those things and watching all these girls that I now have this keen awareness of His presence. I don't go to church, but I believe He's here with us; right here, right now. I just know it. I have no tangible proof, but I just know it.

I know it.

My Life Today

I am now retired from the school district and twenty-five years sober. I continue to head the Pathways to Independence Foundation, which is truly the passion of my life.

I never knew that there were so many kind and giving individuals in the world. I used to be suspicious of virtually everyone. Now I look for the good in people and embrace it.

Even after twenty years, I am passionate about this program and all the girls in it. It brings me great reward and satisfaction to be able to help them.

Ralph Waldo Emerson once said: "It is one of the most beautiful compensations of life that no man can sincerely try to help another without helping himself." Helping these girls has changed my life forever.

I used to be prone towards depression. Not anymore. I see my own "rough childhood" in such a different light. That's why I have such a big heart for these girls in our program who are struggling so much. They're trying their best, and they may not even make it—or it might take a long time for them to make it.

I remember being just like these girls in Pathways. I remember skipping meals when I was in college because there was simply no food to eat. I remember my parents sending me a fifteen-dollar check every month with an apology of, "That's all we could afford. I hope it helps in some small way." And I remember that it did; it made a *huge* difference—even though fifteen bucks was really not much, even back then.

Watching these girls become transformed has transformed *me*.

I will never, ever retire. I want to be completely used up when it's my time to go.

Today, I am so happy and so very blessed.

Pathways Today

Today, we have forty young women in Pathways to Independence. In all, two hundred sixty-three women have been helped by the program.

We have a formula that works. To qualify, they must be poor by government standards and come from significant tragedy or abuse—from their family of origin, self-inflicted, or both. They must have a sincere desire to become educated.

Once they join, they commit to full-time school and part-time work, weekly therapy, and weekly mentoring. In return, Pathways pays for all of their books and tuition, and provides them either housing or a housing stipend. We keep their cars in full repair, and provide them with a doctor, a dentist, and an optometrist.

Every provider is a volunteer. In all, we have over three hundred volunteers and one part-time paid clerk and one part-time paid program developer. This includes all of our management, accounting, legal work, printing, everything. This army of volunteers, which includes fifty physicians, sixteen dentists, forty-three therapists, and many others, is amazing.

The average stay for a Pathways client is three and a half years. During that time, our clients have a truly profound life-changing experience.

The Future of Pathways

The passion I have for Pathways doesn't go away. It gets stronger. It's like a volcano inside me, always wanting to burst out.

If God sent us a lot of financial support, we would grow immensely. Someone asked me the other day just how far would I take this. I said, "We have forty today; I'd take it to forty *thousand* tomorrow."

He looked at me with that *Are you crazy?* stare. I told him I was completely serious.

I actually have a plan as to how that would all work. I would do it in a minute. The future is more of the present, but much larger.

The formula for starting a Pathways program is simple:

1. Form a board of directors (a working board, not just a decision-making board).
2. Admit one client.
3. Ask professional members of your community to help you.
4. Appoint a mentor to the client.
5. Raise some money.

There you have it. This could be done anywhere in the nation, or in the world. In fact, one of our program graduates, Sopie, has started up Pathways to Independence, Cambodia.

Today, half of our board of directors are Pathways graduates. Eventually the whole Pathways board will be made up of graduates. I also think God is sending me someone to take my place—or at least take my place for *half* of what I do, in order to allow me to help the program grow. So I keep looking for who He's sending.

That person—or *persons—will* come.

And the generosity that Pathways to Independence has been blessed with so far *will* continue.

I know it.

The Pathways to Independence Foundation

Providing hope, healing, and guidance to young women in need.

The Pathways Mission

Pathways to Independence commits to making profound changes in the lives of young women who have been neglected and abused by their families and society. We assist these young women in healing their emotional wounds and in getting an education, enabling them to become independent, contributing members of society.

Pathways Roots

Pathways was founded in 1991 by educators Dave and Joyce Bishop, to help a former student achieve self-sufficiency. Monica was the product of a dysfunctional alcoholic family and at age nineteen had a two-year-old daughter and no support. With the Bishops' help, Monica was able to get advanced training and a full-time job with health benefits for her and her daughter.

Pathways Clients

Pathways clients are an underserved population of women who have experienced grievous childhood trauma.

- ♥ Most come from alcoholic families.
- ♥ Many have experienced years of incest, violence, or other forms of abuse.
- ♥ Some have spent years in foster care or even become indigent.
- ♥ Pathways currently serves young women in Long Beach and Orange County, California.

Client Requirements

Clients must be young women (early thirties or younger) who meet the following criteria:

- ♥ Are poor by state/federal standards.
- ♥ Come from a history of family or personal abuse.
- ♥ Have a serious desire to receive an education.
- ♥ Are striving to become socially and economically independent for the first time.

Pathways Benefits

Pathways provides the following services to our clients, to assist them in overcoming past trauma and attaining self-sufficiency:

- ♥ Weekly counseling with a licensed therapist.
- ♥ Weekly interactions with a mentor.
- ♥ Full payment of school tuition and books.
- ♥ A monthly housing stipend.
- ♥ Access to over a hundred healthcare professionals, who donate their services.
- ♥ Access to mechanics, who donate their labor.
- ♥ Access to a wide variety of local professionals who donate services.

Client Accountability

Pathways clients sign mutually developed contracts specifying their commitments to education and personal growth. These agreed-upon commitments include:

- Required frequency of counseling.
- Required frequency of mentor interactions.
- Minimum college credits to be earned.
- Minimum grade point average to maintain.
- Minimum weekly hours of part-time employment.

Mentors and program coordinators hold clients firmly accountable to their contractual commitments and monitor progress on a consistent basis.

Pathways Funding

Pathways to Independence is a volunteer-based organization.

- Pathways relies on financial support from individuals, corporations, foundations, service clubs, and churches. We are supported by over a thousand donors.
- Holds 501(c)(3) status as a public charity.
- Over 93% of the budget goes directly to clients.
- The board of directors and all officers work for free.
- Aside from a part-time clerk and a part-time program development director, no one who manages or administers the Pathways program receives any compensation.

Pathways Volunteer Program: Leveraging what's right in the world!

Pathways clients are supported by over 300 community volunteers. All professional services are donated for FREE!

Professional Services

- ♥ 50+ Medical professionals
- ♥ 40+ Licensed therapists
- ♥ 16 Dentists
- ♥ 4 Orthodontists
- ♥ 3 Attorneys
- ♥ 5 Grant writers
- ♥ 3 Printers
- ♥ 5 Mechanics
- ♥ 2 Accountants
- ♥ 3 Cosmetologists

Volunteer Services

- ♥ 50 Mentors
- ♥ 50 Fundraisers

(The foundation reimburses for out-of-pocket expenses.)

Pathways' Success

- ♥ As of January 1, 2011, Pathways to Independence has served over 250 young women.
- ♥ Roughly 80% of program entrants have succeeded in graduating from college and becoming independent, contributing members of society.

The Pathways Family

"Often, we are thanked by organizations we make donations to; but with Pathways, we always want to say thank you, because you are giving us the opportunity to do something that we think matters."

—Glen and Debbie Bickerstaff,
Key Donors and Volunteers for Pathways

Pathways to Independence is a foundation fueled by two main power sources: donors and volunteers. Both are the driving wheels in its survival and success. And both are comprised of individuals of extraordinary generosity, energy, and talent.

Any charity organization needs funds from heartfelt financial backers to operate, of course. But as Dave Bishop's dream began to materialize, a unique network of super-volunteers also emerged—skilled professionals who took the "What can I do to help?" ethic to an unheard-of level.

This tireless team of financial contributors and hands-on pros have not only changed the lives of so many deserving women since Pathways' inception, they have made the world a better place for all of us, in so many ways.

Glen and Debbie Bickerstaff

Key Donors & Volunteers

Pathways to Independence.

If you live in this building, God has truly blessed you through the generosity of Debbie and Glen Bickerstaff.
When you graduate, pay them back by helping others.

Est. 2009

—Plaque inscription at the Pathways living complex

Dreams do come true.

In 2006, as the Bickerstaffs were talking with Dave Bishop, Glen asked Dave: "If you could have one dream come true as far as Pathways goes, what would it be?"

Dave was quick to answer. His dream was for a facility that could house a number of the Pathways girls during their recovery—a place of beauty, serenity, safety, and mutual community support.

"Consider it done," replied the Bickerstaffs.

Tears ran down Dave's cheeks.

In July of 2009, the doors to the beautiful twelve-thousand-square-foot facility were opened. So far, over twenty-five young women have lived, learned, and renewed their lives there.

Since 2000, Glen and Debbie Bickerstaff's generosity has been instrumental in allowing Pathways to Independence to continue—and grow—its phenomenal work.

They are an exceptional couple in many extraordinary ways.

Glen is a self-made man. He experienced an "ordinary childhood" in a middle-class neighborhood, but his fascination with baseball statistics just *may* have been a foreshadowing of his eventual involvement with the kinds of numbers that are integral to a financial career.

Batting averages and ERAs gave way to more fiscally focused statistics as Glen graduated from USC and joined the Trust Company of the West as a portfolio manager. In 2001, he was one of the top-rated money managers in the U.S., garnering him a cover story in *Money* magazine. Combining his business acumen with a passion toward "giving back," Glen has used his financial savvy to do just that.

Debbie's tireless passion for wanting to help others—especially women and children—was generated early on in her life. Growing up in a low-income alcoholic family, Debbie saw firsthand the effects of hardships and addiction. That passion and *com*passion has driven Debbie's generous participation in over twenty different charities—deserving causes that include mothers2mothers, an African organization that provides healthcare and life-skills training to HIV-affected mothers; the Bickerstaff Pediatric Family Center at Miller Children's Hospital in Long Beach; the Starlight Foundation; Project Cuddle; and the Cameron Siemers Foundation for Hope.

In 2000, Debbie, Glen, and their two children created the Bickerstaff Family Foundation to further their selfless assistance to those who need it most—such as the girls in Pathways. Debbie is the driving force behind that foundation.

"When we started giving to Pathways," explains Debbie, "they had eighteen girls in the program. I believe we have had an impact in Pathways' ability to grow the program and offer more girls the opportunity to benefit—and that was our intention. We knew the program was working and that there were still professionals and volunteers out there, willing to donate their time, expertise, and resources. The program simply needed more funding, and we were able to provide that."

"You hear these girls' stories," says Glen, "and your instinct is to tell them: 'Anything, anything we can offer, we will.' But we always want to be sure that *what* we offer has a direct impact on the lives of beneficiaries. We want to be sure a program works; it's important to us to gain that confidence.

"With Pathways, it was obvious that the program was truly changing the lives of these girls."

"We feel so fortunate to be involved in Pathways," say Glen and Debbie. "Often, we are thanked by organizations we make donations to; but with Pathways, we always want to say thank *you,* because you are giving us the opportunity to do something that we think matters."

And all that the Bickerstaffs do *does* matter. Beyond the couple's tremendous financial support, both Debbie and Glen have become personally involved in Pathways—giving of themselves as well.

"From the start, we were so happy to become Pathways donors, but we had no idea just how *much* we would fall in love with this program," says Debbie. "It became a bigger and bigger part of our giving, and our relationship with Dave grew as well. We have so much respect for him and admire him so much."

However, the Bickerstaffs' first encounter with Dave was one of those "you never get a second chance to make a first impression" situations.

"We laugh about it now," recalls Debbie, "but as we were forming our family foundation, we heard about Pathways and set up an appointment with Dave to learn more. Dave got the date wrong and stood us up!

"So by the time we actually *did* meet him," she continues, "we had researched Pathways on our own and had decided to get involved. In fact, we had already written a donation check, which we brought to the meeting. Dave, of course, knew nothing about it.

"So listening to Dave explain the program was just icing on the cake for us. We thought, *Wow! This is a program that really works. Here is a man who is completely dedicated to these girls, completely committed to helping as many of them as he can.*

"We handed him the check on the spot."

"But Pathways is not a business," explains Debbie. "It's an organization. Yes, we need to raise money because we want to grow the program, but even as the program expands, each individual is given special attention. And that's a big part of why the process works. Pathways has become like a family, in which the total entity is important, yet the needs of every individual are honored. Everyone involved is part of the Pathways family."

A big part of that family is the volunteer network, which provides a "fail-safe" path to success for the girls.

"They literally take away any excuse for them to fail," says Glen. "An entire community of volunteers is involved. The resources are all there.

"Pathways eliminates excuses like, 'I couldn't do this or that because I didn't have a car…' Well, if that's the case, we're going to give you a car and make sure it works...and you don't have to worry about health issues now either."

"Just giving them the kind of support they need medically is huge," adds Debbie. "Some of these girls hadn't been to a dentist since they were five years old—some, not even then. They haven't been to an OB/GYN. They haven't had their eyes examined. The basic things that everybody in a healthy family has, these girls simply haven't had. I think the Pathways network makes them feel like 'Somebody cares about me. My health *is* important. Emotionally, I should be healthy and feel good about myself!'

"And the therapy provided through the volunteer network *truly* helps them begin to feel that way. It is the cornerstone of the Pathways program."

Mentors—the frontline guides who help these girls regain their lives—are a major part of the volunteer network. Both Glen and Debbie have given their own time and love as mentors.

"I came from a very dysfunctional family myself," says Debbie. "My father was an alcoholic who came from a very abusive home, and my mother also experienced significant abuse as a child. So, I am familiar with some of the things these girls have gone through. I have a lot of empathy for them."

"There are five or six male mentors," explains Glen of his role. "But the number is growing. Dave himself has mentored many girls over the years. It can be difficult in the beginning, because the girls are often guarded when they start out. They assume that people—especially men—want something from them. Many have had no positive males in their lives.

"For me, it's simple: I treat the clients as if they were my own kids. You offer support and encouragement; and you call them on things when they get off track.

"Little by little, they come to see that they are cared about and loved because they are deserving of that. Watching their esteem grow is the main reason we stay involved in this program and feel so strongly about it. It's an amazing, wonderful, and beautiful thing to see these girls learn to love themselves and trust the world again."

Another integral aspect of the Pathways family was made even more substantial by Debbie. While the butterfly had been a symbol of the foundation for many years, it was Debbie who formalized the aura and quiet power of the butterfly into a lasting metaphor for all the girls who graduate from the Pathways program.

"I said to Dave years ago," remembers Debbie, "that it would be really cool to give the girls something at their graduation to symbolize their achievement and the process they went through. Someone had given me a gift of a Swarovski crystal butterfly, and I decided I would like to give one of those butterflies to each of the girls who graduate.

"After I had that idea, I found *The Story of the Butterfly*."

"The more Debbie talked about the butterfly," says Glen, "the more we realized it was the *perfect* metaphor for the amazing transformations that the girls achieve in the program. And *The Story of the Butterfly* is an empowering allegory that tells the girls that everything they had to endure in their lives served a greater purpose. Their experiences strengthened them to overcome whatever difficulties they will face in their lives."

"And so every semester at the graduation dinners, I give each graduate a crystal butterfly," says Debbie, "and I read that story. It's a tradition now and it seems to ring true each time."

As both donors and mentors, Debbie and Glen have been able to see many girls blossom—to witness firsthand the profound impact that the Pathways family has had in the lives of these young women.

"I have told Dave many times that the graduation parties are the greatest hook, if you will, to attract new donors and volunteers. The girls are the best possible program advocates," says Glen. "When you go to the graduation dinner, you hear their stories and you see how dramatically the lives of these girls have changed. Debbie and I thought: *How can we* <u>*not*</u> *be part of this...how can we* <u>*not*</u> *try and help in some way?*

"So often you send an organization a check and you really have no concrete way to know what happens with your donation. But at the Pathways graduations, you realize, *Wow, we really did something. We really had an impact.*

"Seeing these girls succeed seems like a miracle. You think, *There is no way they got from there to here in only four years;* it's just mind-boggling. The transition is truly magical.

"And the changes are permanent—as opposed to when someone just hands you something. When you acquire the tools and learn the skills on your own, then that lasts a long time—forever!"

And Glen and Debbie Bickerstaff are an extremely important part of that bright and beautiful forever for the girls of Pathways.

The McMillen Family Foundation

Key Donors

"We don't want to just throw money around—we want to make a difference."

—Karl and Carol McMillen

As Pathways to Independence donors, Karl and Carol McMillen—through their family foundation—have become major contributors to the organization's miraculous ability to change lives.

And as warm, generous, extraordinary human beings, they have found a way to turn a history of personal tragedies into a legacy of selfless aid to countless people in need.

Karl's amazing story of business success is counterbalanced by the emotion-searing deaths of his first wife to cancer, and of both his sons—sons who spent much of their lives battling substance abuse. Karl, too, has struggled with alcoholism and proudly carries his fifteen-year sobriety chip.

Karl McMillen was born in the remoteness of Miami, Arizona, in 1928. In the Depression year of 1929, his family moved west and Karl began to grow up in a young and developing Southern California—learning the plumbing trade and an overall industriousness from his father. This industriousness saw Karl with two paper routes and early business forays, such as selling wreaths at Christmas. It was along those paper routes, as he made deliveries to Cal Tech in Pasadena, that Karl snuck into seminars about commerce and industry.

"I didn't know what the hell they were talking about," said Karl, "but I'd take notes!"

Growing up hardworking but still feeling the effects of the Depression, the advantages of the GI Bill looked good to young Karl. Without the financial ability to attend college, he joined the marines right out of high school—with the furthering of his education always on his mind. After the military, he applied to USC—but was rejected. Undaunted, Karl attended college in New Mexico, eventually qualifying to transfer to USC.

But business became his focus—and his strongest attribute.

His from-the-ground-up development of Alert Plumbing and subsequent ownership of Todd Pipe and Supply are legendary business success stories. Both firms became enormously successful and respected in their field. Both were the result of the power, perseverance, and prowess of Karl McMillen.

But all of Karl's strengths were called upon in a more personal way as his family began to suffer that series of tragedies—a chain of hardships that few individuals ever have to face in one lifetime.

His two champion-surfer sons became involved with drugs in their teen years. What followed were decades of prison stays, rehabilitation attempts, shattered family lives, and the eventual overdose death of Karl's oldest son, Mark, in 1986.

And the nightmare was far from over.

In 1999 Karl lost Thelma, his wife of nearly fifty years, to cancer.

In early 2010, his youngest son, Chris, also succumbed to the ravages of that devastating disease—even as he *continued* his lifelong battle against his destructive disease of drug addiction, which had landed him in and out of prison for most of his adult years.

It was out of these horrors that The McMillen Family Foundation and an almost unprecedented benevolence was born—with a focus on supporting charities that serve people affected by chemical dependency.

Karl's foundation began by establishing The Thelma McMillen Center: a chemical-dependency treatment facility at Torrance Memorial Hospital in California.

"We started out with the Thelma Center where we donated $5.3 million," says Karl. "Then we've gone on to support Pathways, House of Hope, and so many others."

The McMillen Family Foundation continually seeks out new avenues for making a difference in the lives of substance abuse sufferers.

"We've been supporting The Lynn House in Orange County," continues Karl, "and we have just given to The Friendly House in downtown L.A.—the first women's recovery house in Los Angeles County, formed in 1951. We also contribute to The Villa Center, a long-running women's treatment center in Santa Ana.

"One of the more interesting rehab centers that we contribute to is First Step House of Orange County, also known as 'Charlie Street.' We just bought them a three-unit property for about seven hundred and fifty grand—paid in full. And we're going to remodel it for them, plus we're remodeling one of their other houses.

"First Step began in 1952; it's a place where they won't take anyone in unless you've had a drink *within the last twenty-four hours!* They have to *cut* the pants off some of these guys because their zippers are corroded and so filthy. They have a bathroom with a shower in the middle of the room where two guys can *hold up* another guy to get him clean. After that comes the hard part: *drying him out.*"

"Karl has done everything he can," says Carol. "Although the tragedies in his life were terrible, a lot of good has come from them. He has started this McMillen Family Foundation, which is helping hundreds and hundreds and will continue on for years to come.

"Out of tragedy comes some good."

Carol and Karl married about eight years ago. She, too, knows familial heartbreak and dysfunction, having grown up in a poor, alcoholic family.

Carol also was a frontline witness to the terrible losses of Mark and Thelma—having worked with Karl in the office at Todd Pipe for many years. Later, as Karl's wife, she was an integral part of the family when Chris died.

Dave Bishop looks at Carol as being the "heart of the McMillen family—her compassion coupled with Karl's business skills makes for the perfect team."

Carol insists however, that the *true* heart of their family is the McMillen Family Foundation Board. "They're good, I tell you. They work so well together as a team. And everyone's heart is in the right place—they just want to help people."

In addition to Karl and Carol, this *team* is composed of trusted longtime friends and associates, each hand-picked by Karl. "Each board member brings his or her personal and professional experience to the table to accomplish great things," says Carol. "They just gel."

The board includes: Family members Kellie McMillen, Ty McMillen, Shannon McMillen, Lani McMillen, and Jeff Morrow; Dan Patrick, Karl's business partner; Gary Michel, personal and business attorney, and trustee of the McMillen Foundation; Dan Fiorito, personal and business accountant; Merle Countryman, close family friend and Chairman of the Board for the House of Hope; and Dr. Moe Gelbart, head of the Thelma McMillen Center.

The board also includes Dave Bishop.

The respect the McMillens have for Dave and Pathways is apparent. And it's clearly expressed in the McMillens' endorsement for how Dave steers the program.

"There's more help out there for men than there is for women," explains Karl. "That's one of the special things about Pathways. The accountability aspect is also very important.

"Dave sets guidelines and he sees that they're enforced. The clients are accountable for everything. It's a great concept…I think that helps give people ambition and drive.

"So many parents don't do that with their *own* kids; they set rules but don't make them follow them. Dave gives these girls the guidance they need *and* the discipline. His famous quote, 'I love you…but I'll love you right out the door' is part of that; he means what he says.

"In time, these girls become financially independent and give back to society, instead of costing it. In fact, part of their 'contract' is to pay it forward—to help other people. And you see the Pathways graduates doing that. Not only are they productive citizens; many devote their *lives* to helping others. And they all continue to support and help further the program.

"Dave has so many people behind him; he has assembled a support group that is wonderful. He has credibility. I can see Pathways continuing to grow—grow very large!"

With caring people like the McMillens as part of that wonderful support group, the growth of Pathways is limitless.

And that optimism has become a proven fact—The McMillen Family Foundation's generosity is directly responsible for a forty percent increase in the size and impact of Pathways.

And, as a man filled with seemingly boundless drive and goodwill, Karl has come out of retirement and restarted his Todd Pipe business—with a new incentive. "The maximum amount a for-profit company can give to charitable donations is twenty percent," explains Karl, "so that's what we give. Twenty percent of all Todd Pipe proceeds go to the McMillen Foundation to continue funding these worthwhile organizations like Pathways."

As Carol put it best: *Out of tragedy comes some good.*

Sharon Dickson

Volunteer Therapist

"To see the courage of these girls,
to see their willingness to face their demons, to look at the pain,
and to trust in me as they take the risk to change—
it doesn't get any better than that."

—Sharon Dickson

Extreme tragedy and abuse produces emotional and mental trauma that requires therapy of extreme power to overcome. It also requires a uniquely gifted therapist in command of that power.

Sharon Dickson has worked a sensitive healing magic in dealing with the horrors of the Pathways girls' backgrounds.

"I'm a licensed clinical social worker; what I provide the girls is psychotherapy. A mutual friend of Dave's and mine—a former Catholic priest—got me involved in Pathways, and I see about five of the girls. I love the girls. I love being part of this."

Sharon uses that love, along with patience, skill, and dedication, to help Pathways clients confront their harrowing pasts.

"These girls, to achieve their goals," explains Sharon, "*have* to look at their stumbling blocks. They have to get on an equal playing field. For these girls to succeed—for them to become everything they were created to be, want to be, and can be—we have to deal with their family-of-origin issues."

Sharon can relate to the educational requirements of Pathways as well.

"I was a 'reentry' student myself; I went back to school as a mom and a wife. The educational process is *so* important."

But the importance of therapy—focused and extensive therapy—is an absolute *necessity* in resurrecting a normal life for the women in Pathways.

"They can sit in school all day long, but until we deal with each aspect of what they have gone through, in tandem with their education, they're going to have a hard time getting to where they want to go. All the degrading messages, all the traumatic events, all the wounds, all the pain, all the lost self-esteem—it *all* has to be dealt with. There's a lot of undoing to do here in this office."

Like everyone else involved in Pathways, Sharon draws strength in the certainty that what Pathways does tangibly *works!*

"It *does* work," she says. "I've seen it. It gives girls who otherwise wouldn't have been able to evolve an opportunity to become everything they want to become.

"I watched a girl I worked with: She had tattoos, she always wore her dress a little seductively, and she wasn't sure what she wanted to do—and even if she knew what she wanted to do, she wasn't sure she could do it!

"But by my last session with her, this girl had become a teacher. She was sitting across from me, with her hair tied back, wearing argyle socks, a sports skirt, and loafers. My eyes just watered. *My God, look at that!* I thought.

"Now she's out there helping others. I just love that. To see them change. To see their children.

"I'm working with a girl now who has a nine-month-old baby. She brings the baby with her for sessions because she doesn't have child care sometimes. But this baby has a chance now because of what Pathways is doing with her mom."

Sharon also shares in the intense gratification of the other Pathways volunteers.

"The reward that I get is beyond words! To see the courage of these girls, to see their willingness to face their demons, to look at the pain, and to trust in *me* as they take the risk to change—it doesn't get any better than that.

"I get more from these girls than what I could ever give. I mean that from the bottom of my heart."

Dr. Jeff Barke

Volunteer Physician & Medical Director

"Pathways gives me an opportunity to fulfill what I believe to be an important mission in my life."

—Dr. Jeff Barke

Dr. Jeff Barke is pivotal to the medical care received by Pathways clients. For eight years, he has been instrumental in returning Pathways women to the physical health that *must* go hand in hand with the emotional and mental health required to create the entire life-transforming package that the Pathways to Independence Foundation provides.

"I feel very strongly about giving back to the community," explains Dr. Barke. "I feel blessed to be in the position I'm in. And with all that I've been given—health, affluence, and education—I feel an obligation to give back to others who are less fortunate than I am. I have a quest and a desire to fulfill that mission.

"It was through Lisa Jo Mais, a Friends of Pathways fundraiser, that I was introduced to the program. I offered to help, and quickly assumed the role of medical director for Pathways, organizing all the medical care for the girls."

Dr. Barke's "quest and desire" led him to bring other physicians, as well, into the Pathways family of super-volunteers.

"I am a family physician, and I have a medical practice with three doctors; we all provide primary care services to the Pathways girls. In addition, I have a network of about fifteen other primary care doctors who have also agreed to volunteer their time and provide medical care to the girls.

"Each Pathways girl is assigned a primary care physician. We provide everything from annual physicals to treating sore throats to handling any medical emergencies that arise—and we do so free of charge."

Dr. Barke echoes the sentiments of many in expressing how personally touched he has been by Pathways and the incredible women who are its clients.

"From time to time, people tell me how nice it is that I do this. That may have some truth, but the reality is that I *get* as much as I *give.*

"Number one, this gives me an opportunity to fulfill what I believe to be an important mission in my life. Number two, I have learned so much from interacting with these girls. It makes me grateful for where I am, and it humbles me to have others willing to accept my help.

"I've also learned a lot of life's lessons from seeing these girls grow in their struggles into overcoming incredible obstacles—Mount Everest–sized obstacles—in their lives. Many have been sexually molested; many come from terrible poverty and horrible abuse.

"If they can overcome that," says Dr. Barke, "and be successful, there's not much left in the way of obstacles that *can't* be overcome."

Dr. Steve Pakiz

Volunteer Dentist

"I feel I'm in kind of a 'paying it forward' situation:
I'm not just helping the individual in my dentist chair;
I'm helping this individual to be able
to help other individuals."

—Dr. Steve Pakiz

Medical volunteers are vital to the reclaiming-of-life process that Pathways girls go through. Dentistry especially, as the issue of diminished self-esteem is common to so many—if not all—of the clients.

"Those smiles *are* so important!" says Dr. Steve Pakiz, a volunteer dentist for Pathways. "There's a lot of self-esteem wrapped up in your smile, and how you present yourself and how you feel about yourself. It's a very personal part of who we are.

"As a Pathways volunteer, I provide general practice dentistry to the clients; I usually have about five Pathways patients at any given time. My staff and I provide all the comprehensive dental care they need. If they need fillings, if they need crowns, if they need whitening, if they need their smile improved, they get it…anything at all!"

Like so many other volunteers, Dr. Pakiz saw Pathways to Independence as an opportunity to make a tangible impact.

"My involvement with Pathways began about seven years ago," recalls Dr. Pakiz. "A friend of mine invited me to a Pathways charity event. I met Dave and heard about the foundation—how it came to be and what they were trying to do. It seemed like something I would like to be a part of; somewhere that I could truly make a difference. I said I'd like to help—I knew it would be a great opportunity."

As the years have passed, that opportunity has fulfilled its promise as this ambitious foundation's full impact is realized.

"My time as a dentist with Pathways has been so rewarding on so many levels," says Dr. Pakiz. "Some of the young women open up over time, sharing their stories. They are all so amazing—where they have come from and what they've been able to do with their lives.

"And it's wonderful how many of them actually want to give back. A lot of them have gone into social work; situations where they are being of service to other people. It's nice to be kind of a 'behind the scenes' person, listening to them talk about these goals. I feel I'm in kind of a 'paying it forward' situation: I'm not just helping the individual in my dentist chair; I'm helping this individual to be able to help *other* individuals.

"There was this one girl; I had no idea what she had been through. Then I heard her tell her story, about things that had gone on in her life and things she had done. Looking at this person, she bore no resemblance to the individual she described herself as before.

"It goes to prove that if you support people in society—if you show them there are people who care about what goes on in their life—so much can be accomplished. Possibilities abound."

Like so many, Dr. Pakiz appreciates the absolute specialness and quality of the Pathways to Independence program.

"I've been involved with charities before, but Pathways is so well run. I am impressed with all the people involved, up and down the ladder;

everyone seems to be doing exactly what they should be doing. It's been a great experience.

"Let's face it, not *all* charities are managed well, in terms of where the money and the help goes. But Pathways really keeps those who are important—the girls—*way* up front."

Mike Evans

Volunteer Mechanic

"If I can be part of that—
to help somebody else and see their lives being enriched—
it just excites me."

—Mike Evans

Along with the mental and physical renewals that Pathways provides, a third component in the "reclaiming-of-life" process is the supplying of the nuts and bolts of day-to-day living.

Mike Evans is a volunteer who *literally* turns those nuts and bolts on the cars that Pathways provides to its clients.

"I own an auto repair business," explains Mike. "I help the girls by working on their cars. I make sure that they're in good shape so the clients can depend on them and not have any problems."

And reliable transportation to school, to therapy, to work, and to all of the other "accountability" requirements of Pathways is *critical* to the program's—and the clients'—success.

Mike's reward, like every volunteer's, is observing the growth and change in the women over time.

"From the way the girls start out," says Mike, "being discouraged in life and so forth, to where they take their lives, how successful they become, and how motivated they are by what they're given—I'm very inspired by it."

That prevalent theme of "receiving much more than we give" is as key to the master mechanic's work as are his big rolling cabinets of specialized tools.

"When you do something for somebody else," says Mike, "it just makes you feel better. If I can be part of that—to help somebody else and see their lives being enriched—it just excites me.

"I'm more motivated by it each and every day."

Renee Banchiere

Mentor & Treasurer

"I believe deeply in empowerment and support
and togetherness and community—
that's why I believe in Pathways."

—Renee Banchiere

By definition, a mentor is "a wise and trusted counselor or teacher." That's an important role to fill; especially when the *mentees* consist of young women whose lives have been invaded by traumas that could send virtually anyone past a point of no return—where even the *best* counseling could not reach them.

It takes a person of extraordinary wisdom, trustworthiness, and caring to reach out to those in that darkest of places.

Renee Banchiere is such a person.

"I'm a people person," Renee says. "When Pathways offered me the opportunity to mentor, I felt ready and willing to love and encourage without conditions."

And Renee had already proven that she *was* ready and willing to help in whatever way she could.

"In 2003," Renee recounts, "a friend approached me because Pathways needed help with the Treasurer position. I'm a real estate broker, so I do understand finances—but as for a natural gift or a love of number crunching and writing reports? Forget about it! But I said yes because that was where the need was and I knew I could do it. Expanding into the role of mentor was icing on the cake!

"My first mentee and I are now like mother and daughter; she's actually my grandchildren's nanny. I love her to tears. Even long since she's graduated, she remains a part of our family. And now, she too, is a mentor to a girl in Pathways."

The mentor/mentee relationship is yet another critical layer in the "cocoon" of support and guidance that Pathways provides. Therefore, it is imperative—and *required*—that it be nurtured and maintained properly.

"Like any relationship, ours started slowly," says Renee. "We took the time for each other. We listened, and we started to trust each other, and to share more and more, and to spend more time together. It was a gift for me to champion her and to acknowledge all the things she was doing to mature and care for herself—to grow, to learn, and to blossom into the beautiful woman that she is. I am deeply blessed by our relationship.

"I just took on a new mentee. We're just now getting to know each other. It's beginning."

Renee feels that Pathways is just beginning to experience *its* potential as well.

"I believe deeply in empowerment and support and togetherness and community—and that's why I believe in Pathways. The way this program is run, it draws on a strong central community for support. It is really about love.

"I feel the evidence is clear that God supports this program. That's why it's growing. That's why so *many* beautiful women are blossoming through Pathways to Independence. By the time these women graduate, their entire being is shining."

Gayle Wright, Johnna Bryant, and Lisa Mais

Friends of Pathways
Organizers & Fundraisers

"Dave says I'm like an angel,
but I get so embarrassed because he is a saint!
The little teeny tiny bit that I do is the easy part."

—Gayle Wright

"It resonated to me that I'm so blessed.
So I asked myself, 'How can I give back?
How can I empower women?'"

—Johnna Bryant

"From the very first time I learned about Pathways,
I really felt like this is something I would do for life."

—Lisa Mais

One of the most relied-upon volunteer posts in Pathways is that of the fundraisers—those who make the contacts and stage the events that make people aware of just what Pathways is, how it works, and most importantly, how they can help.

Three key members of this fundraising staff—the Friends of Pathways—are Gayle Wright, Johnna Bryant, and Lisa Mais.

The teaming of these three special women goes back over fourteen years.

"A friend of mine turned me on to Pathways," explains Gayle. "She told me of an impending auction, and I offered to donate something or give a check. I never heard back from her, but I *did* hear from Dave Bishop; apparently my friend told him I might be a good fundraiser. He asked me to come to a board meeting, and I was just so taken by everything!

"When I came home, my neighbor, Cathy Richie, was out front doing yard work. 'I just came back from this *amazing* organization!' I told her. I went on and on and on. She attended the next meeting with me and that's how the whole thing started."

Johnna Bryant was also invited to hear about Pathways

"I got hooked that very first night," says Johnna. "I'll never forget it...we all sat around the room transfixed by the story of just *one* of the clients. There wasn't a dry eye in the house. We were all so moved."

"Then we had our first brainstorming meeting," recounts Gayle, "to figure out how to raise some money for this group. We called friends, set up meetings, and got some speakers from Pathways; that's how we started it. We wound up with a core group of twenty-five or thirty helpers.

"Dave came up with the idea of hosting a progressive dinner party as a fundraiser—and it worked. It continues to work. We've done it every year in my neighborhood of Park Estates in Long Beach, California.

The neighbors are wonderful about it—and have been *very* generous. Everyone opens up their homes to it. They love it.

"Over the years, there have been so many women that have given so much time and money and effort—it's been awesome!"

Another one of these women is Lisa Mais—a cousin of Gayle's neighbor, Cathy.

"They asked me to get involved with that first big fundraiser," recalls Lisa. "At the time, there were only nine girls in the program and Pathways was essentially out of money. We raised $38,000 that first year. Last year—fourteen years later—we brought in $270,000."

Financial infusion like that is the direct result of the strong presence and tireless work of these dedicated women, some of whom have been raising money and awareness for Pathways for years.

"It is a very collaborative effort," says Johnna.

And these supporters really *are* so much more than just *Friends of Pathways*; they are the heart that pumps the blood to the rest of the vital organs. And it is a behind-the-scenes presence—a work that, while not always in the spotlight, is such a crucial part of this organization's supporting cast.

"We don't get to interact with the clients that much," admits Johnna, "because the fundraising part of this is so intensive. We don't really have the *time* to interact. We *do* get with the clients on the day of the annual party, and they come a couple days beforehand to help us clean the yard. They work cleanup afterwards, too.

"And I *love* going to the graduations," says Johnna. "I go and I hear the girls' stories all over again from the beginning to the end, and I get all tingly and teary-eyed; I can't stop crying. It's a beautiful transformation. It makes my heart full..."

Although the fundraising end of Pathways may not be as client-interactive as the roles that the doctors and the therapists and the other volunteers assume, there is no way that *anyone* associated with this program in *any* capacity can *not* develop a connection—a personal connection—with the clients and the situations that brought them to Pathways.

"I'm an only child," explains Johnna, "so I always wanted brothers or sisters. When I was younger, I felt that the clients were *like* sisters… I felt so much emotion, so much sympathy and empathy.

"But I couldn't even *imagine* going through what they went through. So for me, it wasn't being able to *relate* to that first client's story that we heard so many years ago that got me *so* excited about Pathways; rather, I was moved because I'd had such a *great* life. I have wonderful parents who are both still alive and well—and who live just three blocks from me! In fact, my mother, Collette Anderson, is now a Friends of Pathways member too!

"It resonated to me that I'm so blessed. So I asked myself, 'How can I give back? How can I empower women?' Give them an education and help them on their way was the answer—and I love that message and that goal.

"The biggest reward is knowing that I'm changing lives. I'm a little cog in a big wheel, but I *am* changing lives. Unlike some other charities I could be involved in, this one gives me the sense that every minute I spend on it and every dollar I contribute makes a *huge* impact on a young girl's life.

"Pathways is something that really works," attests Johnna. "It has a huge success rate. You see it in the girls' smiles and you see it in their body posture. The girls start out looking down a lot, saying 'Ummms…,' and their shoulders are hunched over; but as time goes on, you see such a difference.

"You especially witness that growth when they graduate. It's just amazing! How they hold themselves up now, how they look you in the eye. They have smiles on their faces…they're grateful…and they feel like they can take the world by the tail!"

Once these personal connections with Pathways and its clients set in, it seems to become a 24/7 network that extends in so many directions.

"My brother is a doctor," reports Gayle. "One night in the ER, a patient came in and revealed to him her traumatic story. He called me immediately and said, 'I just met a girl who *needs* to be in Pathways!'

"My brother's patient was Kaysie—and she will graduate this year!"

Like so many of the volunteers, Lisa also shares a *personal* commonality with the Pathways clients.

"I grew up with two parents who love me unconditionally," says Lisa, "but unfortunately my childhood does have some common threads with our clients, in that I grew up in an alcoholic family and my parents later divorced."

And like *all* of the volunteers, Lisa feels as though she receives as much as she gives.

"From the very first time I learned about Pathways, I really felt like this is something I would do for life," says Lisa. "I'm inspired every day by these girls' courage, their determination, and their hope for the future. These kids come from just horrific backgrounds, and they come in so scared. They're not sure why all of a sudden they're getting this gift.

"But they emerge so confident—they know where they're going and they develop their own missions. The change is remarkable. Education is power. The more they learn, the better.

"And there's another thing that just means the world to people: having a family that really cares about you.

"And that's exactly what we are."

Join the Pathways Family

"Act as if what you do makes a difference. It does."

—William James

Pathways to Independence depends on and is grateful for the financial support of individuals, family foundations, businesses, and local charities. But the demand for support vastly exceeds supply.

With no advertising, Pathways has about forty girls active in the program, with almost *twice as many* more on the waiting list—a list that is constantly growing. We *need* to get these young women into the program as soon as possible! In many cases—their lives *literally* depend on it.

And how many *other* girls out there are trapped in a nightmare, struggling just to survive?

With YOUR support, we can throw them a lifeline!

How Can I Help?

Pathways' primary challenge is funding. Every dollar matters! We urge you to give a one-time gift, or better yet, pledge a *monthly* contribution—large or small—to enable us to provide sustained support for these deserving young women.

Just think—if 1,000 people each gave just $10/month, that would allow us to accept more than seven new clients into the Pathways program!

Here's how your monthly contribution can make a difference:

$10 • *Provides* ***school supplies*** *for one client*

$25 • *Provides* ***prescriptions*** *for one client*

$50 • *Provides* ***restorative dental work*** *for one client*

$75 • *Provides* ***textbooks*** *for one client*

$125 • *Covers* ***medical expenses*** *for one client*

$250 • *Covers average* ***college tuition*** *for one client*

$650 • *Covers an average* ***rent stipend*** *for one client*

$1,250 • *Covers* ***ALL DIRECT EXPENSES*** *to sustain one client in the program*

The Path to 40,000...

Dave Bishop's dream is to grow the program from 40 girls today to 40,000 tomorrow.

YOUR generosity will help us reach this goal!

How Do I Give?

To schedule monthly payments or give a one-time gift, visit our secure online donation center at:

www.pathwaystoindependence.org

Or mail checks to:

Pathways to Independence
P.O. Box 43, Los Alamitos, CA 90720

Remember: Your donation is tax-deductible!

Visit the Pathways website to find out more about volunteering and mentoring opportunities, donating items for auction, and more!

Shop Our Online Store!

Support the Pathways program by purchasing from our unique line of **CLOTHING, JEWELRY,** and **MORE** at:

www.butterflytears.net

Your support helps a struggling young woman succeed.
Join the Pathways Family TODAY!